RETHINKING
CRITICAL THEORY

DATE DUE

Rethinking Critical Theory

Emancipation in the Age of Global Social Movements

Larry J. Ray

SAGE Publications

London • Newbury Park • New Delhi

SAGE Publications Ltd
6 Bonhill Street
London EC2A 4PU

SAGE Publications Inc
2455 Teller Road
Newbury Park, California 91320

SAGE Publications India Pvt Ltd
32, M-Block Market
Greater Kailash – I
New Delhi 110 048

British Library Cataloguing in Publication data

Ray, Larry
  Rethinking Critical Theory: Emancipation
  in the Age of Global Social Movements
  I. Title
  301

  ISBN 0–8039–8363–8
  ISBN 0–8039–8364–6 (pbk)

Library of Congress catalog card number 93–083467

Typeset by Photoprint, Torquay, Devon
Printed in Great Britain by The Cromwell Press Ltd,
Broughton Gifford, Melksham, Wiltshire

Contents

Acknowledgements

I would like to express my gratitude and indebtedness to the following people: Martin O'Brien, for his invaluable contribution to the original concept for this book; Nick Abercrombie, Celia Lury, William Outhwaite, John Urry, David Waines and Alan Warde, for advice and guidance on earlier chapter drafts; Chris Quinn, for assistance throughout this project; and, above all, Emma, for tireless patience and support.

Introduction: Marx, Critical Theory and Social Movements

This book addresses social movements in the global arena in relation to the claims of Critical Theory, especially Habermas' theory of communicative action. A central claim of his theory is that the transition from pre-modern to modern social organization released divergent potentials for social organization. The organizational forms which became dominant in systems of monetary and bureaucratic domination, regarded by much sociology as modernity per se, have been continually challenged by an alternative, suppressed potential for rational and democratic communication, whose existence can be reconstructed in various ways. One of Habermas' boldest claims is that this latter modernity, though repressed, is none the less presupposed in everyday communication and makes its presence felt not only in oppositional, protest movements but also in the inherent instability of repressive social institutions. The notion of an historical alternative to existing arrangements, not merely as a utopian idea, but as a movement with real effects, has been a continuous thread in Critical Theory. However, for Adorno and Horkheimer, the horror and tragedy of the twentieth century limited the negative or critical potential to the status of a memory, rather than a concrete historical movement.

Later critical theorists have attempted to rediscover an emancipatory potential, without having recourse to fictitious historical agents. Twenty years ago, Trent Schroyer claimed that critique can restore the memory of blocked potential and anticipate the emancipation of humanity from constraints of repression, and by addressing empirical instances of struggle and ideology can 'begin to define the emancipatory in the present' (1973: 81). Seyla Benhabib wrote of theory 'allying itself with the struggles of those for whom the hope of a better future provides the courage to live in the present' (1986: 15) and recently Douglas Kellner (1989: 225) called for a re-politicized Critical Theory which takes a position on current political issues in the manner of the earlier Frankfurt Institute. Again, Michael Ryan concluded his review of French and German social theory by asking:

> How do we relate this already discontinuous network to problems of popular power in Mozambique, of the anti-feudal peasant movement within the context of a democratically elected communist government in West Bengal, and of the liberation struggle in El Salvador? (1981)

This question is important because it acknowledges that acute social struggles are taking place outside the developed capitalist world, although the latter has remained the focus of analysis for much Critical Theory.

Habermasian theory is taken as a starting point, despite its Eurocentric focus, because this complex and nuanced body of analysis might be used to address the difficult and tantalizing issues which surround contemporary social movements, global crises and new identities.[1] But Habermas has taken Critical Theory (not without controversy) some way from its origins. For earlier Critical Theory the rupture between theory and practice was symptomatic of a flaw in modernity which arose from the linkage between rationality and the domination of nature. Thus for Adorno and Horkheimer the dark side of Weber's instrumental rationality was calculating violence, unreason and authoritarianism, all of which pointed in the direction of total administration – through fascism, Stalinism or the culture industry. Habermas, however, has re-posed the problems of early Critical Theory in ways which permit a reformulation of the limitations and possibilities of the present. He has shifted the grounds of debate from the search for subject-agents of universal values (such as the proletariat) to the inherent potentials for rational and universalistic action inhering in the constitution of the social itself. Whether he has done this consistently and rigorously enough to address a wide compass of contemporary political conflicts will be discussed here.

It is not always clear what is meant by 'emancipation' in Critical Theory, which Alvin Gouldner once described as 'epic rhetoric' which is often accompanied by 'essentially Fabian political practice – when it has any politics at all' (1976: 117). For most people outside the developed world, and for a sizable number within, emancipation means freedom from hunger and degradation and the guarantee of entitlements to physical and social security. This in turn is unlikely to be guaranteed without the stabilization of a democratic civil society within which the arbitrary powers of states are subject to popular restraint through formal institutions. In this context, a common connotation is the achievement of juridical equality for an oppressed group, in the sense of women's or national emancipation. Thirdly, however, emancipation in a Habermasian sense refers to decolonization of the lifeworld – the expansion of democratic social control over markets and bureaucracies through extended public spheres, combined with a critical attitude towards the normative bases of authority. These possible meanings are neither hierarchical nor sequential, and struggles are conducted on each level simultaneously, frequently *within* social movements.

Marxism, Critical Theory or Antitheory?

What is Critical Theory? In some ways this is difficult to answer, since the original concerns of the theory, such as the domination of nature, the demise of a revolutionary proletariat, the culture industry or the expansion of technocratic management, are now widely shared amongst writers who propose quite different responses (such as postmodernists). Moreover, Habermas rejects the style of critique in the *Dialectic of Enlightenment* (Adorno & Horkheimer 1973) and has brought Critical Theory closer to mainstream sociology. Indeed, it might be thought that *The Theory of Communicative Action* (Habermas, 1984, 1989b) concedes so much ground to functionalist or Weberian sociologies that it no longer has a distinctively 'critical' approach. However, this judgement would overlook the way in which Habermas conducts a critical dialogue *within* sociological theory, throughout which he continuously refers back to an emancipatory reason, which is historically and socially grounded in language and communication, as a pointer towards a reformulated Critical Theory and social practice. Of course, the notion of historically grounded reason, which offers both the legitimation for Critical Theory and the impetus behind the resistance of oppression, has become unfashionable in an intellectual milieu informed by relativism and postmodernism. Habermas believes he has found a way of avoiding reference to external narratives (history, the proletariat, etc.) whilst resisting surrender to postmodernist relativism by embedding critical politics in linguistic and moral evolution. In evaluating this claim, two key issues will be addressed: first, the reconstruction of the theory of social action in terms of universal pragmatics; and, secondly, the argument that modern social organization poses problems which cannot ultimately be resolved without recourse to emancipated forms of communication.

The second of these claims owes a lot to the approach, if not the substance, of Marxism, with which Critical Theory has always had an ambiguous relationship. The pessimistic conclusions of Adorno and Hork-heimer were the result not so much of abandoning Marxism (as some of their Marxist critics frequently suggested) but of a logical deduction. Two central propositions of Marxist philosophy are that, first, a society freed from want and injustice is no mere utopia but is implicit in human resistance to oppression; and, secondly, that the conditions for emanci-pation unfold progressively through social struggles which develop an increasingly universalistic focus, culminating in the proletarian revolution. However, when historical development seemed to move in the opposite direction, towards mass destructiveness, the second proposition looked highly untenable. Thus Adorno's comment that Hegel's 'philosophy may well have succeeded in unifying history and truth, but by the same token its validity has diminished as history took a turn for the worse' (1984: 483) expressed the conundrum of a critical philosophy that tied its fortunes to the objective movement of history. Further, even if the first proposition remained true, if the possibility of an emancipated life was implicit in social praxis, then Critical Theory was at best left with the task of remembrance, of locating residues of possible emancipation amongst the wreckage of history.

The crisis of Marxism for early Critical Theory, and indeed for much of western Marxism, was a crisis of the emancipatory subject, which from

Marcuse onwards prompted a quest for substitutes – new social movements, women, the Third World, Eros, intellectuals or popular democratic
fronts (Benhabib, 1986: 352). For example, Joseph McCarney's in many
ways sympathetic Lukácsian critique of Critical Theory recognizes that the
Frankfurt Institute arrived at the conclusions they did because of their
particularly sharp self-consciousness and historical awareness (1990: 176).
However, his claim that they converted Marxism into a normative critique
skates over their central dilemma, whilst his conclusion, 'that the crucial
task of identifying the revolutionary subject has to be performed again'
(1990: 180), merely reiterates it. The reality is that any attempt to pin
utopian hopes on a subject-agent is necessarily elusive. Emancipatory
subjects are defined abstractly in terms of an alleged congruence of
interests ('objective position') whereas in practice there is absolutely no
reason to suppose that commonality of interest will result in commonality
of action, since the latter will depend upon a range of factors such as
structural conduciveness, the organizational capacity of relevant social
movements, the responsiveness of the system to demands, the strength of
counter-movements, and effectiveness of conflict management.

One response to this realization is to abandon any attempt to theorize
political practice, and, as Martin Jay puts it, 'celebrate with a kind of
resigned gaiety, the virtues of fragmentation, non-identity heterogeneity
etc., . . . preached by a wide variety of *soi-disant* post-Marxist philos-
ophies' (1988: 121). Partly in response to the failure of Eurocommunist
strategies in France and Italy in the 1980s,[2] and partly following a more
general crisis of the historical models of socialist organization, postmodernism offered a kind of liberation from the demands of an integrated
theory (Stame, 1984). With Foucault this entailed the replacement of
systematic theory by highly generalized intellectual history illustrating
equally general concepts (Ray, 1989). Since all sites of power were also
sites of resistance, and since power was 'everywhere . . . the name given to
a complex strategic situation in . . . society' (Foucault, 1977: 21), the
question of what *kinds* of resistance, or under what conditions, tended not
to be posed. Postmodern politics expressed the diversity and complexity of
contemporary struggles and rejected the idea (which was attributed to
Marxism) that historical development unfolded according to an emergent
rationality, a view summed up in Lyotard's critique of 'meta-narratives of
historical justification' (1991: 13–14).[3]

As Ernesto Laclau put it, social reproduction and regulation is a
complex and pragmatic process, 'starting from a multiplicity of points in
the social tissue and . . . involving a plurality of social actors' (1991a).
Indeed, Laclau and Mouffe have been closely associated with the view that
the emancipatory project seeks no 'nodal points', and instead is a 'constant
overflowing of every discourse by the infinitude of fields of discourse'
which become the basis for new 'hegemonic articulations' (1985: 161).
This, they claim, opens up the way to a radical democratic politics
constructed around indeterminate and self-posited identities (such as

gender liberation, workers' self-management), or around habitat, consumption and welfare.

However, this renders theoretical critique and structural analysis redundant, to be replaced by what is at root an empiricist view of social reality as contingent and unpredictable. Thus Laclau and Mouffe's attempt to define a radical democratic politics is ultimately vacuous and amounts to an abandonment of theory altogether (as Geras and Mouzelis argue).[4] This difficulty is evident in their discussion of the New Right, which they claim owes its success to an ability 'to mobilize [against the liberal-Left] a whole series of resistances to the bureaucratic forms of state organization'. Thus there is 'a new hegemonic project to articulate the neo-liberal defense of the free market economy' (Laclau & Mouffe, 1985: 175). Again, Laclau claims that if

> the rationalism of modernity, with its ambition of controlling the ground of society, left us the poisoned gift of an unresolved tension between universalism and particularism, the post-modern renunciation of such ground opens the way to a mediation between the two and, in this sense, makes possible the full potential of the democratic revolution. (Laclau, 1991b)

Yet it is not clear why Laclau should believe this if, as he claims, there are no rational grounds for choosing between a multiplicity of particularisms – based on race, nation, class or whatever – whose meaning will be 'pragmatically and hegemonically constructed through social struggles' (1991b). In rejecting the 'rationalism of modernity' *tout court*, postmodern politics, like earlier Critical Theory, fails to recognize the dualism of dominant and suppressed modernity.

None the less, it is quite true that Marxism itself lacked an elaborated account of the political which has given rise to serious analytical problems in the twentieth century.[5] Its self-conscious aim of politicizing economic relations, meant that a general explanatory theory of political practice per se was never elucidated (Mouzelis, 1990). Indeed, in his essay, 'On the Jewish Question', Marx called for an eradication of the boundaries between the state and civil society as a precondition of social democratization, contrasting this 'human emancipation' with the limited bourgeois goal of 'political emancipation'. This view is currently criticized on two counts. First, as economistic: 'by rejecting the notion of politics as a form of activity *sui generis*, and by calling for "the end of politics", Marxism itself tends to marginalize or exclude from politics issues that cannot be reduced to class, such as ecology, gender or ethnicity' (Held, 1991: 6). Secondly, it is viewed as anti-democratic to suggest that the boundaries of civil society should be eradicated in favour of a deep politicization of society. Socialists such as Ferenc Feher and Agnes Heller (1986) or André Gorz (1982) concur with neo-liberals over the need for a plural and independent civil society separate from the state, an issue which has been brought to the fore of these debates by the East European revolutions.

However, born-again liberalism begs too many questions, especially those of fundamental inequalities of power and wealth, and the highly problematic public–private dichotomy. Indeed, there might be some truth in Samir Amin's observation that 'those who proclaim the death of Marxism, far from surpassing its contributions to the understanding of the world, have simply shifted into reverse gear in order to return, without the slightest critical spirit, to the comfortable fold of the constructs that legitimate capitalism' (1989: 118). The objective crises which informed Marxist analysis are as real as ever, and, as Habermas has said, 'it is not as though the collapse of the Berlin Wall has solved a single one of the problems specific to our system' (1990). The long-term failure of Western economies, international debt problems, ecological catastrophe and increasing inequalities between the developed and underdeveloped regions all indicate how prone the modern world is to crisis. If this is the beginning of the 'New World Order' which was evoked to legitimate the 1991 Gulf War, then its parameters and principles of regulation have not yet matured or stabilized, since the world is in many ways less ordered and more crisis-prone than it was during the past four decades.

Moreover, the vacuity of post-theoretical politics is illustrated by its almost exclusive focus on ephemeral cultural forms (consumption, fashion, style, chic, etc.) and its equally fastidious avoidance of material structures of global domination. Under the influence of Baudrillard (1981), 'consumer capitalism' has been understood as a world of spectacle in which everything is symbolic, where the laws of exchange have been replaced by the 'political economy of the sign', and resistance is limited to struggles over the appropriation of meanings. This leaves postmodernism open to the objection that it takes capitalism at face value, as a system of circulating commodity/signs (Callinicos, 1989), but further that it cannot address the conditions for empowerment over production and reproduction, since this would require a fundamental shift in relations of economic and social power. In this context, Sabina Lovibond argues that 'localism and pluralism, the hall-marks of post-modern theorizing', conceal a 'reactionary distaste for modernist social movements', and if feminism aspires to be 'something more than a reformist movement, then it is bound sooner or later to find itself calling the parish boundaries into question' (1989).

In short, a radical theory needs a grasp of the structures which make some outcomes (and struggles) more likely than others, which implies a focus which has always been central to Critical Theory, namely the relationship between social inequalities and the management or regulation of potentially destabilizing conflicts. Early Critical Theory was essentially diagnostic, in that it developed a theory of displacement, an account of the ability of capitalism to off-load crises through closure of the public sphere and the mobilization of authoritarian social movements. The latter provided a release for structural strains whilst protecting the integrity of the mode of domination. In Habermas the theme of systemic management through crisis displacement was taken further, especially in *Legitimation Crisis* (1976), although, unlike earlier Critical Theory, Habermas emphasizes the tenuous and partial nature of systemic regulation as a context within which new conflicts and structural problems arise. This view will be developed here by analysing the ways in which collective struggles are defined by failures of systemic regulation and the search for new system-solutions to underlying problems of unequal access to resources, social power and speech rights in communicative processes.

Before proceeding, however, it is worth noting that the French regulationists (for example, Anglietta and Lipietz) have also theorized capitalism as a regulatory system. Attempting to move away from overly abstract theories of the capitalist mode of production, the regulationists descriptively periodize capitalist development into four modes of regulation: pre-Taylorist, Taylorist-Fordist, full-blown Fordism and post-Fordism, each of which is based upon a temporary crisis resolution and class compromise (Jessop, 1990). Regulation theory requires that we look at a triangular relationship between an industrial paradigm, accumulation regime and its mode of social regulation. The mode of regulation establishes the nature of the capitalist wage–labour nexus, inter-capitalist competition, money and credit relations, the manner of adhesion to the international economy and forms of state intervention. The regulationists, however, are primarily concerned with modes of economic integration, and, as Brenner and Glick (1991) argue, they have relatively little to say about the social institutions of capitalist rule. The present volume offers a social theory of regulation which develops the Habermasian idea that modern systems have evolved mechanisms of crisis displacement and technocratic management of potential conflicts in ways which avoid threatening the identity of the system. In this context, however, an important insight from the regulationists will be deployed, namely their understanding of crises as complex events which might permit a re-stabilization of the system through a new set of consensual arrangements. In these terms, the onset of crises could be viewed as the beginning of struggles towards new forms of consensus, or as exit routes from social arrangements which have become unworkable. Systemic breakdown is then viewed as permitting the release of new problem-solutions and forms of integration, the vehicle of which are social movements, as carriers of new forms of social organization.

Social Movements as Carriers

Critical Theory shares with Marxism an emphasis on structural and systemic processes in social development and situates emancipatory possibilities within this framework. Marxism involves a theory of evolutionary transmission via the social application of stored knowledge. For Marx and Engels, after the initial breakthrough from primitive communism to more complex social forms involving relations of property and gender, social organization has an *inner logic* of which actors have generally been neither aware nor consciously able to control. As these are unequal societies, differentiated by ownership and non-ownership of productive resources, property and gender relations have been conflictual, even if this has been at times latent rather than manifest. Moreover, the transition between one form of society and another has been the result of a combination of internal class conflict and the maturation of new productive forces within the framework of the old order. At times Marx suggested (in Saint-Simonian fashion) that the historically decisive class conflicts were those between old ruling classes (for example, the feudal fiefs) and the 'bearers' of new productive relations.

Social evolution is thus closely linked with the development of pro-ductive and organizational innovations. In *The Poverty of Philosophy* Marx commented that the 'hand-mill *gives you* society with the feudal lord; the steam-mill, society with the industrial capitalist' (n.d: 150 emphasis added). Again, in *Capital*, Marx argued that the co-operative character of the labour process is a '*technical necessity* dictated by the instrument of labour itself . . . *technical* subordination of workers to the uniform motion of the instruments of labour gives rise to a barrack discipline . . . elaborated into a complete system in the factory' (Marx & Engels, 1974: 399–400; emphasis added). Similarly, in the *Grundrisse* (1973) Marx suggested that just as the feudal order had constricted nascent capitalism (for example, through feudal land tithes or guild labour regulation) so bourgeois social relations would eventually impose fetters on the further expansion of productive capacity:

> Beyond a certain point the development of productive forces becomes a barrier for capital. Thus capitalist relationships become a barrier for the development of the productive force of labour. On arrival at that point, capital . . . enters into the same relationship to the development of social wealth . . . as did the guild system, serfdom, slavery and is necessarily rejected as a fetter. (Marx, 1973: 636).

It is at these historical conjunctures that the new order breaks through the confines of the old, not simply as an effect of technology, but as a consequence of social struggles over the stabilization of new organizational forms.

The necessary prerequisites of bourgeois development were 'the clock and the mill (at first the corn mill, specifically, the water-mill). Both were inherited from the ancients' (Marx to Engels, 28 January 1863, Marx, 1977: 526–28). The transition to capitalism was then accomplished through the application of new techniques of appropriating value through the equiva-lence of time and money. The future transition to socialism was likewise prefigured in the productive and communicative potential for social reconstruction in rational planning and management, complex information flows and the autonomous 'productive force of science' (for example, Marx, 1973: 141). Indeed, the transition from one mode of production to another requires the deployment of cultural learning (for example, the measurement of labour by time) which has accumulated *prior* to the transformation. As Timothy Luke (1990: 57–61) argues, historically owning classes develop managerial techniques for intensive increases in production, which develop first in proto-typical forms. In ancient and Asiatic societies this came about because of the perfection of military, bureaucratic and administrative techniques for regulation. With feudalism a network of productive techniques developed from mutual obligations and estate privileges to bind together a decentralized small-scale domestic economy. Capitalism deploys literacy and mechanical time-keeping to set free new relations of time, value and organization, around which new forms of social regulation and discipline, such as the concentration and regimentation and specialization of labour, could develop.[6]

If this account is correct, however, it follows that the development of cultural knowledge is logically distinct from the development of productive technology. As Max Weber's (1974) 'Protestant Ethic' thesis suggests, innovation in sixteenth-century religion (Calvinism), itself the outcome of a process of cultural learning, was transposed into a secular ethos in the form of new techniques of accounting and business organization (the 'spirit of capitalism') and thereby facilitated the new forms of labour discipline necessary for capitalist growth.[7] This congruence of cultural and technical innovation, however, was guided by an 'elective affinity' between Calvinism's implications for social action (the search for evidence of salvation) and the material conditions for capitalism (landless labour, the separation between household and production, mercantile trade and a money economy).[8]

Broadly speaking, this view is advanced in Habermas' critique of Marx, Weber and earlier Critical Theory. His reconstruction of historical materialism develops the claim that 'perhaps the concept of a mode of production is not so much the wrong key to the logic of social development as a key that has not yet been sufficiently filed down' (Habermas, 1979a: 152).

In order to file down the key he reconstructs historical materialism in terms of an evolutionary theory, around the concept of the 'principle of organization'. This involves two levels, that of productive technologies and that of social relations which have independent developmental logics. The evolution of forces of production does not determine patterns of cultural development, rather the stock of cultural knowledge is sedimented into norms, beliefs, standards of judgement, etc., and is transmitted through socialization. His thesis, at this level similar to Weber's, is that social transformations occur when learning accumulated in culture breaks into the logic of technology. For example, he asserts that class societies emerged in response to systemic problems in the kinship structure of neolithic societies – land scarcity and population density – which unleashed new productive forces already present *in an exemplary way* in the cultural learning mechanism (for example, knowledge about cultivation, stock-farming, handicrafts and irrigation). The shift to class societies, then, initiated an evolutionary movement which embodies cumulative learning and more intensified exploitation.

Leaving aside for the moment objections to Habermas' thesis (which will be discussed in Part 1), the evolutionary-learning model can be used to suggest that cultural innovations, such as scientific methods, artistic expression or standards of ethical judgement, whilst feeding into material production, might have the potential for the release of new forms of social organization which reach beyond economic relations. In *The Theory of Communicative Action* (1984, 1989b) Habermas develops this idea through critique of Weber's notion of a long-run cultural tendency towards increasing 'rationalization',[9] through which traditional forms of action, belief and social organization were progressively eroded by instrumental, specialized, goal-specific and secular beliefs and practices.

His objection to Weber, and by extension to theorists like Adorno and Horkheimer who have argued similarly, is that Weber's understanding of rationalization was only partial. For Habermas, Weberian sociology could have moved in three directions – to a consideration of social movements attempting to institutionalize various types of rational action; to a cultural sociology of rationalization; or to an analysis of how one sub-type, purposive rational action, became institutionalized. Habermas suggests that Weber took up only the third possibility, concentrating on origins of instrumental capitalism and bureaucracy, and hence viewed modernity as condemned to loss of meaning (*sinnverlust*) since outside of a religious context there was no ultimate foundation for moral consciousness. Habermas, however, claims that through reconstruction of rules of linguistic interaction it is possible to identify a potentially unified rationality underpinning different cultural value spheres of science, norms and art (an argument which is considered in Chapter 3). This might appear to be a rather arcane point, but its implication is that modernity released the potential for new forms of critical reason and organization, which are blocked by the intrusion of markets and bureaucracies into everyday life. This discursive rationality, the 'unfulfilled potential' of modernity, is both the epistemological grounding for Critical Theory and, most important, the impetus behind the formation of emancipatory social movements. Further, it is argued here that in periods of crisis, when regulatory mechanisms weaken, social movements are released which offer cultural innovations and new potential solutions to systemic failure.

This approach might offer an answer to the question posed above in relation to Laclau and Mouffe, namely by what criteria might one distinguish amongst divergent articulatory practices? Habermas' concept of communicative action attempts to acknowledge the absence of a universal agent-subject, and thus avoids appeal to historical narratives, whilst offering a criterion of what constitutes progress in the evolution of social relations (increasingly open, risk-bearing, democratic structures of communication). However, for this postulate to be more than what Luhmann derides as serving to 'express good intentions, to appeal to good will' (1982: 119), Habermas needs to demonstrate that the expansion of communicative action is a social evolutionary potential which is exemplified in real social movements.

Conflicts in the Periphery[10]

Two issues have been identified so far. First, social evolution is a process through which technical and cultural learning is released into developmental trajectories and stabilized in organizational and productive forms, where it takes on regulative functions. Secondly, systems of regulation are subject to crisis tendencies and generate social movements which offer alternative organizational solutions – exit routes from social arrangements that have become unworkable. It is proposed to address these questions in relation to regulation crises and social movements in the global arena, specifically with reference to three areas – the former socialist bloc, Islamic neo-revivalism and the liberation struggle against apartheid – each of which has crucial implications for the emergence of a new world order.

The discussion has two concerns. On the one hand, there is the question of what insights Critical Theory might bring to a post-Cold War global analysis which is to some extent still tentative. The relevance of such a perspective is illustrated by the growing number of writers attempting to elucidate the implications for the theory and practice of emancipatory movements in the Third World, of the collapse of East European socialism and the post-Cold War order (for example, Adam, 1990; Babu 1991; Saul, 1991; Shivji, 1989). A theme which will be pursued here is interaction between the economic globalization, the crisis of the state in peripheral societies, and consequent social movement struggles over regulation at the periphery.

On the other hand, the analysis of Critical Theory in an unfamiliar terrain will throw some of its own theoretical deficiencies into relief. First, Habermas' whole conceptual framework has a West-Eurocentric focus, whilst major and possibly fateful developments occur elsewhere. Secondly, he conceives of systems of bureaucratic power and the market in terms of the nation-state, whilst in an age of globalization of economic and political structures it is no longer appropriate to analyse social movements solely at the level of nationally defined space. Thirdly, Habermas writes about the transition from pre-modern to capitalist society from the point of view of internal and normatively driven possibilities for cultural rationalization. However, in peripheral formations, where capitalism has by and large come from the outside through colonialism, this mechanism cannot work in a comparable fashion. Fourthly, Habermas' claim that social movements appear at the 'seam' between system and the lifeworld, the point of resistance to bureaucratic and monetary encroachment, presupposes relatively stable social institutions anchored in social values and practices. Where this is not the case, where a modernizing but repressive state confronts a partly modernized, partly traditional society, one would expect acute social conflicts and movements that display erratic combinations of pre-modern and modern identities. This is especially so when the impact of global relations at the periphery has supported state-dominated (étatist) organization and the state is not subject to the constraints of a public sphere. Finally, despite the central role he gives social movements as bearers of new models of social organization, Habermas offers surprisingly little analysis of their formation, impact and relationship with other key processes such as colonization of the lifeworld.

The analysis here therefore, examines how collective action is structured by the different ways in which the global system impacts on local social relationships. 'Global analysis' however, is used in differing ways in current debates, one of which is to suggest that the world is undergoing increasing cultural homogenization, consequent on the standardization of international markets, the increasing density and power of communication, global computer networks and so forth (for example, Featherstone, 1990). But it would be mistaken to imagine that the spread of fast food outlets or satellite television, superficially 'globalized' consumption cultures, indicates increasing world integration in structural terms. On the contrary, capital accumulation in the world system creates less not more structural homogeneity, and the long-term tendency is for the majority of the world's population to fall increasingly behind the standards of wealth set by the West (Arrighi 1991; Clark 1991: 123–6).[11] Actually, the expansion of core cultures, combined with dislocation caused by the global economy, is likely to produce both defensive reactions and *new* cultural forms which provide the grounds for new polarities in the world order, such as nationalism amongst sub-national and linguistic communities.

Regulation and Social Movements

It will be argued that social movements are carriers of alternative forms of modernity within a field of action structured by crises of global regulation, which shifts the focus away from both earlier Critical Theory and the recent Habermas. In relation to earlier Critical Theory, Habermas has shown that its preoccupation with the effects of technocratic manipulation on consciousness meant that it could not appreciate how new critical social forces were bound to arise which expanded the scope for rational consensus. However, Habermas' theory of communicative action at best demonstrates the genesis of resistance, and has next to nothing to say about its impact, or the possible relations between systemic crisis, social conflict and the regeneration of modes of domination. Habermas' theory of steering media offers the outline of a theory of regulation, although its implications need to be taken further, especially in a global context. It is argued that modes of regulation are concerned with the displacement of crisis tendencies (for example, privatization of public issues), constraint of the public sphere, the development of sophisticated systems of strategic action and the creation of sufficient consensus for the continued identity of the system.

When these systems of co-ordination themselves enter crisis, and previously displaced conflicts burst into the public domain, the form of political rule is called into question – as occurred in the Soviet system between 1989 and 1991, in Iran between 1978 and 1979, and in South Africa today. Initially, regulation crises open up the field of political action to new social movements mobilizing social infrastructures and identities, which, as carriers of new forms of social organization, offer exit routes from the crisis and the possibility of stabilizing new conditions of integration. Typically this period is characterized by a rapid proliferation of movements only some of which will be incorporated or consolidated into organizational learning processes. Others will fail and form sub-cultures of suppressed modernity – such as the alternative forms of social organization thrown up during the 1960s – which will either atrophy or thrive underground. Those which survive might offer the basis of critique of the new social order and continue as potential organizational forms which might yet come into their own as the newly stabilized system itself runs into problems.

However, in the context of theories of regulation, the formation and impact of social movements needs closer examination. Habermas describes the lifeworld as 'colonized' by systemic media of power and money, and friction between system and lifeworld creates the ground for the appearance of social movements. But if systems of power and money enter the 'pores of communication structures', as Habermas claims they do, then it perhaps follows that social identities and collective social action will themselves bear the imprint of configurations of systemic colonization. That is, rather than atomize or undermine the lifeworld as Habermas suggests, the steering media of money and power might create new forms of sociality and, indeed, under certain circumstances, preserve old ones. If this is so, however, then the process by which social movements as problem-solutions are incorporated into or rejected from developmental trajectories will to a degree be conditioned by social networks established under the previous mode of regulation. This means that a major crisis in the political system need not exhaust the recuperative powers of the old social order. A case in point might be the ability of the old nomenklatura in the former socialist countries to survive the disintegration of communism and indeed to entrench their position. The conversion of White domination under apartheid into the market power of the same group in a racially plural society would be another. But the issue is more general, pertaining to the relationship between crisis and systemic identity. If crises are means of systemic adjustment then their resolution might take the form of a new consensus of forces which stabilize organizational forms consistent with the continued identity of the system. The question then arises, for a theory concerned with the potential for emancipatory crisis-resolution, what represents fundamental change rather than an adjustment of the mode of regulation? Broadly speaking, the answer is likely to be found in the ability of social movements to stabilize within public spheres which display openness, loosely coupled forms of integration, reflexive examination of identities, and which therefore mobilize resources against the closure of political agendas.

Part 1 addresses the development of a critical theory of society through Adorno/Horkheimer to the later Habermas, raising themes of subjectivity, praxis and social movements. This section begins with early Critical Theory, the critique of technology, mass society and authoritarianism (Chapter 1). Habermas' attempt to identify emancipatory potential in modern societies in terms of the interface of system and lifeworld is discussed in Chapters 2 and 3, and in Chapter 4 a modified theory of social movement impact is developed. Part 2 begins with an account of the state in relation to globalizing systemic forces (Chapter 5) and proceeds to address instances of crisis and struggle in three arenas: the democratic revolutions of Central and Eastern Europe (Chapter 6); the Islamic revolution (Chapter 7); and the crisis of the apartheid state (Chapter 8). This discussion will examine the concept of the lifeworld as a source of mobilizing resources, and the ways in which social identity articulates conflicting interests whilst mediating systemic crisis. It is not assumed that each of these examples will fit easily into the proffered characterization of Habermas' theory, and since this is largely uncharted territory, the analysis will in places inevitably be tentative. Two further caveats are in order. First, as a conceptual system Habermasian theory is most useful for sensitizing analysis to certain complex dynamics of social processes, rather than for deriving formally testable propositions – thus its usefulness in the end will be judged in terms of whether it opens up analysis to productive interrogation. Secondly, Critical Theory is deployed here in ways which seem appropriate to the material in question, and ultimately whether or not it is used in a way which is 'faithful' to Marx, Adorno or Habermas, etc. is quite unimportant. The intention is to push Critical Theory more clearly into engagement with political practices and to clarify the kinds of issues that a critical theory needs to resolve – both about itself and about the external world – if it is to critically address the contemporary reality.

Notes

1. According to Honneth and Joas, 'anyone participating in debate today with nothing . . . to say about this great figure [Habermas] excludes him/herself from the ranks of serious theorists' (1991: 2). Well, no doubt we all wish that our theoretical preferences were more widely shared, but exclusionary practices are hardly in keeping with the spirit of communicative openness!

2. Eurocommunism was premised on the possibility of a 'proletarian' (actually Party) hegemony over broad-based popular movements, a strategy articulated by post-Poulantzian writers such as Laclau and Mouffe, and justified by the assertion that the contradiction between capital and labour had been superseded by that between state monopoly capitalism and 'the people'. With the electoral collapse of the French and later the Italian Communist Parties in the late 1970s, and the departure of droves of intellectuals from their ranks, this 'popular frontism' gave way to a displacement of class struggle from the object of practice, the proletariat becoming one fractured social actor amongst others (in particular the 'new' technical petite bourgeoisie). See Raulet (1983) or Smart (1983).

3. Actually there is plenty of evidence that Marx eschewed the kind of historicism attributed to him by Lyotard and others. For example, 'History does nothing; it possesses no

colossal riches, it "fights no fight". It is rather man, real, living man, who acts, possesses and fights . . . . History is nothing but the activity of man in pursuit of . . . ends' (*The Holy Family* in Marx (1977: 134)). Or his later comment that Darwin's importance was the 'death-blow dealt here . . . to "teleology" in the natural sciences' (letter to Lassalle, 1862 in Marx (1977: 525)).

4. See the somewhat acrimonious debate around Laclau and Mouffe's *Hegemony and Socialist Strategy* (1985) (Geras, 1987, 1988; Laclau & Mouffe 1985; Mouzelis, 1988). Mouzelis (1990) offers a 'non-reductionist Marxism based on the concept of a mode of domination' which he hopes will resolve this controversy. This sees all social institutions as constituted by technologies, structures of appropriation and legitimating ideologies.

5. Indeed, Samir Amin suggests that if social totality is conceived in terms of three dimensions of the economic, political and cultural, one could credit historical materialism with having a theory of the social struggles that underlie economic choices, and an undeveloped concept of the political, but 'as for the cultural dimension, it remains mysterious and unknown' (1989: 5).

6. See also Thompson (1967).

7. This thesis has of course been subject to six decades of continuous controversy which is beyond the scope of this argument. A serious misunderstanding of Weber's thesis, however, is that it attempted to establish the priority of ideational factors over material ones, an interpretation against which he warned readers in the closing paragraph of the final essay in *The Protestant Ethic and the Spirit of Capitalism* (1974). See Ray (1986).

8. Weber's *Economic History* (1981) largely follows Marx in describing the material preconditions for capitalism, whilst Marx himself was aware of the connection between Calvinism and capitalism (see Marx & Engels, 1974).

9. Weber's concept of rationalization is complex. First, it refers to the shaping of all scientific practice according to the model of the natural sciences, and the extension of scientific rationality to 'the conduct of life itself'. Secondly, this is part of the secularization of the modern world, which Weber described as 'disenchantment'. Thirdly, secularization leads to the growth of means–end rationality, whereby social action is increasingly given over to the calculation of means to the attainment of specific goals. Fourthly, there is a growth of rationality in ethics, which are systematically orientated to fixed goals. These are forms of action generally associated with the rise of the market and a capitalist economy. It is crucial to the development of Habermas' theory that Weber argued (e.g. in the *Protestant Ethic* essays) that the rationalization of world-views (e.g. the Protestant Reformation) preceded and created the conditions for the rise of capitalism.

10. In line with world systems theory, the periphery and semi-periphery are understood as regions outside the organic core of early industrializing nations – North America, Western Europe, Australia and New Zealand, and the newly industrialized Pacific Rim (especially Japan). From this perspective, the former socialist bloc, although industrialized, is viewed as occupying a semi-peripheral relation in structural terms.

11. Relative inequalities in per capita GDP between the organic core regions and the periphery have increased by factors of 1.8 in Latin America (2.4 excluding Brazil), 2.6 in South East Asia, 2.7 in the Middle East and North Africa, 4.1 in Southern and Central Africa and 4.6 in South Asia (Arrighi, 1991).

PART 1

1

Authority and Tradition

This chapter discusses some key features of early Frankfurt Institute thought[1] in order to set Habermas' critique in context. Habermas' objection to Adorno and Horkheimer is essentially that they too readily accepted Weber's critique of rationalization, which they generalized into a world-historical condition, so precluding any emancipatory outcome from the present. This left to Critical Theory the task of seeking out the last, tenuous reminiscences of harmony between nature, life and expressive culture (a harmony Adorno called 'mimesis').[2] There is some controversy over this interpretation – with Robert Hullot-Kentor, for example, claiming that, 'as Habermas has become more powerful [in Frankfurt] he has become increasingly confident in making completely implausible claims about Adorno . . . [for example] that the *Dialectic of Enlightenment* was a repudiation of reason when in fact it was a recuperation' (1989). Again, Frederic Jameson argues that *Dialectic of Enlightenment* (hereafter *DoE*) is an 'alternate rewriting of social history in terms of natural history [that is, social relations with nature] which leaves Marxism intact'. Adorno was 'more Marxist than conventional Marxists' in that dialectical reason was premised upon a social organization of future reconciliation (an emancipated society) until which time the resolution of philosophical problems would have to await solution (Jameson 1990: 230–1).

This claim is certainly defensible, but even so they were rather odd 'Marxists'. The indefinite postponement of emancipation left only two options for the critical intellectual. One was to 'lead a private life, as far as the social order . . . will tolerate nothing else' (Adorno, 1974: 39). The other was to find a kind of personal authenticity through critical reflection, to 'lend suffering a voice', by fashioning perspectives which 'displace and estrange the world, reveal it to be, with its rifts and crevices, as indigent and distorted as it will appear one day in the messianic light' (Adorno, 1974: 247). The latter places emancipation beyond the realm of the imaginable present, and is closer to what Loewy describes as 'revolutionary romanticism' than to Marxism.[3] An engaged Critical Theory, then, might give the Habermasian project a chance of proving itself, although it will be suggested that Habermas has accepted more of earlier Critical Theory than one might at first imagine.

Culture, Reification and Resignation

The new techniques of regulation and social integration created a situation largely unanticipated by Marx. The proletariat, which was to have been the bearer of universalism and justice, had been defeated, or incorporated within mass consumer culture, bureaucratic trade unions and increasingly sophisticated techniques of regulation and integration. Early Critical Theory responded with a theory of false consciousness, and a psycho-social account of mass society, both of which drew upon the Romantic critique of capitalism. Initially, however, Horkheimer remained broadly within a Marxist frame of reference,[4] and as late as 1940 invoked the 'trailblazing' tradition of workers' councils going back to 1871. Impatient with Marxist orthodoxy's notions of 'mature conditions' for revolution, he claimed that

> it might be said of past historical enterprises that the time was not yet ripe for them. Present talk of inadequate conditions is a cover for the tolerance of oppression. For the revolutionary, conditions have always been ripe. . . . A revolutionary is with the desperate people for whom everything is on the line, not with those who have time. (Horkheimer, 1973)

The corollary of this spontaneity, however, is the privileging of consciousness as the decisive factor in revolutionary mobilization, combined with implied contempt for the masses, who allow themselves to be duped by the manipulative lure of popular culture, consumerism and the appeal of demagogic leaders. In the *Dämmerung* (Twilight) collection of essays (1926–31) Horkheimer suggested that there was a multitude of 'subtle apparatuses' (such as education or the mass media) working to protect the 'swaying gods' of capitalism against the consciousness of the masses, which 'herald the night of humanity' (1974a). After the Holocaust, the night of humanity, the critique of mass culture which had always been present in Frankfurt thinking became central to Adorno and Horkheimer's analysis, and in *DoE* the whole trajectory of modern reason points towards mass destruction. Universalism gives way to authoritarianism, the Marxist/ modernist project runs aground in the grotesque caricature of Stalinism, and scientific and cultural advance produces the extermination chambers and the neutron bomb. In the liberal democracies, moreover, soporific popular culture is not as innocently facile as it seemed, since this too is the harbinger of new barbarity.

Two dominant themes in this critique are mass society and the effects of scientific and technological domination of nature. The mass society thesis was originally formulated by conservative thinkers such as Le Bon, Ortega y Gasset and Heidegger.[5] Gasset, for example, in *The Revolt of the Masses* (1951) claimed that liberal democracy, built upon the rapid expansion of scientific and technical knowledge, is simply a mass of primitive, uncultured and atavistic mediocrities whose lives are informed no longer by the civilizing influence of traditional culture, but rather by the pragmatic values of modern technology. For Adorno and Horkheimer, mass society was understood sociologically as lacking strong independent social groups and institutions, in which the population grows passive, indifferent and atomized; where traditional loyalties, ties and associations become weak; and coherent publics based on definite interests and opinions gradually disintegrate permitting domination from above, especially by the culture industry. Adorno (1982: 60), for example, cited Spengler's reference to 'a reading mass that storms through the streets', in support of the view that mass literacy had increased popular susceptibility to fascist manipulation. However, the conservatism of the original thesis is given an ironic twist, since

> The sociological theory that the loss of the support of objectively established religion, the dissolution of the last remnants of precapitalism, together with technological and social differentiation or specialization, have led to cultural chaos is disproved every day; for culture now impresses the same stamp on everything. (Adorno, 1974: 120)

In place of predicted cultural chaos, in other words, there was the regimentation of a totally administered society. Even so, the conservative critique of mass culture, albeit used ironically, reflects Adorno and Horkheimer's view that underlying the malaise of modernity was a loss of high culture, a view which conservatives and Romantics had been advancing since the early nineteenth century. Indeed, it could be argued that the opposition between Enlightenment optimism, found in the progressive expansion of technology and reason, and the Romantic sense of lost harmony and meaning (*Bedeutsamkeit*) which had supposedly characterized pre-industrial societies, has occupied a central place in disputes about modernity over the past century and a half.[6]

Adorno and Horkheimer *did* distance themselves from Romanticism, arguing that the past could never be recovered:

> We are the heirs, for better or for worse, of the Enlightenment and technological progress. To oppose these by regressing to more primitive stages does not alleviate the permanent crisis they have brought about. On the contrary, such experiments lead from historically reasonable to utterly barbaric forms of social domination. (Horkheimer 1974b: 127)

However, with no way forward to a more progressive future, and yet no way back to a lost sensibility and sensuality, Frankfurt Institute theorists 'viewed the past with a melancholy nostalgia' (Friedman, 1981: 67). This was an ambivalence they shared with Simmel or Weber, for whom modernity was double-edged, in that increases in personal freedom and scientific advance involved the cost of loss of meaning and sensibility.[7] Aspects of this diagnosis of modernity appear too in the early Lukács,[8] who also placed the critique of reification (*Verdinglichung*) at the centre of analysis, although with different emphasis.[9] Like Adorno/Horkheimer, Lukács concentrated on commodification as the defining character of modernity, but his critique suggested that as a result of the complex integration of mass production (described by Marx as 'detail labour') the consciousness of the proletariat was fragmented, rendering the historical dynamic of capitalism opaque. Meanwhile, drawing implicitly on Simmel,

Lukács suggested that the commodity form had broken beyond the bounds of the labour process and entered all cultural forms, such that capitalist social relations took on a false appearance of facticity, or reification.

However, Adorno and Horkheimer understood reification more in terms of the culture industry, which, being geared to mass markets, permitted the commodity form to enter the very process of creation or composition, though again the central idea is the way reified consciousness has occluded critical reflection. In his 'Perennial Fashion-Jazz' for example, Adorno made four claims. First, that jazz never disturbs the crude unity of its basic rhythm, its improvisations are frills that rehash basic formulae. Secondly, whilst competition in the culture market has produced effective techniques, it has also produced standardization and domination by fads. Thirdly, that jazz establishes a 'vague and inarticulate' division between experts and the mass, which 'recalls the brutal seriousness of the mass of followers in totalitarian states' (1982: 129); and, finally, that the aim of jazz technique is mechanical reproduction of a regressive moment, the 'false liquidation of art' (1982: 132). In other words, by degrading aesthetic harmony, popular music eliminates the critical potential which Adorno believed was inherent in authentic art.[10]

The separation of theory and action, then, had 'become an historical phenomenon' (Horkheimer, 1972: 4) and Lukács' view, that the ideal-typical consciousness of the proletariat resided in the Communist Party, offered no solution. Thus Adorno and Horkheimer sought 'traces' or 'reminiscences' of non-oppressive life in areas of culture still preserved from the commodity form. 'In Adorno's work', says Huyssen, 'the locus of *Vernunft* [critical reason] was the modernist aesthetic, the vantage point from which he radically criticized modernization . . . art and literature were the last refuge of truth and the utopia of redemption' (Huyssen, 1981). Adorno privileged the aesthetic since this permitted a *sense* of disharmonious contradiction which eluded discursive analysis. This critical tension could be located in avant-garde artistic forms, such as Schoenberg's atonal music – the criterion of revolutionary art was that it demanded not contemplation, but praxis; like the Jewish song which concludes the 'Survivor from Warsaw' Schoenberg's music represents the protest of humanity against myth (Adorno, 1982: 172).

The second theme, critique of science and technology, in some ways points towards more recent eco-Marxism[11] as well as a more general anti-positivist epistemology. A common Romantic myth in the nineteenth century, which was enduringly captured in Mary Shelley's *Frankenstein*, was that science would unwittingly invite its own self-destruction. Stewart Clegg (1991) notes that Weber's iron cage of bureaucracy is in some ways a replaying of this myth, and the same could probably be said of the later Adorno and Horkheimer too. Just as Weber had identified rationalization as movement of *longue durée* with its roots in the ancient world, so Adorno and Horkheimer claimed that the 'bourgeois mode of production goes incomparably further back than historians who date the notion of the *burger* only from the end of medieval feudalism would allow' (1973: 45). In German philosophy, the Homeric Odyssey was often thought to anticipate the ideal unity of subject and object (Held, 1980: 43), but in Adorno and Horkheimer it became a tale of the origin of the autonomous, repressive subject. Their Odysseus was the 'proto-type bourgeois individual', whose voyage from Troy to Ithaca epitomizes a 'rational' exchange between survival and renunciation. Like that other lone hero, Robinson Crusoe, Odysseus survives at the expense of the alienation of aboriginal people and nature, whilst both stories express the capitalist ethic of profit as the reward for risk (each traveller after all could have perished against the breakers). Odysseus deploys calculating reason against myth (which symbolizes both nature and pre-modern peoples) out of which is born the modern calculating ego, and the alienation of crews, servants and labourers. The famous encounter with the Sirens illustrates how social domination is already implied in domination over nature, in that Odysseus treated his crew as he treated his knowledge of the weather, as a means to an end. The establishment of a peculiarly modern form of domination, between mental and manual labour, and between high and popular culture, occurs in the sequence where Odysseus is tied to the mast, unable to steer, whilst the crew, their ears plugged with wax, continue rowing, oblivious to the music. Here the enjoyment of art and manual labour break apart as the world of prehistory is left behind.

This draws heavily on the Romantic critique of Enlightenment, and Adorno and Horkheimer contrast intuitive reason against the cold domination of science, which

> does not work by concepts and images, by . . . fortunate insight, but refers to method, the exploitation of other's work and capital. . . . What men want to learn from Nature is how to use it in order wholly to dominate it and other men. That is the only aim . . . for the enlightenment, whatever does not conform to the rule of computation and utility is suspect. . . . Enlightenment is totalitarian. (Adorno & Horkheimer 1973: 6)

Such appeals to intuitive, non-rational, or at any rate non-discursive, forms of argumentation were to draw the criticism that they had given up on the progressive potential of Enlightenment.

Authoritarian Conflict Displacement

Aspects of both themes, critique of mass society and of technology, inform Adorno and Horkheimer's analysis of the authoritarian state. The culture industry was one aspect of the ability of the capitalist system to neutralize conflict and potential subversion, and another was the mobilization of authoritarian mass movements. The analysis of the authoritarian state was one of the most significant theories to emerge from the Frankfurt Institute, and opens the way to an understanding of the dynamics of contemporary social movements in the context of the psycho-social bases of authority. The Institute's members were in broad agreement that the causes of

Rethinking Critical Theory

fascism were closely connected to the inner dynamics of capitalism ('he who does not wish to speak of capitalism should be silent about fascism', as Horkheimer put it) but exactly how they were related was a source of controversy. On the one hand, Neumann, Marcuse and Kirchheimer argued that fascism completed in the political sphere what monopolization and cartelization had already achieved in the economy. In *Behemoth* Neumann argued that a highly monopolized system must be hypersensitive to cyclical changes, and that if the labour market were not controlled by authoritarian means, if raw material supply, price control, and credit and exchange-control offices were in hands hostile to monopolies, then its survival would be threatened. 'In short, democracy would endanger the fully monopolized system' (Neumann, 1944: 290). On the other hand, Adorno, Horkheimer and Pollock, argued that the authoritarian state represented the appearance of a new social formation, a 'post-market society', following Pollock's work on state capitalism. The latter was defined as a social formation where the substitution of the market by state planning turns prices into an administrative tool, turns the capitalist into a rentier (dependent on state policy and contracts) and bureaucratic management takes the place of market-led investment decisions. State capitalism could take either 'democratic' (as in the New Deal) or 'totalitarian' (fascist) forms, but, either way, 'today the forces of production and the relations of production are one . . . material production, distribution, and consumption are ruled together' (Adorno, 1974: 165). Politics was in command (Postone & Brick, 1982).

Much of the ensuing controversy surrounded Pollock's claim (which Adorno and Horkheimer shared with reservations) that state capitalism, in either form, could regulate class conflict and thus ensure its rule for the foreseeable future.[12] However, Adorno and Horkheimer went beyond both sides of the debate, and blended Weberian analysis of bureaucratization with psychoanalysis, to claim that irrationality and violence were inherent in the very genesis of the modern state. Linking these with the mass society thesis, they identified a tendency towards authoritarian politics – a kind of totalitarian drift – within bourgeois society which arose from the deep psychological and social frustrations which bourgeois politics could mobilize.

To appreciate the logic of their thought one needs to understand how, like Weber, they believed that modernity entailed a loss of meaning, a kind of permanent legitimation crisis. The potential force of critical reason, had it been permitted to develop unhindered, would have subjected all unreasonable systems of domination to critique. As Albrect Wellmer put it, Enlightenment demands 'the abrogation of all repressive conditions that could claim no legitimacy other than their sheer existence' (1971: 46). Implicit in this claim was the view that the critique of metaphysical worldviews releases the critical capacity of reason (an idea that later became central to Habermas' theory, although with more promising conclusions). From this it follows that a post-Enlightenment social order is bereft of ultimate sources of legitimation, and could be threatened if it is unable to provide reasonable grounds for citizens' acquiescence to authority. However, this critical potential, manifest in the so-called 'bourgeois' republican and democratic revolutions of the past two centuries, was eclipsed by authoritarianism which from Robespierre through to fascism arose within the context of the modern state. One explanation which Adorno and Horkheimer offer for this is that Enlightenment was incomplete, forced back on to an alliance with traditionalism. Hence, 'the anti-authoritarian principle has to change into its very antithesis – into opposition to reason . . . which allows domination to ordain as sovereign and to manipulate whatever bonds and obligations prove appropriate' (1973: 93).

In removing the obstacles to the market and development of productive forces, the bourgeoisie de-mythologized all previous taboos and bonds of sentiment.[13] However, the liberation of critical reason from the constraints of tradition threatened the existing social order and ultimately the bourgeoisie itself. For example, in the late eighteenth century Mary Wollstonecraft turned the Enlightenment critique of domination against the concepts of public and private domains which were central to bourgeois political philosophy. She argued that there could be no progressive development without a restructuring of private relations, and that this in turn presupposed the transformation of government institutions. Public virtue cannot be achieved until 'the tyranny of man' is ended, thus the emancipation of women is a critical condition of liberty in a rational and moral order (Wollstonecraft, 1982: 318). Following the Enlightenment's commitment to reason she argued that oppression of women could not ultimately withstand the force of rational critique.

This Enlightenment potential, to turn critique against fundamental social relations, was blocked and reason retreated, to permit the reappearance of domination in new forms. Even so, having undermined traditional world-views, the post-Enlightenment social order was deprived of legitimating myths (religion and sacred authority) thus domination appeared within a 'rational' form. For this to happen the compass of rational reflection had to be restricted from critical reason (*Vernunft*) to mere instrumental rationality (*Verstand*). As Weber had indicated, the latter could not provide grounds for civic virtue, and the only rational motive bourgeois society would recognize was the paltry ethics of utilitarianism. Silent about its own domination, and unable to justify even its meagre ethics, Enlightenment in this truncated form left the way open for the return of myth, and the manipulation of traditionalistic bonds and obligations. By admitting no public rationality other than self-interest, questions of fundamental value got shunted off into the 'irrational' realm of personal ethics and private associations, thus escaping public scrutiny.

However, this displacement was unsuccessful, and irrationality returned with a vengeance in authoritarian mass movements. The crucial thing about fascistic regimes was not just their ability to suppress opposition, but their capacity to generate mass support. As Weber noted in his discussion of 'plebiscitary democracy' (*Führer Demokratie*), dictators who emerged in revolutions of the ancient world and modern times (such as Cromwell or Robespierre) sought legitimacy through plebiscite and the recruitment of personal staff, opening avenues of rapid social mobility for 'able people of humble origin' (creating a loyal cadre stratum). Thus whilst destroying traditional, feudal, patrimonial and other types of authoritarian powers and privileges, plebiscitary democracies create economic interests which are bound up with the regime. Meanwhile the legacy of revolutionary or anti-colonial struggle legitimates (at least for a time) a terroristic Jacobin dictatorship, freed from formal procedures, as is the case with revolutionary tribunals, war-time rationing and other cases of limited and controlled production and consumption. (Weber, 1978: I, 270).

In 'Egoism and the Freedom Movement' (1982–3; originally published 1936) Horkheimer develops this analysis in ways which will be relevant for understanding populist movements such as Islamic revivalism. Horkheimer makes three claims in particular.[14] First, revolutionary populism combines defence of tradition with ideological innovation, thus early modern charismatic leaders such as Luther attempted to 're-introduce old customs and to refurbish the glory of antiquity'. Secondly, the bourgeois order establishes a regime of instinctual renunciation, since the dominance of the commodity form ('the narrow egoistic practice in the market place') enters into conflict with the desire for 'happiness' (which Horkheimer understands in the psychoanalytic sense of carefree pleasure, love, libido).[15] Renunciation creates a hypocritical public culture where bourgeois moral asceticism contrasts with 'narrow-minded obscenity and prostitution'. This contradiction between moralism and happiness is manipulated by charismatic mass movements which invoke a 'pathos of justice accompanied by ascetic severity' and 'hostility to carefree pleasure' (1982–3). This leads to the third claim, namely that sado-masochistic dependence cemented relations between charismatic leaders and their followers. Authoritarianism harnessed psychical energies in which repression of desire produced a vicarious enjoyment of the cruelty of the charismatic leader, whose terror pursued a 'rarely admitted' intention to satisfy his own followers by unleashing aggression, for example in war and national mobilization (and especially against 'enemies within'). The Leader permits followers to vicariously participate in the brutality, thus he must appear both as heroic, an exceptional individual, and as a figure with whom people can identify, as one of the 'plain folks'.

In Adorno and Horkheimer's analysis of antisemitism, the mass society thesis was complemented with class analysis, since it was the petite-bourgeoisie, squeezed between monopoly capital and imminent proletarianization, who experienced the full force of psychical repression. By the late 1930s, Adorno/Horkheimer had developed beyond more common accounts of antisemitism as scapegoating to suggest a deep mechanism of psycho-cultural violence, since charismatic leaders appeal to a personality type which is inwardly rebellious but impotent (the infamous 'authoritarian personality'). Politics becomes a struggle between morally irreconcilable forces, where opponents are leagued in secret conspiracy (for example, the 'world Jewish-capitalist-Bolshevik conspiracy'). This generalized paranoia, where all power in a hostile world is concentrated in a few hands, effects a cognitive simplification of repressed psychic conflicts and thus relieves the tension of unconscious ambivalence. Horkheimer had said that 'The concept of the alien becomes synonymous with that of the forbidden', behind petit-bourgeois 'rage over Jewish immorality . . . is hidden a deep erotic resentment which demands the death of its representatives' (1982–3: 53). Or again, the 'masses suppress happiness' but any reminiscence of this loss 'draws down upon itself the destructive lust of the "civilized" '. Thus the 'illusory conspiracy of corrupt Jewish bankers financing Bolshevism is a sign of innate impotence, just as the good life is a sign of happiness' (Horkheimer, 1973: 172).[16]

In other words, capitalism creates dull cultural homogeneity and a denial of pleasure, the result of which is that the repressed longing for a fuller life is turned into aggression directed against Jewishness, which serves as a symbol both of diversity (the forbidden 'otherness') and of modernity itself. Again the latter idea was articulated by Simmel, who argued that financial institutions became associated with foreignness, hence the 'hatred of national sentiment against internationalism, the opposition of one-sidedness which, being aware of its specific value, feels overpowered by an indifferent, characterless force whose essence seems to be personified by strangers' (1990: 226–7). The Jew comes to be both the symbol of modernity (the money economy) and the object of anti-cosmopolitan revolt against colourless egotism. Indeed, Jews were 'the very epitome of Simmel's strangers – always on the outside even when inside' (Bauman, 1989a: 53). This was paradoxical, however, since, as Bauman says, the identification of Jewishness with modernity allowed 'anti-modernist phobias to be unloaded through . . . forms only modernity could develop' (1989a: 46).

As an explanation of fascism this thesis has come under extensive empirical criticism (Kershaw, 1989: Chapter 2), especially concerning the importance of petit-bourgeois support for the Nazis. At most the theory offers an account of predispositions for supporting authoritarian move-ments, and does not address the conditions for their mobilization or the conditions for resistance and disenchantment with populist leaders, which sets in sooner or later.[17] Further, as many commentators have argued, the thesis is overly psychologistic. Adorno and Horkheimer's account of prejudice is premised on the psychoanalytical projection theory, in which emotional ambivalence (the love/hatred syndrome) is converted into cognitive simplicity (antisemitic stereotypes). More recent studies have pointed to the complexity of prejudiced belief systems where ambivalence that is projected on to 'the enemy' reproduces rather than simplifies unconscious conflicts. For example, the antisemitic stereotype displays fear and admiration for Jews, attributing both base characteristics (greed, duplicity etc.) but also extensive power (for example, the 'world Zionist-Bolshevik-Finance conspiracy': Billig, 1978, 1982).[18] Further, this suggests that conspiracy theories are best understood as cognitive world-views, in which antisemitism counters the complexity and unpredictability of modern social systems by personalizing power and simplifying politics. Power is personalized in that an identifiable group is held responsible for every alleged misfortune (and addresses the interrogative question 'Why has this happened?'). It simplifies politics by appeal to the *Führerprinzip*, according to which strong government and rooting out 'enemies within' solves complex problems.[19] In these senses, antisemitism or other conspiracy theories are discursive systems of thought, cognitively articulated and understood, rather than projections of unconscious conflicts.

However, viewed in the broader context of Adorno and Horkheimer's work this account suggests a subtle model of social regulation, in which deep-seated social conflicts are displaced into private spheres removed from critical scrutiny. These repressed energies then provide a mobilizing resource for populist social movements which generally invoke a heroic ideology of self-sacrifice for the Cause. This kind of authoritarian populism might have an apparently revolutionary character, and might be an agent of modernization, but is deeply ambivalent towards modernity and often gives rise to quasi-traditional forms of politcal clientelism (which could be said of Soviet as well as other forms of authoritarianism). This is a theme to which the subsequent discussion will repeatedly return.

Moreover, *DoE* still reads as a powerfully trenchant critique of violence and oppression, and Kate Soper (1989) suggests that there is 'distinct family resemblance' between recent feminist critiques of mainstream epistemology and Adorno's polemic. For Adorno and Horkheimer the birth of the modern was accompanied by new patriarchal violence. The witchcraft trials, coinciding with the explosion of modern science, served to celebrate and confirm the triumph of male society over prehistoric matriarchal and mimetic stages of development (1973: 248). Likewise, Merchant (1983) claims that with the rise of new science and technology (and male scientists as the new high priests) the destruction of nature as an organism had a parallel in the violent attack on women during the witch-crazes between the fifteenth and seventeenth centuries. Similarly, Mies argues that 'we cannot understand . . . our present problems unless we include all those who were "defined into a nature" by the modern capitalist patriarchs: Mother Earth, Women and Colonies' (1989: 74–5).

The bourgeoisie profited from female chastity and propriety (which had pre-capitalist origins) in that women appear in bourgeois society to be vanquished, subsumed under the sign of 'beauty'. 'Behind male admiration of beauty . . . lurks always the ribald laughter, the withering scorn, the barbaric obscenity with which strength greets weakness' (Adorno & Horkheimer, 1973: 249). More recently, Ehrenreich and English (1973) argued that whereas the old patriarchal societies of Asia were 'gynocentric', in that women, though exploited, were crucially important as mothers of sons, with the rise of capitalism as a world-system, nature and col[e] people were placed beyond 'civilized society'.

However, to say that early Critical Theory anticipated some themes or later feminism is not to say that Adorno and Horkheimer had an adequate theory of patriarchy. Jessica Benjamin (1978) argues that Adorno and Horkheimer sacrifice their analysis of the relationship between destructive rationality and nature when they move to discuss present-day conformism. This is because their theory of ego-weakness is dependent on the disputable thesis of the decline of the patriarchal father, made redundant by monopoly capitalism. This, they believed, inhibits moral autonomy, since one must have internalized a strong authority figure to engage in self-reflection which is the condition of emancipation.[20] Not only this, but *DoE*, like Romantic critiques of science and mass society, is premised on the notion of a Fall from totality, rather than an immanent connection with the present. Golden Ages are myths and such a critique hardly addresses struggles within the present for attainable objectives of emancipation. Further, to contrast an alienating and often destructive technological culture with its apparent antithesis in the form of intuitive or non-discursive reasoning is to miss the possibility that there might be an alternative reason which is non-oppressive yet discursive and non-intuitive. This, indeed, is the gist of Habermas' critique, which occupies most of Part 1.

Habermas' Critique

Roughly speaking, it might be said that what divides Habermas from earlier Critical Theory is the former's insistence on what Benhabib calls 'normative critique' as opposed to 'utopian transfiguration'. The former, she suggests, is directed towards fulfilment of what is promised by the official values of society but remains unfulfilled, such as gender equality, or minority groups' civil rights. The latter refers to 'qualitatively new needs, social relations and modes of association' which open up utopian potential as a condition for emancipation (Benhabib, 1986: 14). The latter has also been critically described as the 'politics of redemption', involving 'imma-ture' antimodernist romanticism and totalitarian leanings towards total social reconstruction, as opposed to 'mature' realism about attainable objectives and plural democratic practice (for example, Feher & Heller, 1986; Jay, 1988: 120). Unlike earlier Critical Theory, Habermas' politics are those of fulfilment rather than redemption in that his project for Critical Theory involves completing the still unfulfilled potential of modernity. Even so, his Critical Theory does in a sense draw its legit-imation from a redemptive potential implicit in linguistic communication (which will be seen in Chapter 2).

In *The Philosophical Discourse of Modernity* (1987) Habermas attempts to demonstrate, first, that Adorno and Horkheimer's critique was depen-dent upon Weber's analysis of rationalization; secondly, that Weber's analysis was flawed because it failed to make a distinction between two types of rationalization, instrumentality and the potential for post-traditional ethics; and, thirdly, that therefore Adorno and Horkheimer's cultural pessimism must also be flawed. Habermas' Weber-critique in general will be examined later, but for the moment let us look at his specific criticisms of *DoE*.

Habermas (1982a) argues that in the 1940s Critical Theory entered a political cul-de-sac, in which the possibility of emancipation appeared only as a critical device, or 'regulative principle'. Indeed, for Habermas (1984: 144), Adorno went further than Weber (whose view was ambivalent) in rejecting the consequences of rationalization, since in *DoE* science and technology become media of social repression and are indistinguishable from class domination. This for Habermas is 'a vague notion of an encompassing societal rationality' not sufficiently nuanced to capture the various meanings which rationalization can have (an important point in Habermas' rewriting of Critical Theory).

This 'Weberian thorn still in Critical Theory' (Habermas, 1984: 378) cannot be renewed; it has outlived its own claims because of its attachment to the 'philosophy of consciousness'. The central concept of reification and the proletariat as a (failed) philosophical-subject was woven into a Romantic critique of modernity. Thus a particular configuration of the learning potential of capitalism, bureaucratic rationality and commodification, was mistaken for a complete resolution of its contradictions (another important point). Adorno and Horkheimer are accused of idealism in detaching the concept of reification from exchange value, that is, modern capitalism, and abstracting it to the ahistorical anthropological foundation of the species, the very process of labour itself.

Adorno's inability to elucidate the mimetic impulse leads to Habermas' central objection to Adorno, namely that he abandons the ground of critical rationality and gives up on the 'unfulfilled potential' of western modernity, with three consequences. First, for Adorno and Horkheimer as for Nietzsche or Foucault, the only residual source of truth lies in the mimetic impulse, which cannot be theorized but is none the less the (unexplicated) basis for reconciliation with nature. Critique can only show why mimetic capacity slips from our theoretical grasp and finds refuge in advanced works of art. Thus any attempt to develop a theory would side off into relativism. All that is left is uninhibited scepticism, the consequence of which is that philosophy loses its differentiated space as 'guardian of reason' (Habermas, 1987: 195). Similarly, Benhabib (1981) warns that by simply lamenting the lost opportunity for emancipation, Critical Theory might be no more than a 'messenger of the apocalypse'. From this follows Habermas' second objection, that *DoE* entails a 'performative contradiction' by denouncing what it must none the less assume, namely the critical potential of Enlightenment. This is contradictory because 'if they [Adorno and Horkheimer] . . . still want to continue with critique they will have to leave at least one rational criterion intact for their explanation of the corruption of *all* rational criteria' (Habermas, 1987: 113). The critique of reason gets sucked into a whirlpool of relativism, because it cannot provide any standard against which its own position might be justified.

Most important, however, Habermas' third objection is that Adorno and Horkheimer show an 'unexplained lack of concern in dealing with the achievements of Occidental rationalism'. Under the influence of Nietzsche they were

> Careless of the achievements of Western rationalism the . . . internal theoretical dynamic which constantly propels the sciences . . . the universalistic foundations of law and morality that have been also incorporated . . . into the institutions of constitutional government, into forms of democratic will formation and into patterns of identity formation . . . etc. (Habermas, 1987: 113)

Habermas uses his critique of *DoE* as a vehicle for reiterating his own conception of the values that are at the core of modern communicative discourse. In fact he suggests that Adorno's vague concepts of reconciliation and freedom can be 'deciphered as codes for a form of intersubjectivity' (Habermas, 1984: 391). That is, the Weberian blind alley into which Critical Theory became stuck in *DoE* can be opened

> only if we give up the paradigm of the philosophy of consciousness – namely, a subject that represents objects and toils with them – in favour of the paradigm of linguistic philosophy – namely, that of intersubjective understanding or communication – and put the cognitive instrumental aspect of reason in its proper place as part of a more encompassing communicative rationality. (Habermas 1984: 390)[21]

This critique is in some ways a recapitulation of Habermas' earlier arguments against Marcuse's notion of the New Science and New Technology. Marcuse had adapted Adorno and Horkheimer's critique of Enlightenment to the counter-cultural politics of the 1960s, against which Habermas had offered a limited defence of science and technology informed by Luhmann's concept of 'system boundaries'. The gist of Habermas' argument was that scientific and technological knowledge were not per se harbingers of domination, but rather the danger arose from the inappropriate application of technological reason to questions of value and politics (Stockman, 1983). To convert political and moral value choices into technological goals represented an erosion of the public domain, and indicated covert political domination through technical rationality (Habermas, 1974). An example of this would be the 'medicalization of everyday life', whereby the medical profession acquires the power to arbitrate on matters of ethical and personal choice, a thesis developed by Beck (1992: 204–12) in relation to reproductive and genetic technologies.[22]

Habermas' critique of Adorno and Horkheimer *is* rather heavy-handed and gives short shrift to Adorno's dialectical method, which continually challenges its own results, producing an elliptical text which on superficial reading might appear contradictory. Further, the emancipatory possibility which had vanished in *DoE* returns in Adorno's later work, if only tentatively; for example, 'Rationality is not true and universal until it has stopped subjugating individual being. . . . The establishment of a rational public order hinges on the resistance by conscious individuals, to organization', a possibility which Adorno has clearly not precluded (1984: 422). Moreover, Habermas overlooks Adorno and Horkheimer's own critique of Weber, which his in some respects recapitulates, namely that, first, beneath the appearance of instrumental rationality there developed massive substantive irrationality; secondly, Weber could not conceive of an alternative to capitalism and equated instrumentality with rationality as such; and, thirdly, Weber's neo-Kantianism could not admit any rationality in the choice of ends, but only of means, a position which Adorno and Horkheimer condemned as 'decisionism'. It will be seen in Chapter 3 that Habermas takes issue with Weber on very similar grounds.

It is further worth noting that, notwithstanding his criticisms of earlier Critical Theory, Habermas accepts significant chunks of Adorno and Horkheimer's analytical framework – which Jeffrey Alexander (1991: 59) notes with dismay. In particular, Habermas accepts the notion of a dualistic modernity, bifurcated into action associated with (dominant) technocratic rationality and (suppressed) critical reason. The focus of his theory is 'modernity' as a process with a world-historical trajectory, against which class structures and conflicts occupy a subordinate role. This posture is defended, as it was in earlier Critical Theory, in terms of the political regulation of market forces. Like Adorno and Horkheimer, he regards monetary exchange (commodification) and reification as central analytical categories, rather than the production of value (which he subsumes within a theory of 'mediatization', as will be seen in Chapter 3). Further, he accepts (for example, in *Legitimation Crisis* [1976]) both that traditionalistic sources of meaning have been 'non-renewably dismantled' and that bourgeois world-views cannot in themselves legitimate the modern state ('To date, all attempts at rehabilitating world views have failed': Habermas, 1991: 224). Thus Habermas confronts the same question as occupied Critical Theory's analysis of the state – what are the bases of authority in a situation where traditional solidarity has been exhausted but where post-traditional structures of integration have yet to be established? His answer is different, though, in that it involves tracing the evolution of normative structures whereby authority comes to rest on assent (Habermas, 1989b: 38). Although he replaces Freudian theory with a theory of identity formation (1989b: 389), the Frankfurt Institute analysis of mass society and the displacement of anxiety turn up again in Habermas' concept of 'colonization of the lifeworld'. His theory of social pathologies, and of social movement formation as defence reactions, implicitly trade on the psycho-dynamics of affect and authority.

None the less, these observations should not be taken as minimizing the differences between earlier Critical Theory and the later Habermas. Moreover, Adorno and Horkheimer's thesis was inadequate on several grounds. Their application of the mass society thesis to late capitalism identified a general tendency expressed in the undifferentiated concept of 'totalitarianism', and the authoritarian state then expressed a uniform propensity implicit within all modern societies, irrespective of their manifestly different forms (the New Deal, the 'new Red despots' or fascism). The problem with this, as with later totalitarianism theories of the 1950s and 1960s, is that it could not account for the re-appearance of cultural protest or the new social movements later in the twentieth century (in both capitalism and state socialism).

Resistance and the State

The authoritarian state proper, the one-party monopolistic dictatorship, has tended to appear in the peripheries of developed capitalism (for example, Russia after 1917, Germany in 1933, or later post-colonial dependent societies). Here one finds a particularly explosive combination of violent modernization with traditionalism, against which the local state represents an authoritarian form of crisis regulation.[23] The totalitarian drift hypothesis was formulated in response to a historically specific phase in the restructuring of capitalism early in the twentieth century. As capitalism expanded, technologies of production and social regulation disarmed the proletariat through co-optation and differentiation. 'Fordist' productive organization was increasingly guided by technical and scientific research, state regulation, the reorganization of labour through scientific management, and professionalization in corporate institutions, all of which amounted to more intensive exploitation of labour and resources.[24]

These strategies evolved into the New Deal in the USA in the 1930s with collective bargaining through an administrative apparatus based on federal labour law, social security, consumer credit, home ownership and suburbanization, and corporate health delivery systems. This transition was further illustrated by Keynesian economics, which deployed sophisticated knowledge of fiscal and accumulation mechanisms to ward off cyclical crises by regulating demand. As late capitalism released newly available cultural potential for complex organization and technical innovation, it involved a combination of homogenization through mass popular culture, the privatization of public life (as career structure and personal consumption become central goals for millions of people) and generalized wage-labour to the point that it ceased to constitute the identity of a cohesive social group. Hence what Adorno and Horkheimer interpreted as the historical defeat of emancipatory possibilities was in fact the transitory effect of a particular mode of regulation. The fragmentation and displacement of contradictions which extended technical and managerial organization deep into previously non-commodified spheres resulted in the appearance of new crisis-logics.[25] These arose particularly at the margins of intensive capitalist development, where capitalism had eroded traditionalistic structures, seeking productive bases where costs were lower than in the highly capitalized sectors. This was dependent upon super-exploitation of low-wage sectors of predominantly feminized labour, relying on women's unpaid domestic labour in calculating the 'household wage', as well as expansion into the Third World.

However, this social order began to show signs of stress in 1968, with the worker occupations in France and West Germany, the (largely unrelated) counter-cultural movements, the civil rights and anti-war movements in the USA and the shaking of the French regime by the Paris students' revolt. Already this was far removed from a unidimensional society which could no longer be challenged except from the stand-point of cultural residues, aesthetics or Eros. But so committed had Critical Theory become to the quasi-Romantic critique of modernity that its practitioners either, like Adorno, reacted in horror or, like Marcuse saw this as the revolt of outcasts and self-exiled outsiders.[26] The perturbations of this transition, towards disorganized (Offe) or de-centralized modes of social regulation and capital accumulation, are still working themselves through, both in the core capitalist societies and in the peripheries. Thus one of the tasks of Critical Theory in this context is to identify the emergence of new articulations of protest and emancipation. In so doing, however, one should not lose sight of a central theme in earlier Critical Theory, namely the recuperative power of systems of domination to reproduce themselves through neutralizing and adjusting to social protest. The discussion of Habermas in the following two chapters will outline his efforts to link Critical Theory to the submerged emancipatory potential of modernity.

Notes

1. This will not provide an account of the origins of Frankfurt Institute thought – see, for example, Jay (1973), Held (1980), Buck-Morss (1977), Rose (1978) or Kellner (1989).

2. Underlying this was the classical concept of an original harmony between thought and action, aesthetics and life (*mimetikos*) which was fractured once nature became an object of production. For Adorno *mimetikos* was pre-conceptual – mimetic harmony could never be re-created but was none the less implied by the efforts of both art and science to capture, or 'identify', their object. Aesthetic form was a kind of 'last refuge' of mimesis, an impulse to resemble a reality which it was forced to transcend. For Jameson (1990: 64–5) mimesis is an underlying narrative, similar to that of childhood in psychoanalysis, the memory of which is therapeutic in its own right even though one cannot return there.

3. 'Revolutionary romanticism' is 'nostalgia for precapitalist societies and an ethico-social or cultural critique of capitalism' (Loewy, 1979: 9).

4. Seyla Benhabib (1986: 205) warns against confusing Horkheimer's pre-1937 essays with the psychoanalytical turn of *Dialectic of Enlightenment*, where the genesis of domination is pushed back to such a primordial level that critical categories can no longer be derived. See also Loewy (1982), Raulet (1979–80), Tar (1977: 203), Dews (1986), Dubiel (1985: 93), or almost any standard commentary.

5. For Adorno reactionary philosophers had often seen through the illusory veil of bourgeois society more effectively than liberals, thus Nietzsche is acknowledged as the 'most consistent enlightenment thinker' because he pushed the intention and meaning of Enlightenment to extremes, 'suggesting that truth, the idea of which triggers enlightenment, cannot exist without illusion, even though it consistently seeks to snuff out illusion for the sake of truth' (Adorno, 1984: 394).

6. This is not the place to examine the influence of Romantic philosophy in detail. Recent

studies include Gusdorf (1982) and Blumenberg (1985). George Friedman (1981) discusses the influence of Romanticism on Frankfurt Institute philosophy.

7. One could trace several lines of influence from Simmel through to Critical Theory. For instance, Simmel's fluid and fragmentary style is echoed later in both Adorno and Benjamin's cultural theory, or Adorno's concept of 'unintentional truth' (*intentionslosse Wahreit*), where inessential phenomena, of fashion or style, reveal universal constellations. In the atomized 'cool reserve and anonymous objectivity' in which only self-interest appears logical, Simmel (1990: 457) mourns a wholeness of meaning, whose tragic strain reappears in Critical Theory's aesthetic critique of modern culture.

8. Despite his often polemical denunciations of Simmel, Lukács acknowledged the former's influence on their generation of students, and that he 'saw Marx through spectacles tinged by Simmel . . . this approach brought me closer to Marx' (quoted by Tokei, 1972).

9. Joseph McCarney accurately detects a Lukácsian theme in Horkheimer's work in the 1930s, but regards Horkheimer's 1937 essay, 'Traditional and Critical Theory', as signalling the transition of Frankfurt Institute thought away from Marxism, since 'there is no social class by whose acceptance of the theory one could be guided' (McCarney, 1990: 166–7). But this transition had been made already in *History and Class Consciousness* (1968), indicated by Lukács' resort to the 'standpoint of the proletariat' embodied in the Communist Party, since this implicitly recognized that critique was henceforth dependent on outside agency rather than on the actual struggle of the proletariat.

10. Aesthetic experience is inherently critical, art 'criticizes society just by being there' since to lose oneself in great works of art is to experience the 'discomfiture, more precisely a tremor' of discovery that the truth embodied in the aesthetic has real possibilities (Adorno, 1984: 321, 346–7). By contrast, production for a mass market necessarily standardizes cultural products and reduces their aesthetic *form* to a lowest common denominator (irrespective of whether their *content* is critical). This process is at work in classical music too, where selected highlights from well-known pieces are marketed, which break up the form of the whole score. Adorno's reference to 'false liquidation' contrasts popular culture with the genuine super-session of art which would occur in an emancipated society.

11. Such as Rudolf Bahro (1984), who argues that ecology poses problems for Marxism that cannot be solved within the central elements of Marx's theory; or, conversely, Wolfdietrich Schmied-Kowarzik, (1984), who argues that Marx, despite himself, was really Green. Reiner Grendmann (1991) reviews these debates.

12. Adorno (1968) argued that opinion research indicated the existence of class consciousness, but that it was very weak. Subsequent trends in western countries show further decline in class-political allegiances (see Sarlvik & Crew, 1983, or Dunleavy & Husbands, 1983).

13. Marx had likewise claimed that capitalism continually revolutionized its own conditions of existence, swept aside bonds of sentiment, etc., and was therefore unable to generate any fixed ideology, or 'halo'.

14. Horkheimer also follows Weber's usage of the term 'charismatic leader', although not always in the same sense. For the latter, 'charisma . . . is the specifically creative revolutionary force of history' because it is these movements which effect real changes of attitude and experience amongst followers (Weber, 1978: II, 1116). But for Horkheimer, charismatic movements merely permit the release of introjected emotion into the public sphere.

15. This line of argument was of course developed by Marcuse into a psychoanalytic theory of liberation, in which *Eros* constituted the only remaining form of authentically oppositional practice.

16. The idea that Jewishness symbolizes modernity is a recurring theme in German thought. Marx's commitment to the emancipatory force of modernity, as well as his concern to undermine religious illusion, meant that he gave little attention to the Jewish Question per se. His two short essays 'On the Jewish Question' (Marx, 1977: 39–57) and 'The Capacity for Present-Day Jews and Christians to Become Free' (Marx, 1977: 58–62) are really foils for developing his concept of human as opposed to political emancipation. Following Bauer and others, Marx invests Jewishness with double meaning, the first ethnic-religious, the second as

a metaphor for modernity, hence, 'From its own bowels civil society constantly begets Judaism. Money is the jealous god of Israel . . . The imaginary nationality of the Jew is the nationality of the merchant, of the money man in general' (Marx, 1977: 60). This involves a crude racial stereotype of Jewishness as money-making, or 'huckstering'. See Carlebach (1978) for a discussion of Marxist antisemitism and the Left's analysis of Judaism; or Jay (1980) on the Frankfurt Institute's explanations of antisemitism.

17. Weber of course did have an explanation for the latter, in terms of the routinization of charisma, as personalized rule is institutionalized (1978: II, 1123).

18. Billig notes that this was recognized but not explained by Adorno's co-researchers Ackerman and Jahoda, who noted that 'the patient [an ex-Nazi] attributes to Jews those qualities of superiority which he envies in his father and which he has given up hope of developing himself' (1950: 99, cited by Billig, 1978: 333). Billig (1978) further notes that antisemitism is peculiar amongst racist beliefs, in that it is characterized by conspiracy theory which attributes to Jews alone global cohesion and enormous power. Thus other despised ethnic groups, such as Blacks and Asians, are presented in extreme-Right ideology as tools of an international Zionist capitalist-communist conspiracy to destroy the British way of life. Islamic neo-revivalism makes similar claims in relation to Jews and the Islamic way of life, suggesting that Jewishness serves as a general metaphor of the threat to traditionalism posed by modernity (see Chapter 6 below).

19. This way of thinking is not, of course, confined to the extreme Right, it is displayed also on the Left, for example amongst Trotskyite groups, where antisemitism appears under the guise of anti-Zionism. See Werner Cohen (1991).

20. Freud's theory of narcissism was important here. This claimed that a pathological state in which the ego, unable to form external object relations, itself becomes the object of libido is consequentially unable to engage in self-reflection.

21. In his review of Stephen White's *The Recent Work of Jürgen Habermas*, (1990) Piet Strydom (1990) accuses White of 'over-privileging' the communicative paradigm in Habermas, and suggests that the debate has since moved on to aesthetic-expressive dimensions of experience. However, this quotation and Habermas' 'Reply' to the essays in Honneth & Joas (1991) suggests that the communicative paradigm remains central to Habermas' theory.

22. Scambler (1987), likewise develops a Habermasian analysis of the power of medical expertise, illustrating how technical language is used in doctor–patient interactions when the doctor wants to encourage a patient to agree to a particular procedure (such as an induced childbirth), thereby precluding discussion of other options or the power relationships implicit in the encounter.

23. Seymour Lipset (1959) argued that the decline of political radicalism followed advanced capitalism which diffuses conflicts through social differentiation. Clearly this understated the potential for new conflicts to appear, but might point to the capacities of a complex society to regulate and diffuse conflict potentials.

24. Intensive here is contrasted with extensive, where the latter involves increasing production by extending into previously uncharted territories (e.g. western colonialism or the Soviet exploitation of Siberian mineral reserves). Intensive refers to increasing the productivity of labour through applied scientific and managerial techniques.

25. Marx was of course well aware of this, which is indicated by his comments on India, where 'England has to fulfil a double mission . . . the annihilation of old Asiatic society, and laying the material foundations of Western society in Asia. . . . The day is not far distant when, by a combination of railways and steam vessels . . . that once fabulous country will . . . be actually annexed to the Western world' (*New York Daily Tribune*, August 1853). However, this annexation was to produce a complex combination of 'combined and uneven' development, rather than straightforward westernization.

26. As Pierre Bourdieu (1979b) argued, the Paris students were not outsiders but inheritors (and much could be said of the international wave of protest movements during this period).

2

From Praxis to Communication

A central claim of *DoE* was that although Enlightenment had released the capacity of reason to challenge domination, the very process which had made enlightenment possible, technical control of nature, also released instrumental forms of action which undermined genuinely oppositional forces. Since instrumentality recognized no rational foundation for conduct other than the most efficient maximization of self-interest, ethics of social justice were relegated to the status of personal convictions. This in turn meant that if irrational power politics, as Horkeimer put it, ousted 'enlightened self-interest' in people's minds, then no moralist could object since 'reason had committed suicide' (1974b: 25). Meanwhile, all that was left for Critical Theory was the location of traces or reminiscences of emancipation in those areas of social life, such as aesthetics, yet to be colonized by instrumentality. However, this view was premised on the Weberian notion of instrumentality as a unitary process, whereas the distinction between *Vernunft* and *Verstand* suggests that two distinct tendencies should be kept separate. On the one hand, there was the expanding cognitive power of critical reason (represented in the republican, democratic and feminist critiques of domination) and, on the other, there was the more limited aim of the bourgeois revolutions to secure the legal and cultural reproduction of capital accumulation. Viewed as distinct logics of development, modernity could be seen as two-sided – involving expansion in both technical control of labour or natural resources and facilities of rational critique. Alongside the expansion of capital into a global system there remained an alternative current of modernity which found expression in emancipatory social movements of the past two centuries, with the continuing potential to be activated from underground, so to speak, despite increasingly efficient modes of systemic regulation. This claim will be developed in this and the following chapters through a critical examination of Habermas' theory of communication, which attempts to locate the ever-present potential for critical reason in the diffuse and textured structures of the lifeworld.

Dilemmas of Theory and Practice

It might assist in understanding Habermas' complex and often abstruse work to keep it in mind that he is a profoundly political thinker whose work displays an abiding concern with the possibilities for social democratization. Whilst it would be inappropriate to impose a unity on Habermas' diverse *oeuvre*, fairly clear motifs are there. Jean Cohen (1979) referred to a 'red thread' running through Habermas' work in his attempt to redeem the promise of the classical concept of politics to provide practical orientation to the 'just and good life', without relinquishing the rigour of scientific analysis. Notwithstanding his critique of Adorno/Horkheimer, Habermas has remained faithful to Horkheimer's central claim, that what distinguishes 'critical' from 'traditional' theory is an active interest in advancing a more rational and just organization of social life. As Habermas observed in *Theory and Practice*, 'We can . . . distinguish theories according to whether or not they are structurally related to possible emancipation' (1974: 37), a theme which is still evident in *The Philosophical Discourse of Modernity* (1987) or *The Theory of Communicative Action* 1984, 1989b – (hereafter *TCA*).[1] On one level, Habermas is conducting a dialogue within the Left in which he aims to address the failure of classical Marxist analysis and strategy, whilst keeping hold of the Marxist commitment to emancipation. In this sense Ben Agger's (1991: 122) assessment of Habermas as broadening (rather than rejecting) Marxism to include the critique of distorted linguistic practices seems accurate. His 'balanced' analysis of the positive achievements of modern societies aims to define realistic limits to radical political action, whilst identifying the dangers inherent in capitalism and bureaucratic power.[2]

Roughly speaking, Habermas' targets are exaggerated optimism or pessimism. Adorno/Horkheimer's 'global pessimism' had become outdated in the post-war era of welfare and cultural protest, yet confronted by counter-cultural politics in the 1960s, which for Marcuse celebrated libidinal creativity, Habermas was equally unenthusiastic. This was so, first, because counter-culture politics were unrealistically optimistic about the possibilities for decentralization and local democratization in complex industrial societies; and, secondly, because they showed an immature tendency towards dogmatism and anti-rationalism which compromised the necessary distance between intellectual critique and political action.[3] Neither position took sufficient account of the ways in which modern world-views release the critical potential of reason to challenge dominant forms of legitimation, and open up spaces for social democratization. For Habermas, then, unwarranted pessimism and optimism were two sides of the same coin, which was careless of the achievements of western modernity.

However, whilst attempting to settle accounts with western Marxism, Habermas is conducting a battle on another front too, against three varieties of conservatism. The first is, the 'old conservatism' which, like Romanticism, longs for a return to 'traditional forms . . . of rural and peasant life, or the life of town dwellers and craftsmen, even the plebeian way of life of the agricultural labourers . . . the melancholy charm of irretrievable pasts and the radiance of nostalgic remembrance of what had been sacrificed to modernization' (Habermas, 1989b: 329). There will be occasion to return to this notion in the context of revivalist religious and nationalist movements. The second variety is 'neo-conservatism', which, like the New Right, or Niklas Luhmann's systems theory, accepts the economic and technical features of modernity but strives to minimize subversive elements of cultural modernism. Habermas rejects this as sterile and dominating, an apology for technocratic control. The third variety is 'young conservatism' – a celebration of desire and aesthetic abandonment of reason, which he associates with postmodernism (for example, Habermas, 1989a). Young conservatism illegitimately polarizes instrumental reason against aesthetic expression and, permitting a celebration of the spontaneous power of the imagination, breaks free from the norms of liberal-democratic government and a rational theory of knowledge.[4] By identifying modernity too closely with instrumental reason, philosophers of postmodernity, such as Bataille, Foucault or Derrida, fashion an 'intransigent antimodernism' which throws out the baby of critical reason with the bathwater of instrumental rationality.[5]

Whereas Habermas might agree with the postmodernism of Lyotard in certain respects, his fundamental objection, like that levelled at earlier Critical Theory, is that it denies the very ground on which critique is based, and can offer no compelling vision of an alternative form of social organization. Both Habermas and Lyotard address the role of communication technologies and expert cultures in the legitimation of late capitalism; both regard modern societies as integrated through complex, differentiated spheres of action which fragment everyday experience. For both, the historical subjectivities which were the putative addressees of Marxist theory have fractured, such that, 'even if the historical addressee were not beyond the reach of theory, the relation of the theory to practice . . . would have to be defined differently than it was in the classical doctrine . . . *revolutionary self-confidence* and *theoretical self-certainty* are gone' (Habermas, 1982b: 222; original emphasis). However, despite these areas of agreement, Habermas argues, in a manner which Lyotard (1991: 72–3) finds unacceptable, that the potential for rational agreement is present whether we acknowledge it or not, in socio-linguistic rules of communication. This background rationality, or communicative action, is prefigured in all struggles for justice, civic rights, participation, or freedom from exploitation.

None the less, Habermas needs to demonstrate this rational presence in some concrete form. Before he elaborated the theory of communicative action (which is examined in more detail below) Habermas' work was to undergo a shift in its conception of consciousness and political action. He began with the theory–practice nexus, which he was later to regard as tied to the flawed 'philosophy of consciousness', premised on the isolated actor-subject, rather than the structural context within which actions are constituted. Habermas' alternative paradigm, of linguistically mediated interaction, emerged gradually out of his earlier attempts to revive Critical

Theory through an educative, or psychoanalytical, model of social practice.

Knowledge and Human Interests (1971, hereafter *KHI*), now often
described as a 'failed attempt' (for example, Holub, 1991: 8), conceived of
practice through an analogy with (an ideal-typical) psychoanalytical
encounter. Here social constraint, like the unconscious force of neurosis,
exercises power over subjects which could be broken through self-
reflection (or 'praxis'). In *KHI*, psychoanalysis was interpreted as a theory
of linguistic distortion in which self-reflection was of itself emancipatory, in
that it promised to erode repressive power relations embedded in tradition,
habit or the unconscious.[6] Neurosis was re-described as a deviant
language-game, or a discrepancy between communication levels, and the
transference situation became the restoration of primal conflicts to the
status of public utterances.[7] At this stage, Habermas adopted a neo-
Kantian quest for the a priori grounds of possible knowledge, via
reconstruction of the three 'knowledge-guiding' or 'knowledge-
constitutive' interests.[8] This schema attempted to locate scientific knowledge in relation to 'anthropologically deep-seated' interests of the human
species (1971: 194ff.) in control, understanding and emancipation, which
correspond respectively to empirical-analytical, socio-cultural and self-
reflexive forms of knowledge.[9] However, the schema was subjected to
extensive criticism, which Habermas tried to meet by shifting attention to
the theory of language.[10]

None the less there have been serious attempts to illustrate a psycho-
dynamic or educative Critical Theory, especially with reference to Paulo
Freire's 'critical pedagogy' (which was partly based on work with Latin
American rural workers). Here self-understanding of structural oppression
leads to new forms of self-consciousness and empowerment (Forester,
1985). Stephen Leonard described Freire's critical pedagogy as 'critical
theory in practice' (1990: 167), although, unlike Fay (1987) or Misgeld
(1985), Leonard confines himself to providing an exposition of Freire, and
leaves the connections with Critical Theory largely implicit. The attractive-
ness of Freire is that he seems to address in practical terms the potential of
a therapeutic practice 'to enlighten those to whom it is addressed about
their position in an antagonistic social system' (Leonard, 1990: 42).[11]
Critical pedagogy, or *conscientization*, begins by singling out elements
from people's 'background awareness' in small, intimate cultural circles
where an uncoerced exchange of ideas is encouraged. These begin by
deploying 'codifications', sketches or photos, objects which mediate
discussion, and are decoded through critical analysis.[12]

Again, Brian Fay envisages educative praxis in groups that are 'relatively
small, relatively egalitarian . . . relatively free of recrimination between
members', that is, 'consciousness raising groups' (1987: 111). Transformation takes place when the potential energies of a group of people are
tapped and organized into a counter-agent with its own power to rise up

against its oppressors (1987: 142). For Fay, the women's movement (which he discusses as though it were homogeneous) is an important example, indicating the potential for a movement that abandons the narrowly political domain in favour of a transformation of everyday life: 'If any movement does, the women's movement shows that the existence of a critical theory, combined with a social crisis which the theory itself predicts, can be a potent factor for mass upheaval' (1987: 114). This is so because, first, it has been guided by social theory with an educative intent: to expose and critique oppressive gender relations; secondly, consciousness-raising requires an environment of trust, openness and support; thirdly, it deals with the problem of resistance that any critical theory encounters, in this case, the fact that the majority of women were initially opposed to the movement. Feminist practice has invested consciousness-raising with the power to erode the constraint of patriarchal oppression, suggesting a complementarity with Habermas' early work (Elshtain, 1981).[13]

However, educative praxis of this kind is limited to small groups whose success in a wider social context is likely to depend upon the conduciveness of their environments to collective organization – over which they have very limited control. The praxis model does not therefore exhaust communicative possibilities in societies where publics and other diverse forms of sociality are constituted anonymously and linked through complex communicative cultures. Such complex interactions are transmitted in various ways and presuppose ephemeral, non-repetitive, optional encounters through mass communications – which leaves the scope for the therapeutic construction of identities rather limited! Further, Habermas (1974: 23) himself has acknowledged that carrying the model of psycho-analysis over into social practice might unrealistically invest confidence at the level of rational critical insight alone. It is not clear why emancipation should follow from public utterance since there is no guarantee that insight will be translated into action (Bubner, 1982; Leonard, 1990: 152). The view of emancipation in *KHI* seemed to presuppose the possibility of what McCarthy (1991) describes as an 'almost Fichtean transparency of social relations',[14] a society freed from all sources of conflict and diversity, which is neither possible nor desirable (Leonard, 1990: 244). Likewise, Ian Craib sees in Habermas a rationalist utopia underlying the assumption that psychoanalysis is able to eliminate the irrational. By contrast, Craib (1989: 99) restates Freud's warnings to the effect that the notion of a human state of unbound happiness is a dangerous, wish-fulfilling illusion. Since Habermas himself has abandoned such claims, arguing that praxis philosophy involves the 'untenable premise' of autonomous self-consciousness on a large scale (1991: 260–1), it might not be useful to take this point further. Moreover, Habermas has continually insisted that undistorted communication is a counter-factual ideal, rather than the goal, or *telos*, of self-reflection.[15]

Communicative Action and the Lifeworld

KHI pursued the rather grand (Kantian) goal of clarifying 'the foundations of the sciences once and for all' (Habermas, 1971: 317). Although Habermas (1986: 152), still considers the outlines of this argument to be correct he now accepts that this was over-ambitious. *TCA* shifts the focus of debate to the question of the normative and structural conditions for emancipatory action. It should already be apparent that a unifying theme in Habermas' work is the search for communicative rationality which will serve as the basis for both the critique of sociology and the location of new emancipatory potentials. To this end, Habermas goes to considerable lengths to develop an elaborate concept of communicative action which serves two purposes. First, through the theory of speech acts and social action it aims to demonstrate that the possibility of emancipation is located in the very constitution of sociality.[16] Secondly, Habermas looks for an historical embodiment of communicative action in the social-evolutionary process – located in the lifeworld, a concept initially derived from phenomenology but given a novel twist by linking it up with an analysis of identity formation and the public sphere. These, it should be stressed, are merely the conceptual foundations for a theory of social evolution which will be elaborated in Chapter 3.

Communicative Action

Critical Theory aims to formulate the conditions in which it is still possible to speak of a rational society lurking in the recesses of global domination. To this end Habermas first draws on Weber's notion of the differentiation of value spheres in order to counter earlier Critical Theory's 'total administration' thesis. But secondly, he wishes to demonstrate that the conclusions Weber drew from his theory were unwarranted. Habermas initially follows Weber's depiction of modernity as differentiated into society (legitimate orders through which participants regulate their membership of social groups), culture (the stock of knowledge from which actors derive interpretations) and personality (competences that permit actors to reach understanding and thereby assert an identity). Corresponding to these are three cultural value spheres (the objective, social and subjective worlds) within which specific types of validity-questions can be posed. Thus questions of propositional truth or cognition are embodied in science; those of authenticity or taste in art; and those of normative rightness or legitimacy in morality and law (see Table 2.1). Each sphere is autonomous from the others and is governed by an internally meaningful criterion of validity (exemplified by Weber's separation between the vocations of science and politics) so there could be no over-arching stand-point of universal reason – what was rational from one stand-point might be irrational from another. This underpinned Weber's diagnosis of modernity as entailing an *inevitable* loss of meaning (*sinnverlust*) – a conclusion Habermas believes follows from an incomplete understanding

Table 2.1 *Differentiation of value spheres*

Value sphere	Criteria	Evolutionary potential
Science	Propositional truth	Technical expertise
Art/art criticism	Authenticity/sincerity	Aesthetic experience
Morality	Normative rightness	Political justice/ethical fairness

Source: Habermas, 1984: 23 (adapted)

of the formation of modernity, and which can be corrected through the theory of communicative action. If, as Habermas claims, the same formal argumentative procedures are presupposed by the different particular contents of each sphere, and if these procedures invoke the possibility of a rational and just society, then the first step has been taken in the reconstruction of Critical Theory.

This is a crucial aspect of Habermas' argument, to which later discussion will return. The key distinction here is that between teleological and communicative action.[17] With the former, like Weber's goal-rationality, ends are chosen on the basis of interpretations of others' intentions, and include strategic (or game-theoretic) action. Weber (and much subsequent sociology) regarded this as primary to modern life, especially since it had become institutionalized in bureaucracies and the market. Communicative action on the other hand involves the use of language to reach an understanding to co-ordinate plans, and negotiating definitions to reach a consensus motivated by reason, in which participants acknowledge only the force of better argument (Habermas, 1984: 85). For Habermas, Weber mistakenly regarded teleological action (means–ends calculation) as the quintessence of rationality. On the contrary, even when actors are behaving in a purely instrumental fashion, in the market or in a bureaucracy, their communication must be bound by shared norms and beliefs which can be reconstructed and critically examined.[18]

There are essentially two claims here: first that, whether we acknowledge it or not, linguistic communication implies communicative norms; and, secondly, that since even strategic action uses language it must implicitly deploy the potential for uncoerced agreement which is 'always already' (as Habermas puts it) present in attempts at mutual understanding. With regard to the first claim, Habermas draws on Chomsky's linguistics and Austin and Searle's theory of speech acts[19] to reconstruct the shared nature of rationally motivated rules of conversation, arguing that the elementary units of communication (speech acts) involve validity-claims that are 'naïvely accepted' in conversations. For conversations to occur we assume agreement about grammatical regulation (performative verbs, dependent clauses, etc.) and the illocutionary force of statements (we recognize something *as* a promise, an assertion, an order, etc.). Further, we share assumptions about external reality (the world of objects), normative reality (socially recognized expectations, values, rules, etc.) and inner reality (the arena of intentions).

Since conversations involve misunderstandings and challenges, implicit validity-claims can be called into question at any point, when the truth of a proposition, the sincerity of the speaker or the appropriateness of the utterance can be disputed. For example, consider the potential reactions of a student confronted by a request from a professor in a seminar: 'Please bring me a glass of water.' The student can in principle reject this request under three validity aspects. S/he can contest the normative rightness of the utterance: 'No, you cannot treat me like one of your employees'; or s/he can contest the subjective truthfulness of the utterance: 'No. You really only want to put me in a bad light in front of other students'; or s/he can deny that certain existential presuppositions obtain: 'No. The next water tap is so far away that I could not get back before the end of the session.' (Habermas, 1984: 306). Thus the professor's request can refer to three different worlds, of social normativity, subjective sincerity and objective truth respectively, within which the validity of statements can be challenged. The student might of course comply with the request without demur, perhaps because the professor has a fit of uncontrollable coughing and refusal would appear churlish (in which case s/he acknowledges the legitimacy of a particular social expectation). Again, the request might be complied with, say, because of respect for the professor's status, or out of fear that refusal would result in a penalty such as lower grades, in which case the possibility for raising validity claims has been distorted by power relations.

Entering into dialogue about the validity of utterances involves a specific type of discussion (*Diskurs*) oriented towards examining (or 'redeeming') the consensus, a practice which is infinitely reflexive in that participants can objectify any utterance and attempt to repair the interruption in dialogue (Habermas, 1984: 28). Such practices will be successful, however, only if we assume equality of access to speech acts and freedom to move from level to level in *Diskurs*, since it is only under such conditions that consensus could be motivated by the force of better argument. This enables Habermas to introduce the 'general symmetry requirement' (also called the 'ideal speech situation') which is the nub of the communicative paradigm. That is, if a consensus is to be reached guided only by the force of better argument, then, *whether we recognize it or not*, we routinely assume certain conditions, namely that everyone has an equal chance to deploy, initiate and perpetuate speech acts; utterances are comprehensible; their propositional content is true; what is said is legitimate and appropriate; and it is sincerely spoken.

Habermas realized of course that these conditions of communicative competence are counter-factual and rarely present in actual speech, but it is precisely this which justifies two further claims. First, that the hermeneutic goal of normal communication is disturbed, much like the analogy with psychoanalysis, by power relations which intrude to prevent questions being raised or validity-claims being tested. Secondly, that these constraints on communication are self-defeating since they contradict the underlying assumptions that make discourse possible at all. From this it follows that rationality can be measured by the degree of openness or closure in communication; that the goals of truth, freedom and justice are not mere utopian dreams, but are anticipated in ordinary communication; and that therefore the goal of emancipation is presupposed in the constitution of the species as linguistic beings. Hence, 'we are concerned here with reconstructing a voice of reason, which we cannot avoid using whether we want to or not when speaking in everyday communicative practice' (Habermas, 1991: 244).

However, the most that this reconstruction of communicative norms achieves is to explicate the *potential* argumentative aspects of language. Martin Seel (1991: 37) claims that all Habermas has really established is the *need* for universal rationality, not its existence – a criticism which Habermas attempts to rebuff in several ways. Initially, he wishes to show that communicative action is 'the original mode of language use', which he hopes to establish with reference to Austin and Searl's distinction between illocutionary and perlocutionary speech acts. Illocutionary acts cannot have causally produced effects on hearers because the speaker's aim can be achieved only by stating it openly. Since the illocutionary part of speech permits the addition of 'hereby' (hereby I promise you, hereby I command, etc.), the validity of the utterance is open to debate over the conditions which would warrant agreement or disagreement. However, this is not possible with perlocutionary acts, where the speaker wants to achieve an effect on the listener (to persuade, frighten, embarrass, etc.) which cannot be openly stated. In this case the speaker has a hidden goal external to the surface meaning of what is said. In the example of the student seminar above, the potential challenge that 'You only want to put me in a bad light' asserts that the request had a perlocutionary, or hidden strategic, purpose, since one cannot say 'Hereby I embarrass you . . .' without laying bare a statement's lack of normative validity.[20]

Now, Habermas claims that perlocutionary effects, even if they involve deception, are dependent on communicative norms in that the deception must be concealed within the appearance of validity claims (just as the confidence trickster is parasitic on naïvely assumed trust). But what about direct threats of force, which Habermas calls 'non-normatively authorized commands', where any pretence at asserting a validity-claim has been replaced by a power claim like: 'If you demonstrate the riot police will break your heads'? Even naked threats of this sort do not represent a 'class of speech acts in [their] own right' since the form of such acts is 'borrowed from the conditions under which normatively authorized demands can be used' (Habermas, 1991: 239). What might appear to be non-normatively authorized demands, even where a hidden perlocutionary or strategic effect is present, are dependent on the potential for agreement or dissent (for example, 'This demonstration is a danger to public order and therefore the use of force against participants is legitimate').[21] The assertion that strategic action is parasitic on communicative norms enables Habermas (as will be seen in Chapter 3) to claim that the latter guides social evolution.

It is hardly surprising that a thesis involving several complex and layered stages of argument has been the subject of much controversy since it was proposed in the early 1970s,[22] but for the purposes of the present study two types of objection are particularly pertinent. First, there is the claim that Habermas envisages domination-free dialogue as an attainable state, or a form of life which would characterize an emancipated society, a utopian claim open to objections both of inherent implausibility, and of trivializing social conflicts.[23] For example, Benhabib asked,

> who is the 'we' of the linguistic community? This hypostatized subject of history is neutralized in a semantic gloss on structural processes. Truth becomes discursive argumentation, in which reflection leads to the ability to enter processes of argumentation and adopt the stand-point of others. (1981).

In response to such objections, Habermas has attempted to clarify the role of ideal speech in relation to political theory, and now insists that it was never his intention to offer ideal speech as an image of a concrete form of life, correcting previous statements which might have suggested this (1982b: 262). He now seems more comfortable with Wellmer's suggestion that ideal speech is a 'dialectical illusion' necessary for *imagining* an emancipated social life, since in *TCA* Habermas describes his concept as fallibilistic, such that we can never be certain that we are 'in' *Diskurs*.[24] His discursive project is now a 'minimalist ethics', in that it cannot provide us with unambiguous, substantive norms of justice, but can only direct us towards thinking about fair procedures for adjudicating normative claims (White, 1990: 73).[25]

Indeed, it is important to stress that the consensus presupposed by communicative action is hypothetical, referring to the conditions which would obtain if all conditions of ideal speech were met, which would effectively signal the completion of human understanding. Since no one expects this to occur (!), the concept describes not a real consensus but abstract and formal conditions of argumentation that are common to all specific discourses (about propositional truth, normative rightness, and taste or subjective expression). It might be the case, as Charles Taylor (1991: 34) argues, that formal argumentative procedures are unlikely to bind together real actors, who will look for more substantial ethical commitments when addressing serious social and political problems (such as ecological issues). But Habermas turns the question round, challenging Taylor to show why every concept of rationality must 'remain enmeshed with the substantive contents of a particular form of life . . .?' (Habermas, 1991: 219). The point about the differentiation of validity spheres is not that the same substantive ethics will be present in each (for example, respect for the environment) but that in each specific case statements can be scrutinized according to the same kind of argumentative procedures.

Secondly, there is the charge that Habermas' emphasis on communication and language is idealist and ignores the importance of material structures. Dux understands Habermas to be claiming that social action is communicative as such, whilst it 'is simply not self-evident that social orders are the outcome of an action which has transpired by means of discourse' (1991: 76). Sociality, Dux argues, is formed through conditions of dependence and objective violence which later become institutionalized into normatively binding rules. Again, Brian Fay (1987) suggests that emancipation through rational reflection ('cognitivism') always encounters limitations posed by what he calls 'embodiment'. Cognitivism is deficient because it omits reference to 'somatic learning' in which 'bodies . . . incarcerate conditioned patterns of activity, attitude and response to stimuli' (Fay, 1987: 148). Since identities are inscribed into constructs of the body, it follows that changing our ideas will not change dispositions to behave and feel in certain ways.[26] Authority requires something 'direct, palpable, manipulative and corporeal', and becoming a member of a particular culture involves becoming a certain sort of body. In the formation of gender identities somatic learning is crucially important too, as research has demonstrated how differences in men's and women's uses of gestures and speech confirm relations of dominance and subordination (Henley, 1977). This is an important issue in view of the way feminism has linked political practice to body politics – questions of sexuality, violence, fertility control and reproductive technologies. How can the rather ethereal theory of communicative action address these?

One response would be to argue that even if there are non-linguistic bases of social action (like the encoding of authority in bodies), then human freedom and empowerment is none the less extended by bringing these as far as possible into the public-linguistic realm. Validity-claims open up reasoned debate precisely because they break the unacknowledged spell of hidden power structures by subjecting them to public scrutiny. For example, the politicization of technologies of the body, the redefinition of illness and therapy, or demands for equal recognition of sexual preferences, illustrate potential for the erosion of somatic domination through the forcing of otherwise repressed issues into the public domain. Again, Nancy Fraser (1989: 172) has said that to *name* 'sexism', 'sexual harassment' 'marital rape' 'double shift', etc., creates a social space around which a feminist agenda enters the realm of public contestation. Whilst a response along these lines might be valid, this is not yet a theory of empowerment within conditions of social domination, which addresses the complex interplay of validity-claims with economic and political power. Habermas believes this can be approached through a theory of the social evolution of communicative structures in the lifeworld, and this should now be examined.

The Lifeworld and Identity

Habermas himself says that formal pragmatics is 'hopelessly removed from actual language', a deficiency he hopes to correct by borrowing from phenomenology the concept of the lifeworld. This enables the theory of communicative action to include culture-specific claims, non-verbal understanding, ambiguity, conversation and background knowledge, whilst simultaneously addressing the objective, social and subjective worlds (1989b: 328). In this way Habermas hopes to effect the link between philosophical critique and social evolution, since although 'the theory of communication is intended to solve problems that are rather of a philosophical nature . . . I see a close connection with questions relating to a theory of social evolution' (1979a: 95–6). Habermas stresses the idea of the lifeworld as a medium of social learning, in that language and culture embody a stock of knowledge – the stored interpretive work of preceding generations – that renders every new situation familiar, in that understanding takes place against the background of culturally engrained pre-understandings. The lifeworld is not synonymous with communicative action but rather the one 'feeds off' the other (Habermas, 1991: 221). This somewhat ambiguous formulation might be interpreted to mean that the communicative potential of language described above is gradually released into the structures of the lifeworld as the spell-binding power of traditional legitimations is eroded (Habermas, 1989b: 335–7).

Habermas (1984: 123) draws on the contrast between lifeworld as 'pre-reflective background consensus' and what Husserl described as the 'horizon' against which aspects of the lifeworld become objects of reflection. A central theme in phenomenology is that background meanings and knowledge about the social world can be subjected to reflection (or 'objectified') but that the lifeworld as a whole remains inaccessible to examination. Thus Gadamer (1975: 443–4) described the background consensus which enables speakers in a dialogue to hold together as the 'infinity of the unsaid' or the 'circle of the unexpressed'. Latterly, ethnomethodologists have argued that agreement is diffuse, fragile, continually revised, and only a momentarily successful communication in which participants rely on problematic and unclarified propositions (Habermas, 1984: 100–1). Again, Schutz and Luckmann wrote of the ' "residua" of opacity', which meant that however extensively the lifeworld background was explicated, there would always be reserves of cultural meaning upon which actors would draw, but which would remain inaccessible to conscious reflection (Schutz & Luckmann, 1974: 169). This is a kind of scaffolding or 'conservative counterweight' against the risk of disagreement and unmanageable complexity (Habermas, 1984: 70).

Habermas agrees with Gadamer that we engage in conversations by bracketing off a background consensus of shared understanding and norms without which everyday communication would be impossible. Further, he does not commit himself as to the extent to which 'lifeworldly' contexts might actually be rendered transparent (an ambiguity also noted in relation to *KHI*). But he does wish to show in opposition to Gadamer that as the binding force of traditional world-views diminish, reflection on the background consensus opens the way for critical subjectivities. This departs from more conventional notions of the lifeworld, since for Gadamer our identities are reflexively examined only by employing concepts themselves grounded in tradition, thus there can be neither 'correct' understandings nor 'false consciousness'. We cannot escape our embeddedness in tradition, such as membership of a national culture, and any supposition that we can is 'objectivist dogmatism' (Gadamer, 1975: 30). For Habermas this is unsatisfactory since once it has been made available to public scrutiny, the lifeworld vanishes:

> The lifeworld is that remarkable thing that dissolves . . . before our eyes as soon as we try to take it up piece by piece. . . . The moment this background knowledge enters communicative expression, where it becomes explicit knowledge and thereby subject to criticism, it loses precisely those characteristics by virtue of which it belonged to the lifeworld structures: certainty, background character. (Honneth et al., 1981: 16)

Habermas believes that this claim can be historically grounded, since as early modern societies became more complex and the lifeworld underwent structural differentiation, world-views which had previously exercised binding force were subjected to public scrutiny. That is, aspects of a previously unexamined normative consensus, and sacred legitimations of the political order (such as the divine right of kings) were subjected to argumentative doubt, which released the possibility of posing validity-questions. Moreover, this represented a new stage of social learning, which could potentially be stored in the structures of the lifeworld and transmitted through socialization.

This surely does not mean that critical reflection in itself dissolves power relations, but that once the ability to pose validity-questions has been institutionalized, a different type of power and authority is created. Once the 'spell-binding power of the sacred' was eroded by civil law and democracy, regulative functions could no longer be performed (as, for example, Durkheim thought) by a substitute for out-moded religious symbols (like the 'cult of the individual'). Rather, as social norms previously invested with sacred authority are subject to the argumentative power of language, social action is regulated less by background consensus and increasingly by normative agreement since legitimating norms lose the protected fence of the sacred. Habermas calls this tendency the 'linguistification of the sacred', a learning process in which the power of the lifeworld over the communicative practices diminishes and actors increasingly owe their mutual understandings to their own interpretations. Culture becomes more innovative and differentiated, which in turn requires a sharper differentiation of the contents of symbolic interaction (for example, in science, law, art, politics or education) from the formal argumentative procedures of reaching agreement.

Habermas further links the communicative possibilities of the lifeworld with a theory of identity and personality-formation derived in part from Lawrence Kohlberg. Here human ethical awareness progresses from a pre-conventional level (punishment avoidance), through the conventional stage (group solidarity and the ability to judge conduct with reference to motives), to the post-conventional level where ethical conduct is self-chosen on the basis of universal principles of justice, equality and reciprocity of rights.[27] Combining this with Piaget, Habermas describes the process as one of 'decentration'. This occurs as a child learns to distinguish between itself and external reality, to differentiate between the world and inner subjectivity, so acquiring the ability to 'decentre' the original pivotal place which it gave to itself in its environment. This cognitive achievement is matched by progress towards moral autonomy where norms lose their apparently natural validity and require justification in terms of reasoned argument. This stage is 'post-conventional' since here norms have lost the authority of unquestionable conventions.[28] The outcome, illustrated in outline in Figure 2.1, is that the lifeworld becomes increasingly rational, insofar as there is an expansion of H in relation to B.

Habermas hopes that in this way he can escape the negative conclusions of earlier Critical Theory. It was noted in Chapter 1 that insofar as Adorno and Horkheimer conceived of a rationally autonomous subject, it involved the internalization of the father-authority figure, since the rejection of authority could take place only following its prior acceptance, from a position of ego-strength. Habermas regards Piaget as having avoided this dilemma by pointing out that the 'struggle with the father' never produces autonomy anyway, but only compliance to the law, motivated by fearful

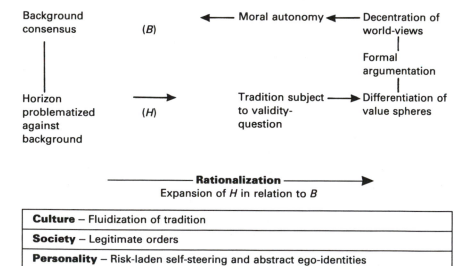

Figure 2.1   *Rationalization of the lifeworld*

submissiveness (Piaget, 1965: 369–70). True autonomy, which is elusive for reasons discussed in Chapter 3, can be learned only in reciprocal inter-action with peers on the basis of post-conventional morality.

Habermas then claims that a comparable process occurs in societal development, where binding myths give way first to global religions (Judaism, Christianity, Islam and Buddhism) and then to the rational critique of traditionalism in which cultural differentiation is accompanied by universalist law and morality. This is also a kind of decentration, since subjects enter a plurality of roles which are defined by specific norms and expectations, as clients, consumers, workers, parents, students, party members etc., none of which individually exhausts the capacity for adopting different identities (Habermas, 1979a: 110). In itself this is hardly an original thesis since role-distancing has been discussed at length by other sociologists such as Simmel, or later by symbolic interactionists like Irving Goffman. But Habermas deploys this idea to claim that the erosion of traditional identities opens up the potential for self-reflexive identities, and hence for a radically transformed relationship between individuals and collectivities. As Gouldner puts it, once freed from the traditionalistic regime of fixed structures and religious dogma, the self 'is viewed increasingly as a rational "subject", a locus of rational social transform-ation' who engages in discourse which is no longer reliant on any authority other than the requirement to offer good arguments (1976: 57). Post-conventional maturity involves both a critical attitude to received tradition and a recognition of the realistic limits to intervention in the world.

Post-conventional identity is thus the medium by which communicative ethics enter into concepts of the self, the conditions for which pertain in the lifeworld, as the stock of accumulated interpretations (tradition) is sub-jected to critique. However, as will be seen in more detail in the next chapter, this is a risky process which is jeopardized by the possibility of reversion to fixed and secure identities (the melancholy charm of irretriev-able pasts). For example, the transfer of sovereignty from personalized kingship to a nation-state increasingly legitimated in terms of bourgeois legality created a tension between the post-conventional ideal of equal citizens and the particularistic interests of the state. Emancipated members of bourgeois society, those with access to the public sphere, could understand themselves collectively as citizens and equal subjects of civil law. However, this was a highly abstract collective identity which was actually better suited to the identity of world citizens rather than citizens of states demanding loyalty (and of course military service) in competition with other states. For a time, this

> competition between two group identities was . . . silenced through membership in nations: the nation is the modern identity formation that diffused and made bearable the contradiction between the . . . universalism of bourgeois law and morality on the one side, and the particularism of individual states on the other. (Habermas, 1979a: 115)

There is evidence, however, that nationalism is no longer a stable solution to problems of collective identity, the erosion of which involves both risk and promise. It offers the possibility of cosmopolitan, fluid and self-reflexive identities; but alternatively the intensification of 'conflicts ignited below the threshold of national identity . . . in connection with race, creed, language, regional differences and other sub-cultures' (1979a: 115). In Part 2 it is suggested that the current manifestation of these conflicts reflects the obsolescence of the nation-state, combined with the difficulties of institutionalizing post-conventional communication.

To summarize then, social differentiation is accompanied by cultural differentiation of the lifeworld into value spheres, which is further underwritten by a de-centred personality structure. The lifeworld is potentially both pre-reflective background consensus, the repository of normatively secured action, on the one hand, and communicatively achieved forms of socially integrated action, on the other. This polar concept enables Habermas to claim that since the lifeworld is linguistically structured, it always contains the potential for the critical appropriation of tradition. Then the argumentative capacity of language offers the potential to break out of the constraints of pre-reflective understanding (B) and release new forms of reflective rational discourse (H), through which relations of domination which have become encoded in unexamined practices and frames of meaning are subjected to critique. Thus when Alexander questions why Habermas should privilege the lifeworld, the site of 'the authoritarian family, religious sect, and peer group . . . *Volk* culture, racism, and submissive beliefs' (1991: 62), he misses the point. It is not that the lifeworld is the source of 'good' communication in a sea of 'bad' instrumental action (as Alexander suggests) but that the lifeworld is the terrain within which these conflicts are fought out. None the less, a number of critics have rightly pointed out that the lifeworld is a diffuse concept which Habermas never defines unambiguously (for example, Schnadelbach, 1991: 17–19). Given the theoretical payload with which it is invested, to serve as the sociological carrier of communicative action and ultimately as the motor of social evolution and social movement formation, this is problematic. It is true that Habermas identifies within the lifeworld a specific component, the public sphere, which acts as a vector for critical self-reflection. But in later work it is unclear through what kinds of institutional norms and structural guarantees the public sphere (roughly approximating the notion of 'civil society') might be constituted. The crucial question, then, is how 'the lifeworld – as the horizon within which communicative actions are "always already" moving – is in turn limited and changed by the structural transformation of society as a whole' (Habermas 1984: 119). This is the subject of the following chapter.

Notes

1. Discussion of every theme in *TCA* is beyond the scope of this book, which will focus on the implications of the theory of communication for social movement formation and impact.

For critical overviews of *TCA*, readers are directed to the excellent summaries by Brand (1990) and Rasmussen (1990).

2. Habermas began work on *TCA* in the 1970s in response to the 'crumbling welfare state' and neo-conservative politics, and does not regard his later work as a disengagement from politics (Honneth et al., 1981: 6).

3. Habermas has recently said: 'Identification with the leaders of nationalist revolutionary struggles in Vietnam, China, Cuba, and South America allowed the students in revolt to transpose the . . . ideal image of the professional revolutionary from the 1920s to the 1960s. This pseudorevolutionary self-understanding slipped like a shadow of the past across the stage', discharging the animosity of the intellectual spectator condemned to passivity (Habermas, 1989a: 93–4).

4. Unlike liberal political theorists, however, Habermas argues that the democratic and rational achievements of modernity have come about despite, as much as because of, the growth of capitalism.

5. His attribution of 'conservatism' to the postmoderns is, of course, polemical, in that it applies to people like Derrida or even Lyotard, who might otherwise be regarded as radicals.

6. The goal of critical praxis was to convert private, repressed languages into public discourse through which previously hidden constraints of domination could be worked over. In psychoanalysis this requires a subject whose ego is sufficiently autonomous from unconscious pressures for self-reflection to take place. It is not clear whether Habermas believed that there were social equivalents to the narcissistic condition, in which (for Freudians) analysis is impossible.

7. Through transference the patient is aided to re-live experiences in such a way that emotions which have been deeply repressed are experienced as present and real. This requires a projection (or transfer) of unconscious hatreds or loves on to the analyst. Habermas' linguistic interpretation of Freud incidentally assumes that the unconscious is operative only in pseudo-communication, not in normal communication. For Freud, however, the unconscious is always operative and is never, so to speak, 'emptied' of symbolic content.

8. *KHI* is Kantian in that Habermas sets philosophy up as ultimate arbiter between practical reason (judgement) and theoretical cognition in order to clarify the foundations and limits of what can be experienced. Habermas later regarded this as over-ambitious, and offers philosophy the more modest role of 'guardian of reason', a position which is still too strong for critics like Rawls (Rasmussen, 1990: 20–1).

9. 'Anthropological' in the sense that the three forms of possible knowledge corresponded to problems encountered by all societies, namely the control of nature, reaching inter-subjective understanding and responding to domination.

10. Critiques include Rorty (1979: 379–85), Keat (1981: Chapters 3–4) and McCarthy (1978: Chapter 2). Whereas the interests in control and understanding correspond to the dichotomy Habermas drew elsewhere between 'work' (or strategic action) and 'interaction' (or communicative action) respectively, the third tier represented by the emancipatory interest has a more tenuous relation to his conceptual framework.

11. Freire (1980: 37) writes of Third World peasants living in a 'culture of silence', unable to see themselves as oppressed, and secretly admiring their oppressor. Acquiescence is not primarily a psychological condition, since an oppressive culture of dependence creates what Freire calls 'necrophiliac behaviour', a destruction of life which destroys any capacity to resist.

12. Codifications might begin by organizing discussion around photographs of the local community, as a focus for articulating power relations embedded in scenes depicted. This verbalization brings aspects of the cultural context of oppression to consciousness. Subsequently, literacy classes encourage participants to manipulate the symbolic codes previously reserved for elites.

13. Other feminist theorists, such as Nancy Fraser or Seyla Benhabib, have strong doubts as to the usefulness of Habermas' work for feminist practice. These are discussed in Chapter 4.

14. Johann Fichte, a late eighteenth-century philosopher, sought to remove the limitations of Kant's doctrine of categorical imperatives, and expounded the view that it is within human

power to achieve radical awareness of independence from pre-existing order through an ever-repeated effort to free oneself from bonds of nature and necessity. Although an Idealist, someone who pursues this goal, has achieved awareness of freedom from objects, ultimate freedom can never be reached but represents a horizon marking a goal towards which infinite progress is possible through education and self-reflection (Fichte, 1971).

15. For example, 'Nothing makes me more nervous than the imputation . . . that because the theory of communicative action focuses attention on the social facticity of recognized validity-claims, it proposes . . . a rationalistic utopian society. I do not regard the fully transparent society as an ideal, nor do I wish to suggest *any* other ideal' (Habermas, 1982a: 235).

16. Since Habermas devotes over a hundred pages of *TCA* to an elaboration of speech act theory, and has recently claimed that sociologists who neglect his theory of formal pragmatics risk a 'prejudiced understanding of my underlying assumptions' (1991: 233), this aspect of Habermas' work ideally deserves more attention here than space permits. A detailed discussion nevertheless would be a diversion from the task in hand, which is to elaborate a critical sociological theory of social change. Readers are referred to discussions of Habermas' (some would say idiosyncratic) adaptation of formal pragmatics in McCarthy (1978), Held (1980: 332–46), Thompson (1982), Honneth & Joas (1991), Brand (1990), Rasmussen (1990), White (1990) and Outhwaite (forthcoming).

17. Initially, Habermas (1984: 75–101) developed a typology of four action types (teleological, normative, dramaturgical and communicative) but subsequently said that he overstated the case to conceive of these as distinct types since each of the first three were dependent on the fourth (1991: 241).

18. Dallmayr (1984: 240) claims that this distinction is never clearly made in Habermas and that both concepts, teleological and communicative, are goal-oriented. Indeed, rather confusingly, Habermas himself says 'the teleological structure is fundamental to all types of action' (1984: 101). Both types are goal-directed although teleological action presupposes an instrumental subject–object relationship, whilst communicative action presupposes mutual subject–subject relations.

19. See Chomsky (1965), Austin (1962) and Searle (1969). Habermas (1984: 278) proposes to 'radicalize' linguistic philosophy by shifting the centre of concern from the propositional content of language to validity claims which are raised implicitly, since the latter are claims to the speaker's authority and legitimacy, and hence invoke power relations.

20. Jeff Coulter (1979: 41) argues that avowals and ascriptions of intentions (illocutionary acts) gain their intelligibility not from some mental divinations, but from the fact that declaring one's intention is to commit oneself to a course of action which is available to public scrutiny.

21. Of course one might not find Habermas' reasoning here persuasive. To claim that threats are parasitic on communicative norms because the illocutionary force is replaced by reference to sanctions seems to beg the question. However, the vast majority of communications contain at least a minimal claim to legitimacy.

22. For example, it is claimed that Habermas privileges communicative functions of language over others, such as irony or aesthetic expression (e.g. Thompson, 1982); that the teleological–communicative dichotomy is untenable since both involve setting goals; that Habermas' attempt to use communicative action as a criterion of truth is flawed because there is no way of knowing whether a consensus is illusory or not (e.g. McCarthy, 1973); that he has misunderstood or misused speech act theory (e.g. Rasmussen, 1990: 37); or that ideal speech displays what Lacanians would call a logocentric desire for perfect presence which has dominated western metaphysics for a millenium (Jay, 1988: 31). For a defence of his concept against these and other critiques see Habermas (1991).

23. 'Moshe Gonzalis' (Paul Piccone), for example, writes of Habermas' 'mystificatory formulation, restricting political participation solely to intellectuals. . . . Social movements have never been constituted by the likes of Descartes or Voltaire making decisions only after exhaustive "domination-free" discussion' (Gonzales/Piccone, 1989). But this objection, like those who accuse Habermas of reducing political struggle to a kind of grand seminar, ignores

his painstaking differentiation between the logic or potential of critical reflection grounded in language, from empirical manifestations of social movements.

24. For example, he quotes Dummett (1976) 'a falsificationist theory . . . links the content of an assertion with the commitment that a speaker undertakes in making that assertion: an assertion is a kind of gamble that the speaker will not be proved wrong', and adds that, 'This I understand as an indication of the fallibilistic character of the discursive redemption of validity-claims' (Habermas, 1984: 318). A not dissimilar view is found in Karl Popper's theory of truth as 'verisimilitiude' – a goal given by our rules of evidence, whose existence we must assume, but never expect to attain.

25. For example, 'the concept of morality is only one of the various general aspects [by which] the rationality of linguistically structured forms of life can be reconstructed . . . ethics can explain only the formal conditions of valid moral judgements . . . not the empirical conditions under which moral views can be put into practice' (Habermas, 1991: 220). Even so, an expanded public sphere as the institutional corollary of communicative action must be capable of actual existence, otherwise it is unclear why Habermas offers his analysis at all.

26. However, Fay does not distinguish between those disciplines which embody relations of power/submission (e.g. when one is entitled to look another straight in the eyes) and those which are innocent (e.g. the vocal formation needed to speak French).

27. Kohlberg (1971). See White (1990: Chapter 3) for a discussion of Habermas' use of Kohlberg, whose scheme Habermas believes he has improved by incorporating it into communicative theory. Since this forms the background rather than the centre-piece of Habermas' theory, no more on this will be said here.

28. Habermas does offer the ontogenetic aspect of his thesis cautiously, since 'we must take care not to draw hasty parallels' (1979a: 102).

3
Communication and Evolution

It has been noted that Habermas' critique of Weber was aimed at effecting a paradigm shift from the philosophy of consciousness to communication, in order to 'remove the Weberian thorn' from earlier Critical Theory. This involved conceptualizing an alternative path to modernity which although present from the beginning had been suppressed by dominant systems of instrumental action. By refusing to regard dominant organizational forms as exhausting the rationality potential of modernity per se, Habermas makes a more strongly universalistic claim than Weber (as White [1990: 96] points out) and attempts to show that the iron cage of instrumentality which Weber regarded as inevitable was actually one-sided and flawed. According to the theory of communicative action, all cultural traditions (and not merely, as Weber thought, those of the West) share formal properties which are capable of rationalization, so the particular route taken by western modernity requires explanation. That is, why did the particular form of occidental rationality, embodied in the market and bureaucracy, emerge out of a field of cultural innovations some of which pointed in different directions to that actually taken? Moreover, how does the presence of this suppressed modernity reveal itself in the formation of contemporary social movements which challenge dominant organizational forms of the present, with an image of a more progressive future?

The argument hinges on two distinctions in *TCA*: first between rationalization of the lifeworld and rationalization of the system; and secondly between the logic and dynamics of development. Regarding the former, a 'lifeworld can be regarded as rationalized to the extent that it permits interactions that are not guided by normatively ascribed agreement but – directly or indirectly – by communicatively achieved understanding' (Habermas, 1984: 340). This Habermas regards as 'wholly positive' (Honneth et al., 1981) and should be distinguished from the contrasting tendency towards rationalization of the system. Here the regulation of action through money and bureaucratic power increasingly encroaches upon (or 'colonizes') the capacities for critical argument, which leads to a 'cultural impoverishment' of the lifeworld, and the appearance of increasingly visible pathologies (Habermas, 1984: xl). Habermas believes that the analysis of society in terms of both system and lifeworld (an idea which originates in Lockwood's critique of Parsons) has advantages over both earlier Critical Theory and contemporary sociologies, in ways which are elaborated below.

Secondly, Habermas distinguishes between the *logic* of potential but unrealized communicative possibilities and the *dynamics* of actual historical development,[1] a distinction he believes Weber overlooked. The logic of development derives from the structural differentiation of the lifeworld into the three cultural value spheres (science, norms and art). If allowed to proceed uninterrupted these would progress towards post-conventional identities and the erosion of domination. However, this process *is* interrupted and empirical development takes the distorted forms of a lifeworld restricted by the global capitalist economy and bureaucratic-military state. This hiatus, between the logic and dynamics of evolution, or between potential and actual development, in turn requires a theory of social selection to explain why only certain communicative possibilities are institutionalized.

Habermas' social-evolutionary framework, which was anticipated in *KHI*, follows the schema that was briefly outlined in the Introduction, and its core conceptual components are sketched out in Table 3.1. Whereas natural evolution is regulated by objective criteria of successful stabilization (organisms either survive or they do not) social evolution is exosomatic (detached from biology) and occurs through language, culture, communication and theories which offer solutions to problems. Exosomatic evolution follows multilinear lines of potential development and proceeds along dimensions of production, where nature is appropriated for human needs; socialization, where inner nature (or personality) is adapted to society through communicative action; and system maintenance through steering capacity, which increases with successful adaptations to environmental disturbances. Successful adaptations are those which are consistent with the continued identity or goal state of the system and protect its core social relations. This involves, as will be seen later, the problematic task of locating those structures which define the identity of the system (such as the capital/wage labour relation) and those which are adaptive mechanisms (such as the welfare state).[2] But the point is that learning capacities are not one-dimensional and open up different kinds of potentials along the dimensions of production, socialization and systemic regulation. Each of these dimensions represent stages of learning in which

> the development of . . . normative structures is the pacemaker of social evolution, for new principles of social organization mean new forms of social

Table 3.1 *Evolution, socialization and system*

Logic	Production	Socialization	System
Dimension	Outer nature	Inner nature	Goal state
Medium	Technical rationality	Communication	Steering capacity
Learning capacity	Success in organization of labour	Normative validity	Altering boundaries
Learning potential	Quantitative expansion	Practical discourse	Flexible adaptation

integration; and the latter in turn make it possible to implement available productive forces or to generate new ones, as well as making possible a heightening of social complexity. (Habermas, 1979a: 120)

Habermas follows Marx in looking to historical evolution to demonstrate not only the concrete possibility of an emancipated form of life, but also that structural problems encountered within modernity can be resolved only through the release of new emancipatory potential.[3] In order to reconstruct historical materialism within the framework of the communicative paradigm, Habermas seeks to demonstrate that social evolution has represented stages of the unfolding of cognitive-moral as well as technical development, and that the transition between stages involves two conditions. First, within the world-view of the old order the potential arises for a higher level of learning (the significance of which might only be apparent in retrospect). Second, this reservoir of learning potential will be released at the point where systemic crises have accumulated within the old order and call its identity into question.

In his earlier work Habermas defined the regulatory mechanism of social evolution as the 'principle of organization'. This determines the limits within which structural changes can occur, defines to what degree the available capacities of productive forces can be socially deployed or new forces stimulated, and how far the complexity of a system's steering capacity can be raised (Habermas, 1979a: 153). Thus social change from one form of society to another takes place when the following four conditions are met. First, new cognitive potential and productive techniques are transposed from world-views in which they had been latent into social institutions (for example, prior to capitalist development new cognitive capacities had accumulated in medieval universities and organizational techniques in the monasteries). Secondly, this transposition occurs when systemic problems of the old order overload its steering capacity and throw it into crisis (for example, the disintegration of medieval feudalism). Thirdly, new rationality structures (both cognitive and technical) are stabilized in institutions (for example, the market and modern bureaucracy). Fourthly, new capacities for resource-mobilization can be deployed (for example, the application of techniques of labour-time management to the production process). Moreover, the stabilization of problem-solutions itself brings to the fore new systemic problems (such as class conflict or economic crisis tendencies). These dynamics are illustrated in Table 3.2.

For example, Habermas claims that state societies emerged in response to systemic problems of land scarcity and population density, in the kinship structure of neolithic societies, which unleashed new productive potentials (cultivation, stock-farming, crafts and irrigation) which were already present in the learning mechanisms of kinship societies in exemplary ways. But concomitant with the development of technical learning was the expansion in moral-cognitive learning, from pre-conventional moral and legal systems (arbitration and feuding) to conventional systems where

Table 3.2 *Evolutionary problems and solutions*

	Crises	Innovation	Selection	New problems
System	Overload [e.g. markets and urbanization under feudalism]	Release of latent technical capacities	Wage-contract Bureacracy Goal-rational action	Class conflict Tendency of the rate of profit to fall
Lifeworld	Exhaustion of learning capacities	Differentiation of value spheres	Suppression of alternate modernities	Resistance Anomie Pathologies

punishment was linked to consequences of action and authority was embodied in the figure of the father-ruler (Habermas 1979a: 95–129). Modern societies by contrast are in the throes of a complex and problematic transition, in which the binding force of conventional and traditional authority has been broken, but in which post-conventional norms cannot yet be stabilized. However, Habermas' somewhat idiosyncratic attempt to resuscitate classical sociological notions of social evolution requires examination, especially since his own defence of the theory is rather sparse.[4]

The Logic and Dynamics of Social Evolution

Separating the logic from the dynamics of social development requires, first, the identification of alternative trajectories towards modernity which were latent within lifeworld structures and represented new forms of potential cognitive and moral learning. Habermas suggests that although 'the counter-factual line of inquiry is unusual for an empirical sociologist', we know 'in an exemplary way' how the possibilities of expanding cognitive, moral and aesthetic knowledge would look from our modern perceptions (1984: 210). This is presumably because modern lifeworlds are sufficiently rationalized to offer a glimpse of what society would be like if communicative action were more thoroughly institutionalized. Secondly, it requires analysis of the process by which instrumental organizations became dominant in the evolution of modernity.

However, it is somewhat paradoxical that although Habermas provides very little analysis of social movements (nor does he anywhere say clearly what they are), they are accorded the role of central actors in the social-evolutionary drama. Indeed, social movements are 'carriers' of cultural innovations which are released during periods of social transformation and affect its course (Habermas, 1979a: 125).[5] This is illustrated in Habermas' critique of Weber's sociology of religion. In the Introduction it was noted that previously isolated cultural innovations, such as the clock and the water mill, entered the productive process with the birth of capitalism, which similarly deployed latent cognitive and organizational capacities. For example, Randall Collins (1986: 52–4) has argued that medieval monastic orders such as the Cistercians combined ascetic withdrawal from the world with refined techniques of accumulation, such as new hierarchies of mental and manual labour, as well as the most economically effective productive units of the time – mills, water technology and wool production. The Cistercians' isolation from the European medieval economy was beneficial to their survival in that it enabled them to circumvent the immobility of capital and labour in the secular economy. These latently stored innovations were released into societal development when the constraints of the feudal order on both economic and scientific development began to weaken. Such constraints would include serfdom, which restricted labour mobility, or ecclesiastic control of natural philosophy, which inhibited scientific-cognitive innovation.

Such a theory of cultural transmission is present in Weber's sociology of religion, which suggests that the ascetic life-style of religious orders broke free from the monasteries and entered social evolution via the early modern Protestant sects. Calvinism's orientation to worldly asceticism was incorporated into social evolution because of an elective affinity between the Protestant ethic of self-discipline and the spirit of rational capital accumulation. Although Habermas accepts this account to an extent, he reconstructs Weber's thesis in order to argue, first, that the structure of the Calvinist world-view admitted only a partial rationalization of the life-world, and, secondly, that an alternative modernity was present in seventeenth-century religious social movements. These claims can then be developed into a theory of the ways in which historical outcomes are the result of interactions between social movements and systems of domination.

Habermas accepts Weber's argument that complex religious world-views address the problem of theodicy, which arose as relatively egalitarian kinship societies clashed with early state societies in the ancient world. The appearance of new forms of domination and inequality posed the problem of how to render ethically meaningful the inequity of suffering. That is, theodicy addresses the question, 'if a wise and just God exists then why is there evil?' (Turner, 1981: 148), which is further bound up with the legitimation of unequal social relations. Problems of theodicy were common to all world religions, even if the content of their answers differed, as between western theocentric and eastern cosmocentric religions.[6] In addressing this problem, world religions offered two cultural innovations, the significance of which 'Weber did not pursue very far' (Habermas, 1984: 201). These were, first, the idea that individual misfortune might be undeserved, and that the individual might cherish the religious hope of being delivered from evil, sickness or poverty; and, secondly, the formation of religious communities, of magicians and priests, whose counsel could remove or expiate suffering.

The appearance of religious communities, dedicated to understanding the meaning of the cosmos and the social world within all-embracing moral and cognitive systems of thought, opened up further dimensions of cultural learning. It was possible to subsume the world under categories of thought and to adopt attitudes (or 'world relations') towards it. The profane world was set against the community of believers for whom it was judged ethically flawed. This separation of the world as an object of judgement in turn permitted a matrix of attitudes (see Table 3.3) of world-rejection (monasticism), world-affirmation (salvation religions), world-mastery (Judeo-Christianity) or contemplation (Greek philosophy or Confucianism). These world relations opened up multiple potentials for the evolution of world-views in the dimensions of ethics, cognition and personalities, only some of which were incorporated into the dynamics of development (Habermas, 1984: 201–13).

Despite these differences of attitude towards the world, however, it is not obvious that the occidental tradition contained any unique preconditions for rationalization. On the contrary,

> the Chinese, from the first century BC to the fifteenth century AD, were evidently more successful than the West in developing theoretical knowledge and in using this knowledge for practical purposes. . . . The essentials of a rationalizable world-view are as little lacking in Confucianism and Taoism as they are in Greek philosophy. (Habermas, 1984: 210)[7]

If this is so (and a similar argument could be made for Islam) then it is necessary to explain why rationalization of world-views proceeded further in the West than in the East; and why in the West the dominant structures of rational action took the limited forms of the market and bureaucracy? Weber's analysis did not address these problems adequately because it assumed that advanced capitalism represented the only possible outcome of rationalization and attributed the specific forms of western modernity to the internal structure of its world-view ('the specific and peculiar rationalism of Western culture' [Weber, 1976: 26]). Not only this, but Weber falsely identified one aspect of occidental development (goal-rationality) with rationality per se, because he omitted a crucial stage of selection which occurred between the Reformation and the birth of capitalism.

Early modern Protestant sects addressed the tension between the ethics of Christian communities and the unscrupulous, cut-throat ethics of business (that is, a variant of the theodicean problem). In the past, this tension had been resolved by inner-worldly withdrawal and mysticism, which kept rationalized conduct locked out of societal development

Table 3.3 *Attitudes towards the world*

Evaluation of the world	Ways of seeking salvation	
	Active	Passive
Rejection of the world	World-mastery: Judaism, Christianity	Flight from the world: Hinduism
Affirmation of the world	Adjustment to the world: Confucianism	Contemplation of the world: Greek metaphysics

(Habermas, 1984: 226). With the development of merchant capitalism, however, the tension between world-affirmation and retreat became more sharply defined since the market tended to neutralize the very difference between the ethics of internal and external relations upon which the possibility of other-worldly withdrawal was based. Thus the religious extension of 'brotherliness' (or social solidarity, perhaps) came into sharper conflict with the extension of market impersonality. The crucial role of the Protestant ethic was to resolve this tension in an historically novel way, if only temporarily, by renouncing universal love in favour of a personal relation with God and a practical attitude towards the world. The latter arose out of the so-called 'predestination paradox' – the uncertainty amongst Calvinists as to whether they were amongst the elect – which prompted the search for evidence of salvation in worldly success. This, Habermas suggests, was the origin of an instrumental attitude towards ethics, which sought validity in outward signs of success, but it was the product of a distorted and highly irrational sect, whose values won the day largely because of their compatibility with the demands of the market.

Calvinism, then, represented only one amongst a number of potential solutions to the conflict between ethics and business. Indeed, Habermas (1984: 186ff.) suggests that Calvinism had meagre potential as a carrier of modern rationality, if this is understood from the stand-point of communicative action – refusing to recognize any exemptions from the critical power of hypothetical thought. Against this criterion, Calvinism's cognitive potential was limited since its dogmatic foundations (concepts of 'God', 'being', 'nature', etc.) were protected from critical interrogation. Explaining the form taken by dominant modernity therefore involves an additional step in the transposition of rationalization from culture to society (Habermas, 1984: 214). On the one hand, the Calvinist notion of worldly success as a sacred vocation was transposed into the secular instrumental ego, suited to commerce and bureaucratic careerism. On the other hand, cognitive innovations which prepared the way for the scientific revolution and subjected traditional world-views to argumentative doubt did not come via the Puritans, but from the medieval universities, amongst the Scholastics and Humanists, and especially from the Renaissance, which 'released potential stored in cognitively rationalized worldviews' (Habermas, 1984: 216).

Calvinism, in other words, released potential for goal-rational conduct in the narrow field of commercial ethics, but did not contain any cognitive advance over pre-modern world-views.[8] Moreover, from the early modern period there were competing religious social movements which attempted to solve problems of ethics and practice in more universalistic ways. For example,

> those Protestant sects that, like the Anabaptists, wanted to institutionalize the universal ethic of brotherliness with fewer reservations . . . [and] did not want to divert the potential of ethically rationalized worldviews onto the tracks of disciplined labour *by privatized individuals*, but wanted to convert it into

social-revolutionary forms of life, failed in this first attempt. (Habermas, 1984: 232; original emphasis)

The Anabaptists represented an alternative path to modernity, in which ethics would not have been instrumentally divorced from politics and social life.[9] They failed because their social ethics were blocked by capitalism which 'permits post-traditional action orientations only in a restricted form' (Habermas, 1984: 233). The emergent order of domination incorporated into the dynamics of development only those social movements which were compatible with its own identity, with a resultant partial rationalization, 'world domination and unbrotherliness'. Thus instrumental rationality 'surges beyond the bounds of' state and economy, to create a 'jagged profile of modernization' within which universalistic ethics could find no foothold and went underground. However, this was soon to create new problems for capitalism, since subsequent conflicts 'had to arise' in the form of social movements, like socialism, claiming the heritage of this unfulfilled potential of modernity (Habermas, 1984: 241).

This is a suggestive account but Habermas makes some major and unexplained leaps in the analysis. Whilst his suggestion that socialism had distant roots in dissident religious sects like the Anabaptists might be defensible, the rather casual assertion that subsequent conflicts 'had to arise' is not illuminating, and the mechanism by which the rationalization potential of certain social movements is released remains opaque. If the nascent structure of capitalism selects compatible 'solutions' to the crisis of late feudalism out of a range of potential innovations, then the weight of explanatory power rests with the social environment, not with social movements nor with the communicative structure of the lifeworld. Further it needs to be shown how communicative ethics that were excluded from the developmental trajectory of early modernity might be institutionalized now, despite Habermas' view that systemic aspects of capitalist modernity are inescapable features of complex social organization.

For example, by 'progress' Habermas means increased capacities for instrumental mastery and consensual resolution, not 'orders of happiness' (1982b: 228).[10] Irrevocable systemic advances occur at a cost to happiness, such as the surrender of primal egalitarianism which followed the transition to complex societies, and 'in spite of the destructive side-effects of the violent process of capital accumulation and state formation, the new organizational forms gained wide acceptance and considerable permanency on the strength of their greater effectiveness and superior level of integration' (1989b: 321). If capitalism was stabilized because it was an improvement on earlier forms of organization, despite the presence of an alternative potential route to modernity, then why should latent communicative potentials come into their own now? The solution to this paradox might be that expansion of the systems of power and money into the lifeworld will have ultimately self-defeating consequences, unless they are matched by an expansion of moral-cognitive learning processes in the socio-cultural sphere. This hardly sounds like a call to the barricades, but it does suggest in post-Marxist fashion that there is a core contradiction within modern systems of accumulation and organization that neither systems theory nor postmodernism can grasp.

Steering Media and Colonization

This argument can be developed with reference to Habermas' theory of 'steering media' and colonization of the lifeworld. A central idea here is that strategic action is stored within technologies and self-regulating systems – the market and bureaucracies – which become progressively detached from the lifeworld which they retroactively 'colonize' (Habermas, 1989b: 335). Colonization of the lifeworld, however, is a pathological extension of the functionally necessary process of the uncoupling of system and lifeworld, so let us briefly examine this first.

As a result of the 'linguistification of the sacred' (see Chapter 2), the co-ordination of action increasingly occurs through negotiated consensus, rather than through the spell-binding power of the sacred. However, the more lifeworld horizons (H) expand in relation to background consensus (B) (see Figure 2.1) the more societies confront the problem of co-ordinating increasingly complex anonymous interactions. Habermas suggests that this overloading of communication structures results in the initial separation between the lifeworld and sub-systems of strategic action. The latter permit impersonal social exchanges released from the need for consensus, the paradigm for which is the market, where actions are co-ordinated through the intermeshing of unintended consequences of action, such that its effects appear to occur naturally and inevitably.[11] These regulatory systems are thus progressively 'uncoupled' from the lifeworld and encode purposive-rational attitudes which influence actors' decisions while by-passing processes of negotiation and agreement (Habermas, 1984: 183).

The model for the uncoupling of sub-systems of strategic action from the lifeworld is derived from Marx's critique of commodified labour. However, for Habermas, Marx missed the point that interconnection of the capitalist economy and modern state might represent a 'higher and evolutionarily advantageous level of integration by comparison to traditional societies' (1989b: 339). Every modern society, whatever its class structure, has to exhibit a high degree of structural differentiation, but Marx envisaged the proletarian revolution bringing the autonomous process of economic growth back into the horizon of the lifeworld. Further, the concept of alienation could not separate this increasing social complexity from the repressive uprooting of traditional forms of life, since both were evaluated against 'the nostalgically loaded, frequently romanticized past of pre-modern forms of life' (Habermas, 1989b: 342). Marx was unable to see that the commodification of labour was merely a specific case of the separation of system from the lifeworld.[12] This process expands as the money economy is supplemented by the state, which in turn segments the lifeworld into a private sphere of employees and consumers, and a public sphere of clients and citizens (more will be said on this in Chapter 4).

In order to broaden Marx's concept, Habermas (1989b: 265) adapts Talcott Parsons' concept of 'steering media', which must exhibit three properties: they can be measured, they can be alienated in specific amounts, and they can be stored. These are routine exchanges no longer dependent on linguistic interaction and are hence removed from the critical potential of *Diskurs*. This is not to say that the market and bureaucracy are literally devoid of language, but that they produce highly formalized systems where action is oriented to the consequences of others' action (for example, an increase in supply of a commodity after a rise in price) which circumvent the need for consensus. That some aspects of market behaviour are automatic (or, for Habermas, 'self-referential') might be exemplified in the way in which share prices can fluctuate according to pre-programmed computerized responses, which do not require direct human intervention. Power, by contrast, does not permit the same degree of 'de-linguistification' as money, but bureaucratic decision-making is none the less 'systemic' because it permits automatic responses and commands that are not subjected to validity-questioning (Habermas, 1989b: 262). Weber suggested something similar when he claimed that the bureaucratic order impinges on 'the masses from the outside', and 'merely replaces the belief in the sanctity of traditional norms by compliance with rationally determined rules and by the knowledge that these rules can be superseded by others, if one has the necessary power' (1978: II, 1117).

However, Habermas' (albeit critical) use of systems theory has been controversial. How usefully might Critical Theory be accommodated with the (often) conservative, teleological and reified accounts of social processes developed by the opposing camp of functionalism? Hans Joas (Honneth & Joas, 1991: 107) has argued that there was no justification for turning to systems theory in order to account for the unintended results of action, which can be understood well enough by theories of collective action. McCarthy (1985, 1991: 137) makes a similar point and suggests that by flirting with systems theory Habermas runs the danger of being seduced by the scientistic illusion to which he claimed Marx had fallen (by scientism he refers to the illegitimate extension of the methods of natural science to sociology) (1991: 124). Further, even if the market is 'norm-free', its relations are grounded on the rule of law, basic human rights, popular sovereignty and other 'moral practical' consensus foundations.[13]

Again, Michael Schmid argues that Habermas 'willingly concedes to the Parsons–Luhmann system theory that steering mechanisms can be explained by a process of differentiation' (1982: 162–80). His evolutionary theory is premised upon identifying a developmental logic of cumulative 'stages, phases, and steps' defined by an intrinsic structure and invariable sequence, in which each successive stage is dependent on that which came before. Habermas (1979a: 74) does add the caveat that the developmental process is 'discontinuous' and 'crisis-ridden', but for Schmid this merely compounds the difficulty because Habermas then explains deviations from the developmental logic with reference to 'regressions' – a term full of 'normative-descriptive ambiguities' which adds no theoretical problems or empirical information. Certainly, regressions from potential communicative competence require explanation, which might be addressed through the theory of colonization, elaborated below. But Schmid implicitly raises an important question, which has dogged all sequential theories of development, including Marx's, namely does a society need to recapitulate each developmental sequence of 'more advanced' societies, and by whose criteria might this be measured? This is a question to which the discussion in Part 2 will return.

However, Schmid is wrong to claim that Habermas concedes the Parsons–Luhmann thesis, since he explicitly states the contrary (1979a: 125; 1989b: 173). Indeed, his principal counter to Parsons or Luhmann is to insist on the autonomy of the lifeworld from systems of co-ordination and regulation, and the central thesis of *TCA* is that the normative structures of the lifeworld cannot be converted into steering media in the way Parsons suggests in *The Social System* (1991). Habermas offers two kinds of arguments to justify this view. The first is an a priori claim that areas of life that primarily fulfil functions of cultural reproduction, social integration and socialization, or mutual understanding, cannot be replaced by media, because these activities cannot be 'bought' and 'collected' like labour and taxes (Habermas, 1989b: 267). Secondly, this irreducibility of the lifeworld accounts for the empirical appearance of pathologies when areas of cultural reproduction are treated *as if* they could be 'mediatized'. Yet Parsonian functionalism, which fails to distinguish system and the lifeworld, can offer no explanation of these pathologies (Habermas, 1989b: 199ff.).

However, Habermas has conceded ground to functionalism in that he accepts that some degree of systemic steering is necessary in order to manage the complexity of modern lifeworlds, and indeed that it represents an evolutionary gain. Hence,

> there is no longer much prospect of the democratic reshaping from within of a differentiated economic system solely by means of worker self-management, in other words by switching from money and organizational power *completely* over to participation. (Habermas, 1991: 261; original emphasis)

Habermas insists that this does not imply a surrender to the capitalist market and state, but on the contrary requires new forms of democratic participation aimed at curbing economic and administrative power. Even so, in these new structures the question of forms of ownership of the economy will be less important than finding means of 'curbing' the state and market, and Habermas (1990) does not indicate what shape these structures might take. For McCarthy (1991), this illustrates how, under the influence of systems theory, Habermas can no longer specify what types of democratization are possible. Moreover, much of Luhmann's critique of Habermas invoked the inevitability of vertical and horizontal differentiation as means of reducing what would otherwise be unmanageable complexity. Thus for Luhmann, talk of truth and justice 'retain only symbolic functions, . . . serve to express good intentions, to appeal to good will . . . [but] degenerate into ciphers of indeterminate and unspecifiable complexity' (1982: 119–20) – a critique which Habermas now seems to turn on opponents whose politics he considers over-optimistic.

Ultimately the adequacy of Habermas' theory should be evaluated against the amount of insight it offers into social processes, a discussion which will be conducted in Part 2. But for the moment an account of the critical use which he makes of systemic analysis might assuage fears that he has gone over to the other side. McCarthy's point is that the distinction between a normative lifeworld and norm-free system is untenable because the lifeworld and system are actually interpenetrated. But this is surely taken account of, since 'production relations and class structures can in no fashion be adequately grasped by means of systems theory, because modes of production and social formations depend on *the manner in which mechanisms of system integration are institutionally anchored in the lifeworld*' (Habermas, 1991: 262; emphasis added) and the difference between lifeworld and system is not absolute but one of degree (Habermas, 1989b: 194–5). What this means is that market forces or state power must be embedded in supportive social, organizational, institutional and normative frameworks. Norms, organizational and institutional forms, social networks etc., ensure the conformity of private economic actions with the overall requirements of continued economic growth. Likewise, the exercise of state power extends beyond its institutional boundaries to secure legitimacy through political cultures, the public sector, voluntary associations, etc., whilst creating new forms of sociality dependent upon it (through social welfare, for example).

Indeed, that steering media (money and power) have to be anchored in the normative structures of the lifeworld engenders a pivotal contradiction. On the one hand, systems of regulation never entirely escape the possibility of rational interrogation, and since late capitalism remains an order of coerced inequalities it continues to engender legitimation problems. These are intensified by the absence of 'functional equivalents for the spent traditions' (Habermas, 1976: 75) where secularization and differentiation of the lifeworld preclude the possibility of social integration based on a dominant ideology.[14] On the other hand, steering media have developed forms of regulation which serve as a kind of substitute for ideologies, by rendering some domination invisible (Habermas, 1989b: 229). To the extent that steering media escape the validity-claims inherent in linguistic communication, they must also limit the capacity to pose legitimacy-questions, and structures of domination then slip from public view. Thus the potential transparency of the lifeworld implicit in the expansion of H is offset by the effects of power and money which remove problematic issues from public agendas. For example, the fragmentation of reason which Weber (and in a way early Critical Theory) had regarded as inevitable, resulted from the fact that along with the three value spheres had arisen 'expert cultures' within which increasingly specialized forms of

argumentation become the guarded preserve of experts and thereby lose
contact with the understanding process of the majority of people. Like the
process of reification, the insulation of expertise has a deforming effect on
everyday life since the possibilities for democratic participation in decision-
making is constricted (Habermas, 1989b: 351–6). This process must by its
very nature remain unseen, hence,

> [t]he reproductive constraints that instrumentalize a lifeworld without weaken-
> ing the illusion of its self-sufficiency have to hide, so to speak, in the pores of
> communicative action. This gives rise to a structural violence that, without
> becoming manifest as such, takes hold of the forms of intersubjectivity of
> possible understanding. (Habermas, 1984: 187)

In the colonized lifeworld the dominant principle of everyday consciousness is no longer ideology as such but fragmentation, through which late
capitalist societies have found 'some functional equivalent for ideology
formation', namely 'preventing holistic interpretations from coming into
existence . . . everyday consciousness is robbed of its power to synthesize:
it becomes *fragmented*' (Habermas, 1989b: 355; original emphasis). However, this process is contradictory because fragmentation occurs at the cost
of disrupting the processes through which membership of social groups and
identities are confirmed and renewed, provoking crises manifestations: loss
of meaning, withdrawal of legitimation, confusion of orientations, anomie,
destabilization of collective identities, alienation, psychopathologies,
breakdowns in tradition and withdrawal of motivation (Habermas, 1989b:
322). The effects of these can be illustrated with reference to the public
sphere.

The Public Sphere and Pathologies

Thus far, the potential for communicative action has been discussed in
abstract terms, but a link with more concrete social processes is made
through the concept of the public sphere. Habermas suggests that this
arose within early bourgeois society (but only in a proto-typical way) when
the developing market economy extended beyond the bounds of private
authority and constituted a sphere of public opinion, where argument
proceeded according to rules of public debate (as opposed to prejudice or
custom). Private individuals, such as merchants, were excluded from
political institutions and became concerned with the government of
society, promoting public debate through newspapers, journals and political clubs. By the end of the seventeenth century, periodicals began to
appear not merely with trade information but also with educational
instructions, literary reviews and political comment; and during the
eighteenth century a critical public opinion had formed in centres like
London and Paris.[15] In fairly orthodox Marxist fashion, Habermas argued
that whilst this public sphere was thought to represent the general interest,
its social basis in private property meant that its commitment to rational
self-determination was never fully realized, and the liberal-bourgeois ideal

of free speech was always at some distance from reality. This discrepancy increased with the development of the capitalist economy, and the subsequent commercialization of mass media eventually excluded political and practical questions from large areas of the public sphere. Indeed the irony which informs Habermas' account of the public sphere is that it was most critical and seemingly most reasoned when its participants were most homogeneous – in gender, class, ethnicity, religion and style of life. As the potential constituency of the public sphere widened with mass democracy, so access to debate was limited partly through ideological strategies of exclusion which drew on bodies of 'expert knowledge' (such as beliefs in 'congenital' pauperism, criminality, illness and 'feeble-mindedness' and the constitutional inferiority of women, the working class and colonial peoples).[16] The upshot of this was that issues of poverty, sexuality, citizenship or women's rights entered the public domain heavily loaded with moralism and prejudice dressed up as scientific argument.

Politics as rational and unconstrained debate was replaced by publicity and public opinion research, through which political parties 'extract' loyalty from the public sphere in an instrumental fashion (Habermas, 1991: 258), concomitant with which was the rise of expert cultures and what Russell Jacoby (1987) calls the 'decline of the public intellectual'. Moreover, the commercialization of the mass media coincided with two developmental trends in late capitalism – increasing state intervention in everyday life, and the growing interdependence of research and technology, as the Frankfurt Institute had noted. The result was the process of 'technicization', whereby questions of moral value and political controversy were converted into managerial, technical or planning processes. However, colonization has the paradoxical effects of both regulating conflicts but also giving rise to new crisis tendencies, which can be illustrated with reference to the welfare state.

On the one hand, the welfare state in post-war western societies was the result of the mass organization of social democratic and labour movements, and represented an achievement of social movements against the monetary-bureaucratic complex. On the other hand, the corporatist state was a systemic response to crisis tendencies within the classical form of capitalism, in that welfare and Keynesian economic regulation pacified traditional class conflicts. Once selected into the developmental trajectory of late capitalism, the corporatist state intervened in the capitalist economies in order to fill 'functional gaps' left by the market and to offset the tendency of the rate of profit to fall.[17] Thus, 'late capitalism makes use in its own way of the relative uncoupling of system and lifeworld' (Habermas, 1984: 348).[18]

This was initially functional for capital, since class conflict is diminished, but in the longer term welfare state intervention gives rise to two types of crisis tendencies. First, as he argued in *Legitimation Crisis* (1976, hereafter *LC*), state intervention *re*-politicizes the previously apolitical realm of the market, thus demonstrating that resource distribution *can be* available to rational planning (social welfare becomes 'the political content of mass democracy'). This in turn engenders demands from trade unions, political parties, welfare-rights groups and the public sector itself for the further extension of planning and administration, a tendency which capital eventually resists as a drain on profitability. Since the welfare state itself is not a 'source of prosperity' (being dependent on fiscal revenue) and cannot guarantee employment security as a right, it is subject to conflicting demands for its preservation or dismemberment (Habermas, 1989a: 57).[19] Clearly this controversy has been of crucial significance in recent politics in all the developed capitalist societies, where the neo-conservative op-ponents of welfare (Reaganites, Thatcherites, etc.) gained hegemony over the political culture (at least for as long as it took to restructure the mode of state intervention).

Moreover, the welfare state goes beyond pacifying class conflict lodged in the sphere of production and spreads a net of client relationships over private spheres of life, which results in both a bureaucratization and a monetization of core areas of the lifeworld (Habermas, 1984: 364). The role of employee loses its 'debilitating proletarian features' with the continuous rise in the standard of living, but is simultaneously 'neutralized' into the role of participant-citizen, or 'client' of welfare state bureaucracy (which is 'the model case for colonization of the lifeworld': Habermas, 1989b: 322). This 'juridification' (*Verrechtlichung*) of social life means that while the welfare state is intended to serve the goal of social integration, it nevertheless promotes disintegration of life-relations (Habermas, 1989b: 143).[20] The displacement of systemic crises (for example, recession and unemployment) into spheres of social integration (for example, socializ-ation and legitimation) creates new forms of instability. Thus one arrives at the crucial formulation: 'along the front between system and lifeworld, the lifeworld evidently offers stubborn resistance . . . when functions of symbolic reproduction are in question' (Habermas, 1989b: 351).

The decline of the welfare state actually creates opportunities for the reappearance of autonomous critical public spheres and self-organization, such as regionalist, feminist or ecological movements (Habermas, 1989a: 67). However, although colonization of the lifeworld creates potentials for the formation of emancipatory social movements, it also gives rise to pathologies. These contradictory tendencies can be illustrated with refer-ence to the appearance of socialization crisis which has both positive and regressive aspects. Extended adolescence, more egalitarian families and increased education create potential for what might be called the demo-cratic rather than authoritarian personality, since appeal to discursive ethics rather than to duty or unquestioning obedience offers the basis for more fluid (post-conventional) social organization. However, the forma-tion of autonomous individuals remains only a potentiality, since disturb-ances in socialization are also manifest in apolitical withdrawal, feelings of emptiness, isolation and futility, pre-Oedipal rage and anxieties concerning the intactness of the self (Habermas, 1989b: 388). Indeed, as Whitebook

(1984) or Lasch (1978) argue, mass consumer capitalism might promote regressive behaviour such as the marked intensification of the pursuit of material success, power and status, a preoccupation with youth, health and glamour, combined with difficulties in forming ongoing relationships with emotional depth.[21]

The over-expansion of steering media then, gives rise to pathologies for which Parsons did not have the 'wherewithal to provide a plausible explanation' (Habermas, 1989b: 202). These pathologies restrict further advances in social learning capacity, since actors' stocks of social knowledge cannot cover the need for mutual understanding that arises with new situations. However, there seem to be two not entirely separate consequences of this. One is withdrawal into 'career/familial privatism', which suggests an apolitical atrophy of public life. The other is that personality systems preserve their identity by means of defensive strategies detrimental to participating in social interaction on a 'realistic' basis (Habermas, 1984: 140–1). Here the melancholy charm of the past serves to compensate for loss of community, or, as the Mitscherlichs argue: 'World redeeming dreams of ancient greatness arise in peoples in whom the sense of having been left behind by history evokes feelings of impotence and rage' (Mitscherlich & Mitscherlich, 1975: 11). The second reaction, unlike the first, suggests a re-engagement with (conservative) political activism.

Although this might appear to be a re-playing of *The Authoritarian Personality* (1969), the focus is not on psycho-dynamics so much as communication structures, which through socialization transmit collective defence reactions to future generations. These 'regressions', from the point of view of communicative competence, then, are adaptive defensive reactions which are stabilized through learning processes in the lifeworld. Klaus Eder (1985: 62) has argued that social privatization, or atomization, separates people from historical memory, which gets mythologized in an uncritical identification with authority. Similar notions appear in Habermas' contribution to the 'Historian's Dispute', which focused on connections between 'normalization' of the Holocaust within German history, an inability to come to terms with the past, and neo-conservative politics (Halfmann, 1985).[22] The conservative historians are important 'in so far as they participate in a cultural climate that . . . endeavours to form a national consensus on conventional identity' (Holub, 1991: 185). Of course, in the very act of conserving 'tradition' something new evolves, and it will be seen that traditionalism is rooted in the dilemmas of the present.

Colonization of the Lifeworld: A Summary

In summary, then, what Weber regarded as an inevitable consequence of the differentiation of the cultural value spheres is for Habermas a specific effect of colonization of the lifeworld. It has been suggested that the logic of modernization presupposes evolution from conventional identities to post-traditional communities, but this is only partially effected because the

dynamics of capital accumulation select into mainstream social development those cultures and personality types most conducive to its own
reproduction. Rationalization of the lifeworld succeeds in eroding traditional bases of identity and authority sufficiently to release stored
learning potentials (previously locked away in monasteries, universities or
religious sects). With the expansion of these new cognitive capacities, the
spell-binding power of the sacred is 'non-renewably dismantled' in the
sense that societies can no longer be integrated through world-views
(which become matters of personal conviction). However, in place of
legitimating ideologies capitalist social relations have been protected in
two ways. First, participatory decision-making has been limited by expert
cultures and the public sphere has degenerated into electoral mobilization
(for example, a preoccupation with image and marketing campaigns rather
than genuine participation). Secondly, in complex social systems, action is
co-ordinated by steering media which are to some extent freed from
requirements of normative consensus. This is self-defeating, however, for
at least two reasons. First, the two media to some extent work against one
another, so that the welfare 'solution' to problems of late capitalism places
a burden on capital accumulation which ultimately deepens rather than
alleviates crisis tendencies. Secondly, both power and money have to be
anchored in symbolic reproduction in the lifeworld, which is exactly what is
disrupted by colonization, so that social dislocation (loss of meaning and
identity) is expressed in crises of motivation, socialization, meaning and
legitimation. The following chapter will discuss what kinds of social
movement theory might be derived from this analysis.

Notes

1. The distinction between logic and dynamics was signalled in *Legitimation Crisis* (1976),
where Habermas developed a set of hypotheses concerning the possible (i.e. logical)
legitimacy crises that could arise as a result of state intervention in the market in advanced
capitalist societies.
2. Further, what constitutes 'success' in social organization varies depending on the ways
in which 'environments' are appropriated through frames of meaning and systems of values.
Meyer and Rowan (1977), for example, refer to 'rational myths', organizational forms and
practices that are recognized as having prestige, ceremonial value and legitimacy, regardless
of their actual efficiency.
3. Although this follows Marx's view that no social order ever perishes before the full
potential of its productive forces has been realized, Habermas (1979a: 223 n.11) insists that
social evolution is not unilinear, there is no uninterrupted development and regressions are
possible.
4. It is perhaps telling of the uncertainty with which he approaches evolutionary theory
that of the eleven papers in Thompson and Held (1982), the only one he declines to answer is
Michael Schmid's critique of social evolution (1982: 162–80). White's suggestion that this
debate be put on one side, since the 'controversy over the theory of social evolution yields
more heat than light' (1990: 170n), is not satisfactory. Evolutionary logic and development
are offered as explanatory concepts and deserve proper consideration.
5. Other sociologists have made the same claim. Eisenstadt (1980) argues that modes of
cultural perception, symbols of collective identity and modes of legitimation are stored
amongst cultural, educational and political elites, and transmitted to societies under
conditions determined by the type of relationship between their core and periphery. This is

not quite the same, however, as viewing social movements as carriers of new social identities, an idea elaborated by Touraine (1977).

6. World religions have provided three types of answer to the problem of theodicy – eschatological belief in future justice; dualism between Good and Evil; and karma, the transmigration of souls. This abbreviates a more complex discussion in Weber on types of theodicy and 'the religious propensities of different social orders' (1978: I, 468–88, 518–28), elaboration of which would digress from the matter in hand.

7. Joseph Needham's (1979) classical study of the relationship between social structure, world-views and the growth of science in Europe and China lends support to Habermas' claim. The argument that Weber over-emphasized internal cultural as opposed to external and material factors in his comparison of eastern and western societies is hardly peculiar to Habermas (see, e.g. Turner, 1984). The issue is raised again in Chapter 7, in relation to Islam.

8. On the other hand, it has been argued that the Calvinist belief in predestination was an intellectual precursor of the scientific concept of causality. Once the cosmos had been subsumed under immutable laws, it was possible to view it as a self-regulating system subject to invariant natural regularities. See Zilsel (1942) or Foster (1934, 1935).

9. A sect within the Radical Reformation, Anabaptism split from Zwingli in Zurich 1525 (over infant baptism) and was developed by Menno Simons in the Netherlands later in the sixteenth century. Denying the legitimacy of both *corpus christianum* (the organic unity of church and society through the state) and Luther's stress on the divine origin of the state, Anabaptists refused to obey laws which conflicted with religion, or to participate in state institutions. Anabaptists viewed the church as an alternative community (*Gemeente*) of believers based on sincerity and love, and in some cases (e.g. the Hutterites) property was held in common. They advocated social justice and tolerance of other religions (George, 1988: 260–301).

10. This is in response to Agnes Heller's criticism that Habermas has an inadequate sense of the tragic. Like Horkheimer, she argues, 'no future will give back the lives destroyed in their youth, no future can make us forget the horrors, the miseries, the bloodshed and the tears of the present' (Heller, 1982: 40).

11. The relationship between normative and monetary regulation is perhaps more complex than this (admittedly highly abbreviated) summary of Habermas suggests. Anglo-Saxon *wergild*, for example, indicates that in early medieval Europe money served as a measure of human worth, since homicide could be atoned for by payment. Later concepts of human dignity rendered this type of monetary reparation unacceptable, which suggests that money has in some areas been superseded by normative-legal regulation.

12. The claim that Marx was nostalgic for pre-capitalist society is idiosyncratic in view of his celebration of the passing of traditional society (e.g. in the *Communist Manifesto* [Marx & Engels, 1969]) and his admiration for the technical accomplishment of detail labour in the factory (Marx & Engels, 1974: Part 4).

13. This incidentally, is a point which Durkheim (1979) made in relation to Simmel.

14. The existence of a dominant ideology in the sense of over-arching integrative beliefs or values has been challenged from other points of view, of course, notably Abercrombie et al. (1980).

15. Habermas implies that a comparable process occurs within the labour movement, which well into the nineteenth century was a traditionalistic defence of endangered ways of life. Once the movement took shape, communicated through leaflets, etc., it became self-reflexive and reached outside the boundaries of its lifeworld (Honneth et al., 1981), which suggests that micro-public spheres form within social movements themselves which presage future organizational forms.

16. Late nineteenth-century medicine, for example, claimed that intellectual capacities, poverty, criminality and illness were transmitted via the somatic 'constitution', a belief later popularized amongst expert cultures through eugenics.

17. For Marx, this was the underlying crisis tendency of capitalism, expressed in the formula $s/(c+v)=p$, where the ratio of surplus value (s) to the cost of production is equal to the rate of profit (p). As the organic composition of capital rises, that is, as the fixed costs of raw materials and machinery (c) rise relative to variable costs (v) the denominator ($c+v$) must rise relative to the numerator (s) and the rate of profit must fall in the long run. This remains the logical tendency of capitalism, even if it is 'offset' in the short term by factors such as colonialism, state intervention or international trade. The hypothesis is difficult to test, given the complexity of global capital and the variation of necessary labour-time and rates of exploitation in different parts of the system.

18. Although this sounds conspiratorial German abstract nouns are more capable of agency than are English, and Habermas is referring to the process of selection outlined above.

19. Claims also advanced in O'Connor (1973, 1987) or Offe (1985). As Lash and Urry (1988: 229) point out, the role of welfare budgets in provoking the neo-conservative reaction should not be over-stressed since their agenda also reflected the global restructuring of capital from the late 1970s onwards. On this see also Jessop (1990).

20. 'Juridification' refers to 'legally supplementing a communicative context of action through the super-imposition of legal norms – not through legal institutions but through law as a medium'. This in turn has the consequence of 'bringing about increasing dependence. Emancipation within the family is achieved at the cost of a new bond' (Habermas, 1984: 368–9). This idea was already present in Horkheimer's account of the encroachment of instrumental culture into nurturance.

21. Christopher Lasch, (1978: 388) argues that the decline of the authoritarian father leaves individuals with an obscure sense of discontent, a heightened version of normality, formed through careful protective shallowness, and difficulty with intimate relationships which threaten uncontrollable rage. The modern pursuit of mass consumption, success, etc., serves as a narcissistic symptom of defence. Habermas (1989b: 388) seems to suggest something similar when he notes the reduction in hysterical symptoms relative to the rise in narcissistic disturbances.

22. The *Historikerstreit* of the late 1980s was largely initiated by Habermas' attempt to link the disparate work of Andreas Hillgruber, Michael Stürmer and Ernst Nolte. For Habermas, what linked these writers was their notion of the historian's responsibility to assist in the renewal of national self-consciousness by providing *positive* images of the past. Hence Nolte claims that mass murder by the Bolsheviks was both logically and factually prior to that of the Nazis (thus the singularity of Nazi atrocities is denied) and that the 'so-called [sic] annihilation of the Jews was a reaction to their earlier disloyalty to the German state'. Again, Stürmer calls for 'empathetic identification' with the *Wehrmacht* defending Germany against the Red Army, even though the survival of the Third Reich meant the continuation of the death camps. For further debate see Rabinbach, 1988.

4

Social Movements and the Lifeworld

Two components of Habermasian theory have been discussed thus far, which will now be elaborated into a more detailed model of social conflict and regulation. First, there is the general theory of social change and modernity, addressing three levels of explanation: systemic crises, which release latently stored cultural learning; selective stabilization, of organizational forms that are isomorphic with the social environment; and consequent patterns of colonization and resistance. The second component is a specific theory of social movements which arise initially 'in defence of endangered ways of life', but, like nineteenth-century socialist and feminist movements, subsequently develop critical attitudes towards tradition as well as universalistic forms of organization through public discourse. Underpinning both of these levels of analysis is the claim that the structure of linguistic communication anticipates an emancipated society in every attempt to reach an understanding. The link between this philosophically derived proposition, on the one hand, and social practice, on the other, is made through the concept of rationalization of the lifeworld, which entails the separation of the three cultural value spheres. It was seen in Chapter 2 that social interactions become more rational and less determined by tradition when agents can pose validity-questions within three 'world-relations' (truth, normativity and sincerity). This structural differentiation of the lifeworld is at the core of modern social processes in that it permits social and individual learning and adaptation along three dimensions – natural and social science, rational-legal procedures and aesthetic expression. However, capitalist modernity has involved an over-extension of monetary and bureaucratic systems which have inhibited the formation of fluid, decentred, non-authoritarian types of communication. Rather, 'colonization of the lifeworld' generates distortions or pathologies in social reproduction including loss of meaning and disorientation, which in turn provoke two ideal-typical value-orientations amongst social movements. At one end, 'defensive' social movements will be concerned with the preservation of traditional ways of life, and at the other, 'offensive' movements will create conditions for 'communicative socialization' – reclaiming the lifeworld for autonomous identities.

However, Habermas has presented these claims in a tentative and provisional way, and in order to develop a model which might illuminate global social movements, some critical amplification is necessary. Although *TCA* attempts to describe the sociological conditions for the emergence of a critical politics, Habermas has not elaborated this image in any detail, as White (1990: 126) observes. The theory is constructed largely around blocks of power–money and system–lifeworld (Joas, 1991: 176) and emphasizes the effects of one upon the other, rather than the internal dynamics of each. Further, it is questionable whether the colonization thesis is a satisfactory explanation of social movement formation for two reasons. First, it relies heavily on notions of social strain, anomie and the critique of mass society (as did earlier Critical Theory); and, secondly, it is not clear why the same process of colonization should provoke two opposing types of social movements (defensive and offensive).

It will be suggested that these problems arise from gaps in the theory of social movement formation and impact which Part 2 addresses in more detail. This will be done through two theoretical manoeuvres, the first of which suggests that crisis displacement is more complex than Habermas implies, in that social movements can be avenues through which the system is protected as well as challenged. The second examines ways in which lifeworld and system are interpenetrated such that ascriptive social rela-tions (for example, gender divisions) might be reinforced and reconstituted by colonization. Habermas' discussion of power only with reference to the system is problematic since power and domination must inhere in lifeworld backgrounds, otherwise pre-modern societies, prior to the uncoupling of steering media, would have to have been 'power-free'. Developing this notion involves opening up the lifeworld to look more closely at its internal architecture and the ways in which this is affected by different types of systemic colonization. The discussion here first examines Habermas in the context of recent social movement debates, and secondly discusses feminist critiques of Habermas which, challenging his division of the public and private spheres, point to the intersection of symbolic and material and structures within the lifeworld.

Habermas and Social Movement Theory

This section identifies key problems with Habermas' theory of social movements (some of which are shared with other social movement theorists) and suggests a modified model. It is argued, first, that the tendency to designate some movements as 'new', because of their concern with symbolic rather than material goals, is ahistorical; and, secondly, that the characterization of movements as offensive or defensive, whilst useful, only partially accounts for their origin and impact. Combining the notion that social movements are carriers of new organizational forms with insights from resource mobilization theory, it is proposed to develop a systemic model of the relationship between social movements and social environments.

However, the discussion has so far continued as if the meaning of 'social movements' were clear, although they are actually difficult to define because of their diversity in scale, level of organization, and relationships with political parties and official channels of interest articulation. For example, social movements appear at neighbourhood, city, regional, national or even international levels, and exhibit a continuum of organizational forms. For Chris Pickvance (1992), their 'common feature is the relative exclusion of the movement's standpoint from the prevailing political agenda'. However, this is hardly a defining characteristic, since social movement agendas tend to be selectively incorporated into programmes of political parties (as occurred with ecological issues, for example). The contrast between social movements and political parties is greatest when one compares single-issue, loosely coupled local action committees (such as Greenpeace) with tightly structured national political parties contending for government and advancing comprehensive programmes. Social movements tend not to command individual loyalty in the same way as established parties, and a high proportion of new movements fail (Zald & McCarthy, 1987: 35).

However, at other levels the contrast is less marked. Smaller political parties such as the Greens have features that are also present in social movements, such as a loose organizational structure and the goal of influencing agendas and broad currents of opinion rather than the pursuit of political power. Some social movement organizations (such as Oxfam, Third World First or the League Against Cruel Sports in the UK) have routinized membership involvement and become adept at using official channels of communication such as Parliamentary lobbying. In relatively stable political settings social movements act as conduits for interest articulation, as well as satisfying the affective needs of their members through constructing identities and a sense of solidarity. However, in periods of political crisis and transformation, social movements might be proto-political parties whose formation has an important impact on subsequent events. A classical example of this is the evolution of trade unions, co-operatives and other movements of workers' self-defence into the British Labour Party at the end of the nineteenth century, although more recently the broad democratic coalitions in Eastern Europe have formed the basis of subsequent political parties. In other words, social movements are ambiguous phenomena which lack a clearly definable form or trajectory, and are better understood with reference to the social environments or opportunity structures in which they operate (Kitschelt, 1986).

In common with a number of social movement theorists, Habermas has argued that contemporary movements differ from earlier forms of collective action in that they address symbolic rather than instrumental needs, and that the transition from industrial to post-industrial society is marked by post-class social movements. Related to this is the belief, widespread in the social sciences, that western capitalism has entered a new phase of development, which is variously called 'post-industrial' (Bell, 1974; Melucci, 1989); 'post-Fordism' (Aglietta, 1979), 'post-modernity' (Lyotard, 1991), 'high modernity' (Giddens, 1991), 'disorganized capitalism'

(Lash & Urry, 1988); or 'programmed society' (Touraine, 1981). Whilst not suggesting that each of these amounts to the same thing, there are common themes concerning the diminution of bi-polar class conflict, the growth of tertiary sectors, expansion of cultural, consumption and leisure activities, and especially new types of social protest.

Habermas reflects these concerns when he argues that colonization of the lifeworld provokes the formation of new forms of social protest, the goals of which are (somewhat tortuously) defined as

> protect[ing] areas of life that are functionally dependent on social integration through values, norms, and consensus formation, to preserve them from falling prey to the systemic imperatives of economic and administrative sub-systems growing with dynamics of their own, and to defend them from becoming converted over, through the steering media of the law, to a principle of sociation that is, for them, dysfunctional. (1989b: 375)

In other words, social movements appear at the seam between the lifeworld and system in a kind of ongoing boundary dispute over the limits of systemic intrusion. They address the 'grammar of forms of life' – equal rights, individual self-realization or participation – rather than the 'old politics' of wages, housing, economic policy, trade union rights (Habermas, 1989b: 392). Although Habermas sometimes implies that trade unions or struggles for economic justice are 'left-overs from the social movements of an earlier type of society' (Cohen, 1982a), more recently he has moderated this view by emphasizing a continuing role for trade union and social democratic politics (Habermas, 1989a). None the less, much of his thesis is premised on a secular decline in the cohesion of working-class politics, which has been superseded by the politics of identity.[1]

This resonates with much contemporary social movement literature. Melucci, for example, argues that

> sociological analysis must abandon the traditional view of movements as characters moving on an historical stage . . . [where they] are cast as figures in an epic tragedy, as heroes or villains who are moving toward some grand ideal or dramatic destiny. (Melucci, 1989: 24)

Rather, social movements are 'nomads of the present', 'submerged networks and laboratories of experience' where 'new answers' are invented and tested (Melucci, 1989: 208–9). These display a diffuse continuum of organizational forms, from loose associations of consciousness-raising or alternative therapy, for example, to national associations with a formal membership and hierarchy. As fluid currents of opinion, their degree of visibility will vary at different times, although periods of latency do not indicate inactivity[2] – an idea similar to Mayer Zald and John McCarthy's (1987: 6) notion of 'affinity group structures' which are susceptible to mobilization by formally organized movements. Having diffuse goals, movements might simultaneously be focused on political rights and cultural identity, for example with gay and lesbian campaigns against discrimination, Aids/HIV awareness or Black self-defence against police harassment.

The novelty of the 'new' social movements lies in their objectives, and the dominance of symbolic over material considerations, related to which are arguments about the predominance of consumption cleavages over productive divisions (for example, Urry, 1981). Melucci writes of 'social movement sectors' as loosely bound, sympathetic friendship networks, involving consciousness-raising, and opportunities to reconstruct life-histories according to new standards, where the formation of identities is more central than specific aims or objectives.[3] Examples of these are women's presses, alternative theatres, small manufacturers of environmentally safe products, women's groups, gay activism, community initiatives or Black consciousness. Echoing Baudrillard, Melucci (1989: 203) suggests that social movements 'operate as signs' through which they construct an organization for expressive not instrumental ends, and display a new consciousness of their global context.[4] Feher and Heller (1986) suggest that whereas earlier social movements (trade unions or women's suffrage) were centred on questions of citizenship, 'new' social movements centre on cultural issues (life-style, mobilization of civil society) and do not have the 'seizure of power' as their aim. Again, Offe (1984) claims that movements such as alternative health, psychotherapy or New Age 'by-pass the state' and defend civil society against inner colonization. This approach attempts to move beyond the state/civil society polarity and its narrow equation of politics with the system of national parties, to grasp the ways in which social movements are embedded in fluid systems of action and identity.

Although these accounts rightly draw attention to the importance of identity politics in social movements, it is not obvious why this should be regarded as new, nor why expressive motives should be more important than instrumental ones. First, claims to novelty are exaggerated and ahistorical since most contemporary demands have long histories, and movements like environmentalism, pacifism, feminism, were significant around 1890–1900 or before. Secondly, the distinction between identity and interest is over-drawn, since it is not obvious that earlier social movements such as workers' education, the Chartists, the Co-operative movement, the Temperance Movement, non-conformist Protestantism or the women's suffrage movement were concerned with interest to the exclusion of identity.[5] Thirdly, this literature tends to privilege social movements within late capitalism which have their base predominantly amongst the middle class, as some commentators otherwise sympathetic to social movement analysis have pointed out (for example, Benhabib, 1986: 251; Eder, 1985; Kellner, 1989: 220). Fourthly, whilst it might be true that actors derive symbolic gratifications from social movement involvement, many movements have an explicit grievance base, such as civil rights or anti-racist campaigns, pro-choice defence against anti-abortion legislation, or defence of sexual preference. For others, especially nationalist or ethnic movements, the politics of identity is clearly central although generally shaped by historical economic and political domination (Gellner, 1991).

Thus the polarization of identity politics against instrumental goals

actually occludes the fact that the agenda of emancipatory social movements is to widen the scope of the political to embrace what were
previously regarded as private or cultural (as opposed to political) matters.
Whereas Melucci implies that social movements are successful simply by
virtue of existing, identity politics is unlikely to be indifferent to strategic
questions of success or failure. Finally, the 'new' social movement
literature is Eurocentric in that outside the organic core nations there
appear deeply polarized conflicts arising from conditions of exploitation
and the impact of the global system on local social relationships.

In addition to the old/new dichotomy which to some extent informs
Habermas' theory, he further identifies emancipatory social movements
which might complete the unfinished project of modernity. This involves
locating proto-typical forms of emancipatory structures and the conditions
under which new learning capacities might be tested and stabilized
(Habermas, 1989b: 314). This is a theory of learning capacities, or formal
properties of communication, rather than of privileged social locations
such as classes – a distinction which is overlooked by critics who suggest
that Habermas 'has painted himself into a corner, . . . unable to posit a
group whose way of life is reasoned in all aspects, he is left only with an
idealized standard of discourse' (Sciulli, 1992: 104).[6] Emancipatory movements are those which advance a resolution of the welfare-capitalist crisis
which would involve the 'decolonization of the lifeworld'. This would
involve the withdrawal of system-integration mechanisms from some
aspects of symbolic reproduction; the replacement of (some) normatively
secured contexts by communicatively achieved ones; and the development
of new participatory-democratic institutions which would regulate
markets, bureaucracies and technologies.[7] Offensive movements represent
in proto-typical form the potential for advanced cognitive-moral learning
associated with post-conventional morality. Purely defensive movements
by contrast are particularistic, they 'conquer no new territory' for the
lifeworld, and are orientated towards 'the defence of traditional values and
social rank' as opposed to trying 'out new ways of cooperating and living
together' (Habermas, 1989b: 394).[8] Offensive movements will eschew
grand revolutionary schemes, but will also resist being integrated into
established institutions (1989a: 15).

This distinction is a useful way of approaching the orientations of
collective actors – whether or not they re-politicize the public sphere by
salvaging practical questions from inner privatism (value decisionism) or
de-politicized administration (technocracy).[9] The offensive/defensive
dichotomy might, for example, differentiate amongst the global and
disparate movements of religious revival – with reference not so much to
their content as to whether they permit reasoned debate or close off critical
publics through authoritarian traditionalism. In this regard, it has been
argued that the Christian messianic churches, which are evangelizing
world-wide (but especially in the Third World) advocate fatalism and inner
withdrawal (Gifford, 1991), whereas 'liberation theology' (especially in

South America) is empowering, in that it opens up issues of dependency, transnational capital, and local autonomy (Casanova, 1984; Leonard, 1990).

However, the offensive/defensive distinction connotes an organizational tendency rather than a movement per se. Thus feminism is offensive rather than defensive, since it is primarily aimed not at 'defending and restoring endangered ways of life', nor merely 'eliminating male privilege', but at 'overturning concrete forms of life marked by male monopolies' (Habermas, 1989b: 393). It seeks to 'conquer new territory', because it 'follows the tradition of bourgeois-socialist liberation movements' in calling upon modernity's unredeemed promise of equality and justice.[10] Even so, Habermas (1989b: 394) claims that feminism tends towards particularism arising from the historical subordination of women in the bourgeois nuclear family.[11] Peace and ecology movements are likewise 'ambiguous' in that here too there is a tendency to withdraw into particularistic identities which leave the economic and state systems intact. Habermas writes of a 'spectrum' of offensive to reactive tendencies within social movements, so that just as there will never be a state of perfect communicative discourse, perhaps neither will there ever be a purely emancipatory movement. Collective action might occupy a broad continuum, from defensive neo-conservative protests to campaigns that expand fluid, post-conventional identities.[12]

None the less, Habermas does not provide much detailed analysis of the ways in which colonization of the lifeworld engenders social movements. It is not clear to what extent the relationship between colonization and social movement formation is causal, since as Berger (1991: 170) points out, he writes variously of 'necessary condition', 'opening up options', 'inner logic', and at times claims merely to describe or interpret. Implicit in his reference to the Anabaptists (Chapter 3) is the idea that once the process of rationalization has been released, the potential for communicative action remains latent in the lifeworld, albeit in subterranean storage and truncated by dominant systems of strategic action. Thus, despite the extension of steering media into the lifeworld, there remains the counter-weight emancipatory potential 'built into communication structures themselves' which promote oppositional movements. However, more specific theorizing will be required to explain the formation and direction taken by particular social movements.

Habermas deploys a model of anomie and social-psychological reaction-formation, illustrated in his reference to the 'reaction of those who are put to flight or aroused to resistance by fateful conflicts, who are driven to sickness, to suicide, or to crime, or to rebellion and revolutionary struggle' (1982b: 227). This is because 'the personality system can preserve its identity only by means of defensive strategies that are detrimental to participating in social interaction on a realistic basis' (Habermas, 1989b: 141). Of course, social strain and anomie have been widely used in the explanation of social movements. Majkowski (1985), for example, argues that strains in Polish society (atomization, poverty, economic dislocation, hostile church–state relations) account for the rise of workers' organizations and ultimately of Solidarity. Again, Mardin (1978) argues that urban political violence in Turkey between 1973 and 1977 was a result of cultural dislocation consequent on secularization, which in the absence of new structures of social integration disturbed adolescent socialization such that aggression was displaced into the public sphere.

However, this is a rudimentary model of collective action which just as 'successfully' accounts for organized protest around ecology, for example, as it does for alcoholism and fatalistic withdrawal. As Melucci (1989: 197) argues, social strain or colonization theses are of limited explanatory value because collective social action is always *constructed*, at cognitive, affective and organizational levels, rather than simply reactive. Moreover, movements can 'turn colonization creatively against itself', for example, by appropriating state welfare resources like health education, for their own purposes. John McCarthy (1987: 55), one of the founders of resource mobilization theory (RMT), has proposed a 'post-mass society' thesis which emphasizes the importance of social infrastructures – pre-existing organizations and communications based in cohesive, ongoing, face-to-face groups like churches, colleges, voluntary associations and parties – as resources which can be mobilized by social movement organizations.

Indeed, the sensitivity of the theory to empirical complexities might be enhanced by deploying an insight from RMT. This might appear to be an odd manoeuvre, since RMT is often condemned as having no theory of the social environment within which social movements operate (Scott, 1990: Chapter 5) or as revolving 'around premises of rational choice theory' which harbour the 'undisclosed assumption . . . that movement élites . . . manipulate their mass following' (Sciulli, 1992: 36). These criticisms are valid, but they overlook what is most interesting about RMT, which is the focus on the relationship between the organizational capacities of social movements and their ability to link into pre-existing social infrastructures. This implies that reasons for the success or failure of social movements to shape public agendas need to be sought not only in their organizational abilities or orientations but also in the structural conduciveness of social networks (or the lifeworld) whose resources they attempt to deploy.

A central idea of RMT is that a movement organization has greater chance of success if it can mobilize the resources – labour, materials, money and communication technologies – of tightly linked established networks such as churches, colleges or voluntary associations. Further, the existence of grievances per se does not account for the appearance of social movements, since many potential preferences for change are under-represented in social movement organizations (SMOs) whilst there is 'enough discontent in any society to supply the grass roots support for a movement if it is effectively organized and has at its disposal the power and resources of some established group' (Zald & McCarthy, 1987: 18). Constituents, then, are not pre-given, but are mobilized by 'issue entrepreneurs' capable of converting loose associations into SMOs and mobilizing adherents (who share the movement's preference structure) into constituents who will be actively involved. In the USA, for example, Black civil rights organizations, such as the NAACP or Congress on Racial Equality, were able to deploy organizational and material resources of the churches as building blocks for organization. Once in existence, SMOs store organizational learning about networks and strategy which filters into other groups – like the Fellowship of Reconciliation which since the early twentieth century has served as a store-house of information about pacifism and non-violence (Zald & McCarthy, 1987: 75).[13] The ability of SMO to gain access to public political agendas will depend on the extent and integration of these social resources. Thus the recent relative success of anti-abortionists in the USA is a result of their ability to mobilize traditional associations, whereas pro-choice groups have been dependent on 'thin' infrastructures of professional associations, mailing lists and weak communication structures. (Zald & McCarthy, 1987: 49–66). This suggests that the nature of social networks will play an important role in selecting and stabilizing social movement initiatives.

It is quite true that RMT is overly voluntaristic, and does not have a satisfactory theory of the issue entrepreneurs who initially define and channel grievances into SMOs. Nor does its deployment of rational choice theory entirely account for social movement participation. It assumes that one of the key structural determinants governing participation in SMOs are the 'costs' to individuals or groups in allocating resources to a social movement (Zald & McCarthy, 1987: 26) so that political repression, for example, would greatly increase the costs of participation. RMT might explain the success of Polish Solidarity once it linked up with both the traditional structures of the church and networks of dissident intellectuals, for example, KOR (Komitet Obrony Robotników, Workers Defence Committee, the intellectual nucleus of Solidarity). However, rational choice would have more difficulty accounting for the success of Solidarity during 1980–1 when the costs of membership could be high (arrest, imprisonment or physical injury) compared with its relatively poor performance after 1989 (membership having fallen from 10 million in 1981 to 1 million in 1992) when the costs of involvement had diminished. To account for the appearance of social movement innovation, and for its success or failure in setting agendas, one needs to examine whether or not lifeworld structures are susceptible to the new organizational forms and learning capacities embodied in the SMOs. Attention to social infrastructures opens up research agendas which might assist in clarifying the ambiguities of Habermas' theory, since the question which needs to be answered is what are the factors which promote political opportunity structures conducive to offensive or defensive social movements?

We can begin to answer this question by examining the conditions which are likely to promote or retard the formation of social networks in which post-conventional ethics and rational argumentation might develop. The above analysis might suggest that this has two aspects: first that proto-public spheres are sufficiently vibrant to withstand colonization, and secondly that social conditions are conducive to the release of new learning capacity. For example, Habermas has tentatively suggested that higher education is a kind of repository of communicative structures, in that the egalitarian and universalistic content of academic values illustrates the rational procedures which are required by modern societies if they are to 'reach an understanding about themselves'. Higher education is at best a proto-public sphere which expresses only the norms of scientific and scholarly activity, not those of society as a whole (Habermas, 1989a: 125). A properly developed critical politics would require an alert and informed public sphere, the minimal requirements for which are a 'halfway functional constitutional state' and public recognition of universalist values. (Habermas, 1989a: 87). However, if higher education were able to preserve its communication structures from colonization, then its learning capacities would become relevant for wider society in the context of a societal crisis, to which such values had the potential to be stabilized as crisis-solving.

Yet the continued existence of higher education as a proto-public sphere is threatened, as Bourdieu indicates in his account of the 'politics of the universal'. This suggests in effect that rationality, freedom of information and argument justified only on its merits rather than by appeal to higher authorities, are values which are at least implicitly present in academic discourse. These values are threatened, however, when higher education is subjugated to commercial values (quasi-marketization, performance indicators, etc.) or when personal integrity is compromised in the pursuit of success, since extraneous norms are replacing those particular to higher education's field of cultural production. It is not that critical intellectuals have any privileged access to universalistic values by virtue of their work situation, but rather the (idealized) academic norms of free speech, rationality, unrestricted information flows, etc., derive from the potential for communicative rationality which is implicit in modern cultures.[14] This suggests that the first objective of critical practice is, as Ben Agger (1991: 103–4) suggests, to struggle within the academy against the 'positivist definition of scholarly legitimacy – surveys, computers, grants, value-freedom', which insists instead on opening up dialogues which, grounded in the ethics of 'betrayed liberalism', prefigure a discursive polity.

However, systems of regulation might be more adept than Habermas suggests at displacing public issues into socially isolated sub-cultures. One should be wary about celebrating the autonomy of social movements which 'by-pass the state', since this might underestimate the recuperative power of regulatory systems to neutralize protest by marginalizing it into alternative life-styles. Anthony Giddens (1991: Chapter 7) argues that new social movements such as ecology or feminism 'bring to the fore' a 'life politics', or the politics of self-actualization, which are complementary to the emancipatory politics of the public sphere. Life politics 'call for a remoralizing of social life and they demand a renewed sensitivity to questions that the institutions of modernity systematically dissolve' (1991: 224). However, as Hay (1993) suggests, the privatization of public issues that this implies could involve a displacement of crisis tendencies from public to private spheres, even when individuals are apparently empowered. This might occur for example, where ecological issues are reduced to 'green' consumerism.

Thus the appearance of life-style politics, which Melucci and others regard as central to the appearance of new social movements, might have the effect of marginalizing critical issues from the public sphere. Paul Piccone and Timothy Luke have argued that the diverse counter-cultural movements of the 1960s broke through standardized cultural homogeneity only to be manipulated by the 'state-corporate social formation', which 'artificially nurtured its own negativity'.[15] This was done in two ways. First, the emergence of originally subversive movements, like ethnic consciousness, environmental and consumer protection, alternative health or local media, were incorporated by the culture industry in the form of segmented markets for low circulation journals, chapbook production, small film recording companies, etc. Secondly, the state permitted a 'tentative reopening of the public sphere', for example, in regional cultures or local political participation, which served its own agenda of withdrawing from public sector welfare and encouraging 'traditional' (especially family) support structures (Luke, 1990: 174–5).[16] Again, Cohen (1982a) argues that: 'The sovereign power of the state and the coercive power of the capitalist economy [social movements] hope to by-pass have a nasty habit of returning to frustrate their projects.' That capital has appropriated the slogan, if not the substance, of ecological demands confirms Marcuse's thesis that there are no absolutely subversive demands under late capitalism.

This discussion leads to the tentative conclusion that we should not expect social movements to arise automatically from grievances or from social dislocation: rather, protest will be initiated by SMOs competing for the mobilization of resources. However, these act in a wider social context of opportunity structures, which have been shaped by the intersections of colonization, system problems and social networks. To understand the appearance of social movements it is first of all necessary to analyse how system crises release social carriers of potential solutions (the paradigm for which is the release of new cognitive and normative social learning in the formation of capitalism). However, the resource-base to which movement initiators appeal has been structured, by steering media on the one hand, and the extent to which rationalization of the lifeworld has proceeded, on the other. Put another way, the likely success of offensive social movements to effect the link between proto-public spheres and the institutionalization of new learning capacities will depend upon the opportunities which exist for testing alternative forms of social organization (such as co-operatives and trade unions in the early phase of industrialization, feminist urban cultures in the 1970s and 1980s, or the illegal underground networks in state socialist societies). However, social protest (such as ecological consciousness) might be displaced into marginalized social spheres which regard themselves as empowered, but by abdicating from conventional politics actually protect the identity of the system. Thus the question of social movement impact needs to be examined more closely, and with reference to systems of social regulation. These points will be developed in Part 2, but first we need to take a closer look at Habermas' concept of the lifeworld and its interface with steering media.

Opening the Box: Gender and the Lifeworld

Habermas tends to theorize the lifeworld and system as 'black boxes', which correspond to the symbolic and material realms respectively, thus social movements which resist colonization are concerned with normative and symbolic questions – the grammar of social life – rather than with narrowly defined interests. True, he insists that the lifeworld 'by no means offers an innocent image of "power-free communication"' (Habermas, 1991: 254), but he *does* separate the household from the economy along the public–private axis: 'The institutional core of the private sphere is the nuclear family, relieved of productive functions and specialized in tasks of socialization: from the systemic perspective of the economy, it is viewed as the environment of private households' (Habermas, 1989b: 319). In turn he suggests that, prior to colonization, the household is a sphere of communicative consensus: 'in these spheres of the lifeworld [school and family] we find, prior to any juridification, norms and contexts of action that by functional necessity are based on mutual understanding' (Habermas, 1989b: 369). Subsequently, juridification or monetization have the effect of formalizing relationships so as to reduce the scope for negotiation or re-definition of norms and identities.

In this context Nancy Fraser (1989) has made four criticisms of Habermas. First, his dichotomy between symbolic reproduction and material reproduction implies that women's unpaid child-rearing counts as 'symbolic' since it serves socialization needs. In reality, she says, this is a 'dual aspect activity' that is both symbolic and material – food and object production is never purely material but rather simultaneously produces social identities. To imply that one can consign patriarchy to the sphere of symbolic relations is to reproduce the ideological division between the public and private. This in turn bears on the problematic notion that the aim of emancipatory practice is to reconstitute the 'private' as a defence against bureaucratic encroachment. Similarly, Susan Okin argues that the idea of a separation between the public and private (the cornerstone of liberal political theory) 'can be sustained only if very persuasive arguments of feminist scholars are ignored' (1991: 65). Once the significance of gender is understood, neither the public nor the domestic realm – their structures and practices, assumptions and expectations, division of labour and distribution of power – can be discussed without reference to one another (Bergmann, 1986).

Secondly, Habermas establishes a dichotomy between socially integrated and system integrated action, yet the household as much as the work-place is a site of labour. Habermas does not make visible the fact that in both women are ghettoized in distinctively feminine sexualized occupations, nor that relations within the family (whether handling of finances or domestic violence) are 'thoroughly permeated with money and power'. Thus Habermas' dichotomy obscures an analysis of families as sites of labour, exchange, calculation, distribution and exploitation, and it was a 'grave mistake' to restrict the term 'power' to bureaucratic contexts (Fraser, 1989: 121). Rather one should distinguish between domestic-patriarchal power and bureaucratic-patriarchal power. Further, to regard juridification as an instance of colonization actually suggests a natural order that presupposes women's domination, since women's liberation is dependent not on the preservation of the lifeworld, but, on the contrary, on freeing child-rearing from non-monetized lifeworld contexts.[17] Similarly there is the question of whether affirmative action/equal opportunities should be regarded as emancipatory or as juridification which offers an illusory (technical-bureaucratic) 'solution' to racism and sexism.[18]

Thirdly, structuring the public/private distinction around roles of consumer, citizen, client, worker, occludes a gender sub-text – the role of 'worker' is male since women are generally in super-exploited locations outside the work-force, and remain primarily wives and mothers who 'happen to be working', whilst the 'consumer' role is premised on the femininity of consumption. The 'citizen' role is male-dominated, which is confirmed in the division between the defender of the polity and protector of women, children and the elderly who allegedly cannot protect themselves. The masculine citizen-soldier-protector role links the state and the public sphere not only to each other but also to the family and to the paid work-place. For Fraser, Habermas misses how the citizen-speaker role in turn links the state and the public sphere to the family and the official economy. He thus misses how the worker-breadwinner role integrates the family with the economy and the state, confirming women's dependent status in each. Finally, he misses how the feminine-childrearer role links all four to each other by overseeing the construction of the masculine and feminine gendered subjects needed to fill every role in classical capitalism.

Fourthly, Fraser (1989: 128) argues that this reveals male dominance to be intrinsic rather than contingent to capitalism because the institutional structure of this social formation is 'actualized' by means of gendered roles. She agrees with Habermas that welfare-state capitalism emerges as a result of systemic crisis tendencies, but again argues that Habermas fails to see that the new client role has a gender, that it is 'paradigmatically female'. She follows (with reservations) Carol Brown's discussion of welfare in terms of a transition from 'private patriarchy to public patriarchy'. Welfare measures do have a positive side (they reduce women's dependence on individual male breadwinners) but their negative side is that they increase dependence on the 'androcentric state bureaucracy'. Since the channels of influence between system and lifeworld institutions are multidirectional, there is a battle-line more basic than lifeworld/system, namely that drawn by the forms of male dominance linking system to lifeworld to women. Critical Theory needs gender-sensitive categories in which 'gender, politics, and political economy are internally integrated'. Since gender identity *structures* paid work, state administration and political partici-pation, the interface between system and lifeworld works in both direc-tions, that is, colonization as posited by Habermas (system → lifeworld) and the gendering of systemic roles (lifeworld → system). In this case, gender is *the* structuring category that overrides and permeates the social relations of capitalism.

The problem with Fraser's critique is that it blurs the distinction between the symbolic and the material which is central to Habermas' critique of colonization. His argument is not that money and power are absent from domestic relations (although he does not make power within the lifeworld very visible) but rather he deals with power and money specifically as steering media (bureaucracy and the market) where they are largely devoid of communicative negotiation: 'the roles of consumer and worker are abstracted in a manner suitable to the medium in question' (1989b: 322). Because domestic relations are located in the lifeworld they are not governed by the same degree of strategic non-reflexive exchange as are money and power, and are *at least potentially* sites of linguistically mediated negotiations over roles, values, appropriateness, sincerity, etc. Fraser says that families 'are sites of egocentric, strategic, and instrumental calculation as well as sites of usually exploitative exchanges of services, labour, cash, and sex' (1989: 120). However, unequal exchange within the household, based on stereotyped identities and normative expectations, is analytically distinct from unequal market exchanges based upon the invisible extraction of surplus value. The ways in which money enters household relations is structured by patriarchal forms of control, but in complex ways that vary over time and with social class (Pahl, 1990) and in this context Fraser's allusion to the 'handling of finances' does not help much. That there are diverse forms of control indicates that household relations are available to variation in ways that mediatized interactions are not. Fraser's argument is based on typicality not systemic regulation – not all consumers are women nor all workers male – and she assumes that the traditional patriarchal family remains the dominant form, thereby minimiz-ing the influence of feminism itself on the crisis of socio-cultural reproduc-tion.[19] Central to Habermas' theory is the notion that normative integration does not equal power-free or consensual integration and that struggles over resources or speaking rights in the public sphere involve organizing against both systemic power and lifeworld hierarchies, con-ditioned by 'the material substratum to the lifeworld' (1989b: 231).

However, Fraser's stress on the interaction between the lifeworld and system is important and moves away from the idea of a timeless lifeworld distorted by colonization towards one in which social relations with the lifeworld – including those of gender – are constituted by capital and complex organizations, and then dynamically act upon one another. Rather than treat concepts of the citizen, consumer, employee or welfare recipient statically (as actually both Fraser and Habermas tend to), we need to examine how phases of capitalist development (or colonization) have involved specific articulations of gender, work and class. Whilst Habermas tends to assume that colonization erodes the normative context of the lifeworld, the converse might also be the case, that capital and organizations harness and sustain pre-modern non-commodity relations in the pursuit of lower reproduction costs.

Hartmann (1979) and Walby (1986: 52–3) argue that gendered job segregation is the primary mechanism in capitalist society that maintains male superiority over women, because it forces lower wages for women in the labour market. Low wages keep women dependent on men because they encourage women to marry and perform domestic duties within a domestic division of labour which further weakens women's position in the labour market. Thus the hierarchical division of labour is perpetuated by the labour market and vice versa. Again, Mies (1989) analyses 'house-wifization', a global process of lowering the reproduction costs of capital through the deployment of domestic labour. Since women's labour is not formally free (because of economic dependence on men) it is exchanged cheap (especially in the Third World but also in the low-wage sectors of developed economies). The more welfare in developed countries is in crisis, the more women as unpaid carers will carry the burdens of managing austerity, which in turn lowers the reproduction costs of capital. The concentration of women (along with migrant workers) in low-wage sectors of the economy, where organized labour has weak or non-existent links, has established new segmentations of the labour market and a marginalized under-class, including the feminization of poverty. This in turn provokes resistance; Arrighi argues that by the 1970s and 1980s, 'acquiescence gives way to open rebellion in which the social power of women and immigrants is turned against the rising tide of mass misery at the core' (1990).

The two sides of the theoretical coin, system and lifeworld, become increasingly interwoven as systemic intrusion both erodes and reconstitutes complex identities, some of which originated in pre-modern forms of sociality. This is illustrated by Dorothy Smith (1983), who argues that by the end of the nineteenth century, as property became corporate and bureaucratized, so 'ruling' became differentiated and detached from an identifiable local ruling class. As the dominant class was organized first nationally and later internationally, consumption divisions became markers of local patterns of social difference. Smith suggests (in the manner of Bourdieu) that from the end of the nineteenth century fashion became symbolic of the organization of the ruling class, as a set of visible signs of class status. Similarly, the suburb became a site in which extra-local relations of classes were constituted. These signs constituted persons as a kind of currency whose value was determined by style, related to which the family appeared as a consuming unit, within which women, already marginalized from productive relations, took on supportive roles in relation to their husband's career. The middle-class domestic world became privatized (cf. Hart, 1989) and domestic labour as personal service was subordinated to the enterprise. The male career became a means to private accumulation for the household whilst vast areas of consumption were feminized (such as cosmetics, detergents, packaged food, pills, baby/child products, etc.).

However, these relationships came under strain as the bureaucratization of capital reduced barriers to women's entry into the professional-managerial middle class, since education and technical skills became more important criteria of entry than family property. In response, women's exclusion was reinforced ideologically, by medicine and other 'expert' authorities (cf. Doyal, 1979), to create fictional mirrors for images of femininity which marked the exclusion of women from market competition with men, whilst reaffirming the subordination of women within a newly constituted domesticity.[20] Moreover, there is a process complementary to this, in which masculinity and male status is expressed in successful separation from subordination to the sphere of women, but this is all fragile and increasingly subject to critique. The wage relation creates an uncertain title to male status, and the unemployed male finds that his masculinity 'was not really his after all'. Meanwhile, the increasing participation of women in the labour market in the later twentieth century 'points to the diminishing power of the domestic economy', while individual authority of the male is weakened by inflation and unemployment.[21] This is over-layed by a gradual displacement of the work-place from its earlier central location in social conflicts by two developments in particular – the partial separation between income and wage-labour, through welfare systems, and the appearance of consumption divisions as principles of social differentiation in their own right. Patterns of home-ownership, for example, create new socio-spatial fractures and patterns of political identification (Warde et al., 1987).[22]

The upshot of all this, in western societies, has been the creation of diffuse patterns of collective action around welfare and employment rights, resistance to patriarchal expert cultures, and life-style politics, which arose from a lifeworld along lines of fracture in part constituted by the dynamics of global capital. This suggests that the lifeworld is the site on to which contradictions from the systems of money and power are projected and within which they are fought out. The public sphere is vitally conducive to the empowerment of oppositional identities, but this will be eroded by systemic regulation which both reinforces and reflects communicative distortion, unless the vicious circle is broken.

Two points have emerged so far in this discussion. First, the lifeworld is not a homogeneous black box, but rather has a composite structure of material and symbolic relations. Secondly, the relations between the lifeworld and the system are multi-directional in that, for example, gender relations embedded in the lifeworld pattern the dominant forms of the market and bureaucracies (for example, in the gendered division of the labour market). These multi-directional relations can have complex and contradictory effects – colonization can erode traditional gender relations through the expansion of women's welfare entitlements, or through affirmative action programmes; conversely it can sustain gender oppression through the marginalization of women in segmented labour markets, or through the reproduction of gender identities through 'expert' professional cultures. Thus one needs to develop a model of the effects of interactions between the system and the lifeworld, as well as the competing effects of money and power, whereas Habermas tends to examine colonization in terms of a single dimension of money/power. These combined effects of the system and lifeworld in turn structure the emergence of political identities and movements, in ways which will be examined later.

Crisis and Regulation

Before moving on to the analysis of crises and social movements in Part 2, the threads of the discussion so far should be pulled together. Habermasian theory sets out the conditions for a Critical Theory of society through the communicative paradigm, which gives evolutionary priority to the argumentative functions of speech. These remain latent within complex worldviews until they are released through the rationalization of the lifeworld, which creates the conditions for learning and adaptation in organizations and socio-cultural life. However, these learning capacities cannot yet be institutionalized on a wide scale because money and power enter 'the communicative pores' of the lifeworld, inhibiting the formation of postconventional public discourse. Normatively regulated action is replaced by strategic management, and public issues are displaced into expert or privatized cultures. However, colonization is never successful in that it gives rise to social pathologies, and to resistance which might be manifest in new social movements. These are carriers of new learning capacities, proto-public spheres which offer potential solutions to systemic crisis in that they presage more fluid and democratic types of organization. However, Habermas does not offer much detailed analysis of either their development or their impact. Following Zald and McCarthy's RMT it has been suggested above that neither social disorganization nor grievance is a sufficient condition for social movement formation. Rather, the focus of analysis moves to the organizational capacities of movements and their ability to tap into pre-existing social infrastructures. What is most interesting about RMT is that the explanation of outcomes moves from focus on SMOs themselves to social infrastructures which act as selectors of success or failure. The ability of movements to deploy these social networks will determine whether their goals are successfully institutionalized, or fail and enter sub-cultural memories in the lifeworld, in the form of marginalized proto-public spheres.

Further, it was suggested that systems of regulation and the architecture of the lifeworld are co-determining – for example, gender relations are both structured by and structuring of markets and bureaucracies. Thus the terrain on which social movements attempt to mobilize will be structured by complex layers of sectional interest, attachments to the past, mini-traditions inscribed in the collective memories of sub-cultures, and quite different ways of appropriating cultural contexts. Habermas' broad differentiation of social movements into offensive and defensive postures does not entirely address this complexity, nor does it explore the capacities of systemic management to incorporate and neutralize social protest. It will be seen in Part 2 that colonization of the lifeworld not only invokes nostalgia for threatened ways of life, that is, reactions to modernization, but also creates attachments to the institutions of regulation themselves, where these have created sectional interests and identities. For example, the collapse of the corporate institutions of state socialism produces not only nostalgia for pre-communist pasts (religious revivals, the return of old national boarders, etc.) but also a tendency to re-create the corporate networks of patronage and dependence instituted by the former system. Moreover, this tendency is exacerbated when post-socialist governments embark on 'fast track' marketization which further threatens such fragile forms of solidarity as continue to survive. Thus the process of systemic collapse and regeneration is complex and its eventual outcome highly uncertain. If social pathologies are reproduced through socialization, as Habermas suggests, then in crisis situations they might be mobilized, for example in predilections for authoritarian movements. The examples discussed in Part 2 will examine the ways in which systems of regulation run into crisis and how the disintegration of the system in turn creates a context more favourable to certain types of social movement organization than others.

It will further be argued in Part 2 that crises of social regulation appear when an existing set of institutions is incapable of generating sufficient legitimacy or scope for innovation to continue fulfilling its fundamental goals. However, it has been seen that modernity releases multi-directional possibilities, and the appearance of crisis does not necessarily spell the end for existing institutional arrangements. On the contrary, it might be a means through which core structures are reproduced in new forms that offer more flexibility and preserve core elements of the system – a kind of repressive modernization where more emancipatory potentials are suppressed, and the transition is managed by dominant powers. On the other hand, crisis-solutions might result in participatory modernization – new institutional arrangements that expand learning capacities, broaden participation in organizational structures, permit a fluidity of roles and initiative, and provide access to social resources on a more egalitarian basis. In this context, with the disintegration of institutions of regulation, the direction of the outcome is likely to be crucially affected by the presence or absence of organized channels of collective organization, and the types of affective and cultural resources SMOs are able to mobilize. These ideas will now be filled out through an analysis of crisis and conflict in the global arena.

Notes

1. In the UK, membership of campaigning social movements is running ahead of that of the Labour Party (the traditional locus of social protest). For example, when Greenpeace was founded in 1971, the Labour Party had 699,522 members and it would have seemed improbable that by 1990 an organization concerned with the marine environment could have overtaken it, but by 1988 Labour Party membership had fallen to 265,927 and Greenpeace's membership had risen to 323,000 (in the UK).

2. For example, the British Campaign for Nuclear Disarmament arose in the early 1960s and then apparently declined, although its resurgence fifteen or twenty years later indicated that the values and organizational experience of the earlier period had merely gone into latency (and perhaps had re-appeared in other social movements in the meantime). Likewise the peace camp at Greenham Common (the site of a US cruise missile base in England) in the 1980s was the product of a confluence of feminist and pacifist cultures and organizational experience, which has entered the diffusely stored collective knowledge of a generation of feminist activists. See Roseneil (1992).

3. Melucci uses the term 'social movement sectors' in a different way from resource mobilization theorists, for whom this refers to the grouping of movements into 'industries' which compete for support from the same preference structures; for example, Greenpeace and Friends of the Earth 'compete' for resources amongst constituencies concerned with environmental issues.

4. The theme of globalism is also taken up by Giddens (1991), for whom the defining characteristic of the present is the new and permanent relationship between the local and global, in which spatially separated events have an influence on individual life through electronic communication.

5. Eder (1982) suggests that social protest movements are phenomena directly related to modernization from the seventeenth century onwards, which would further question the novelty of 'new' movements.

6. Habermas did suggest that the 'interests of the carrier stratum' determined the extent to which Reformation sects could become carriers of lifeworld rationalization. But if interest were to be the main predictor of adopting an emancipatory attitude towards post-traditional institutions, Critical Theory would need to locate subject-carriers with universal interests, and would be led full circle back to Marx's problem in the *Critique of Hegel's Philosophy of Right* (1844), of defining an historical agent of emancipation – that is, straight back into the philosophy of consciousness.

7. It was noted in Chapter 3 that Habermas regards *some* systemic steering as unavoidable in complex societies, and therefore advocates a 'balance' between steering media and communicative action. It is unclear, however, as Brand (1990) argues, at what point the former ceases to be nefarious (perhaps when it no longer causes pathologies?).

8. Habermas has in mind differentiating movements with universalistic reference (e.g. peace or anti-racist movements) from middle-class, not-in-my-back-yard kinds of protests which are defensive in posture (even if they campaign against hazards such as nuclear waste).

9. This point is completely missed by Scott (1990), incidentally, when he criticizes Habermas for having only a 'partial understanding' of new social movements, on the grounds that whilst some movements demand an extension of rationality, others (notably Green mysticism) are anti-rational. This is precisely Habermas' point.

10. The notion of feminism as the immanent critique of modernity is contentious, in that radical feminism calls into question the deep structures of modernity and rationality. Mies, for example, says that the 'demands of the French Revolution no longer constitute the core aspirations of the new feminist movement. Most feminists do not want even to be equal to men in the patriarchal system', but rather struggle for 'a non-hierarchical, non-centralized society where no elite lives on exploitation and dominance over others' (1989: 37). However, she offers no evidence for her claim to know what 'most feminists' want. Fraser (1989), on the other hand, defines the goal of feminism in terms of participating 'on a par with men in all types of social interaction, including political deliberation and decision-making', but also defends cultural separatism as a short-term necessity.

11. Perhaps Habermas is advocating what Ben Agger (1991) parodies as 'Girl Scout' feminism, as opposed to 'bad feminism', which is 'man-hating lesbian separatism'. On the other hand, Kate Soper (1989, 1991) insists that feminism invokes universalistic values, since 'one cannot seriously engage with gender "bias" or offer grounds for defending the call for it to be corrected, except on the assumption of an impartial and objective mode of relating', which seems closer to Habermas' view.

12. See Scott (1990) and Elkins (1989–90) for accounts of 'deep ecology' as a movement which attempts to invoke traditionalistic and anti-rational conceptions of nature and intuition.

13. Another example would be the way gay activist social networks which had been built during the 1970s, such as Gay Switchboard, subsequently formed the nucleus of defensive, educational and support groups in response to Aids/HIV.

14. Frank Adler (1990–1) regards such views as 'hopelessly naïve' since real academic communities are characterized by 'nasty internal power relations'. Precisely – the force of this critique is a call to arms, to resist the incorporation of critical theories in academic careerism and the intrusion of commercial criteria of efficiency.

15. 'Artificial negativity' claims that by the 1960s intensive rationalization of production through Fordism and an extensive public sector bureaucracy had reached its accumulation limits and become counter-productive. The system then began to implode, since opposition through counter-cultural movements came from within (i.e. from the universities, the professional intelligentsia, etc.). This 'negativity' was artificial in that it could be regulated, and turned by the system to its advantage (Luke, 1990: 159–78). Put as strongly as this, however, the thesis is open to Habermas' criticism of earlier Critical Theory, that it predicts in advance that almost all social protest will be neutralized.

16. Similarly the anti-psychiatry movement of the 1960s, in the UK and USA, was taken over by the state (without its counter-cultural aspects of course) in the programmes of mental hospital closure during the 1980s.

17. Kate Soper makes a similar point: 'the "Symbolic" will not recommend itself to those women who have yearned for a bit more "systemic" encroachment into their cherishing preserve in the form of proper public child care, not to mention wages for housework' (1989). Habermas is endorsing the lifeworld not as a kind of natural economy, however, but rather as its potential site of communicative ethics.

18. Paul Piccone (1990–1) for example, claims that affirmative action is bureaucratic deformation which substitutes categories (quotas) for moral subjects, and, rather than bring about a more egalitarian society, re-invents, reifies and reinforces racial and gender differences which result from class domination, social inequality and marginalization of women and ethnic minorities.

19. Challenging assumptions in the sociology of the family, Ben Agger points out that 'fewer than one-seventh of Americans today live in the definitional nuclear family. If the concept of family is meant to include people who may fall outside traditional patriarchal marriage, but who nonetheless share an enduring intimacy, then the text has a responsibility to make this clear' (1991: 55).

20. As women challenged male monopolies over the professions and campaigned for suffrage, especially from the 1860s, the belief in women's constitutional inferiority gained ground in expert cultures like medicine. Similarly, the era of mass politics and colonial expansion was accompanied by beliefs about the congenital inferiority of colonized peoples

and the working class, who were often alleged to be at a comparable level of evolutionary development.

21. It is possible, however, that this is temporary and cyclical, related specifically to recession. As long ago as 1844, in *The Condition of the Working Class in England*, Engels described the inversion of roles between men and women in north-west England as a result of male unemployment. This was hardly the beginning of the end of patriarchal divisions within the industrial proletariat!

22. Indeed, struggles around the labour process, then, can interact with broader emancipatory struggles. Aronowitz (1981: 75) gives the example of the radicalization of US public servants in 1960s, which he suggests was based on a number of material factors: first, the relatively privileged position of workers in the private sector; secondly, the entry of young Black women into public service; thirdly, the erosion of ideology of 'public service'; fourthly, the combined effects on these of civil rights and women's movements.

PART 2

Introduction

Part 1 has dealt with some complex questions and it would be useful briefly to review the ground covered and the ways in which the substantive analysis in Part 2 has a bearing on the discussion so far. Habermasian theory begins with a highly abstract reconstruction of the possibility of a Critical Theory, which makes a decisive turn away from earlier Frankfurt Institute thought whilst accepting some of its concerns (such as the negative effects on critical politics of commodification or technocratic planning). Like earlier Critical Theory, Habermas' diagnosis of modernity addresses fragmentation of the lifeworld, although this is understood no longer in terms of the reification of consciousness (as it was by Lukács or Adorno), but rather as the restriction of possibilities for communicative discourse. Habermas believes that the shift of focus in Critical Theory from consciousness to communicative structures is a promising framework within which to re-assess the emancipatory possibilities of the present.

Fragmentation of the lifeworld arises from the partly inevitable but also partly nefarious co-ordination of social action by steering media of money and power. The co-ordination of action through the partially norm-free mechanisms of the market and complex organizations is inevitable to the extent that they reduce the risk of modern communicative structures being over-burdened with the requirement of agreement. Hence Habermas argues that it is no longer realistic to envisage an emancipated society *simply* in terms of autonomous self-managed collectives or soviets, since this would involve unmanageable communicative complexity. Rather, resource allocation and planning would still require the co-ordinating systems of money and power (even though these would be subject to democratic regulation, in ways which Habermas does not specify).

However, even if some degree of co-ordination through money and power is unavoidable, Habermas links Critical Theory to a critique of the effects of their over-extension into the lifeworld, which causes dislocation and social pathologies. The task of Critical Theory is to identify those social potentials which resist colonization, and attempt to reclaim the lost integrity of the lifeworld from bureaucracies, technocracies, élitist expert cultures and market forces. This might appear paradoxical, since it is precisely anonymity and individualization, that is, the fragmentation of social life, which permits the disintegration of sacred world-views. Yet, paradoxical or not, this is more or less what Habermas does. Having used Weber against Marx and earlier Critical Theory, Habermas now uses the

Hegelian-Marxist notion of a reunification of reason in order to criticize Weber.

Habermas agrees with Weber that it is the differentiation of social life into value spheres of science, normativity and aesthetics which permits actors to raise validity-claims and to separate personal concerns or beliefs from the formal procedures through which we reach consensus. Although he was alert to the negative consequences of instrumental rationality, Weber was reluctantly prepared to settle for the inevitable loss of all-encompassing systems of meaning (*Sinnverlust*) as the price to be paid for the freedom to live as private citizens pursuing personal interests. However, Habermas takes issue precisely with Weber's view of the inevitability of *Sinnverlust*, which he regards as the result of his insufficiently nuanced concept of rationalization, an error he hopes to correct through a two-tier concept of society as system and lifeworld.

For Habermas, Weber conceded too readily to the inevitability and uniformity of instrumental (or system) rationality, a mistake which was then repeated in an even more extreme form by Adorno and Horkheimer. Instead, Habermas wants to locate an alternative, liberating rationality, which he believes can be found in universal pragmatics. By adapting Searle and Austin's speech act theory, Habermas attempts to reconstruct the rational procedures and types of argumentation (the conditions of reciprocity or the ideal speech situation) which will be valid within each substantive area of social life. Irrespective of the content of discourse – which will obviously differ in scientific, normative/legal or aesthetic fields – it is possible for participants in dialogue to suspend judgement on (or bracket) other speakers' claims to validity, and enter a specific kind of debate (*Diskurs*) where statements are challenged with respect to whether they are existentially true, normatively right, or sincere. If permitted to proceed unhindered this would result in consensus (although it was emphasized that this refers to a hypothetical not an actual consensus), and since these conditions are given in the communicative structure of language itself they constitute the inescapable prerequisite of linguistic competence.

If the conditions of ideal speech are inherent in language then we unavoidably presuppose them in any attempt at reaching an understanding (although they can be disregarded, as they are in strategic, manipulative or openly coercive behaviour). Moreover, once communities have attained a self-reflexive understanding about themselves, once they are no longer bound by taken-for-granted traditional norms, and authority has to be justified, there is no way in which this learning can be 'forgotten'. Structures of domination will attempt to deflect the potential for critical reason in various ways, which will include technocratic management, the re-invention of traditions, or naked repression, but there can be no going back to an unreflective acceptance of sacred authority. Moreover, for Habermas, strategic or even coercive behaviour is parasitic upon communicative norms (for reasons outlined in Chapter 2) which in turn allows him to claim that communicative norms have evolutionary priority in social development.

This is again a paradoxical claim since Habermas suggests that although communicative norms are always latent, they are none the less causal in historical development. However, Habermas is suggesting not that 'ideas' determine evolutionary development, but rather that the development and deployment of productive resources entails prior expansions in cognitive and moral learning processes. Moreover, the release of these learning potentials further required the more general precondition of differentiated and rationalized world-views which would permit hypothetical questioning of established beliefs and norms. By characterizing social development as a learning process in which only some potential advances are incorporated into the dynamics of development, Habermas hopes to revive social-evolutionary theory with a critical edge. Drawing upon Kohlberg and Piaget's developmental social psychology, he claims that the break from pre-modernity offers the potential for post-conventional forms of authority and socialization. Whereas a conventional orientation to authority, fixed rules and right behaviour consists in doing one's duty, post-conventional morality presupposes a decentred ego able to take the stand-point of others, aware of the relativity of personal values, and procedural rules for reaching consensus. Although this is the 'official' morality of liberal-democratic constitutions, modern societies have only partially realized the communicative possibilities which post-conventional reasoning offers. Nevertheless, Habermas insists that the break-through to modernity liberated the (suppressed) potential of critical reason as well as the (dominant) instrumental reason of markets and bureaucracies. Indeed, and now we get closer to a sociological thesis, the former has always constituted a kind of counter-culture of modernity, a permanent opposition to the dominant forms of instrumentality – which was apparent first in the Radical Reformation and has since then surfaced in emancipatory social movements, notably socialism and feminism. At this point, Habermas the Marxist comes to the fore and argues that suppressed modernity got suppressed because the organization of emergent capitalism incorporated into development only those structures which were compatible with its interests. That is, dominant modernity is a partial, jagged and restricted rationality which Weber and early Critical Theory incorrectly equated with modernity per se. The task for Critical Theory, then, is to locate those social movements which are potential carriers of new learning potentials, which offer the capacity of widening the scope for a critical politics whilst defending endangered ways of life against systemic encroachment.

So far so good, but beyond these rather general statements a detailed analysis of the formation of social identity and collective action is largely absent. The paradox remains after all, if one wants to argue on the one hand that communicative norms are inherent in the structure of the lifeworld and have evolutionary priority, but on the other hand that they keep getting zapped by power and money. It is a peculiar kind of evolutionary priority which is persistently over-ridden by other forces. Of course, one could argue that this is a process of *longue durée*, and that the underlying drift of modern societies is towards the continuing erosion of traditional socialities and the expansion of critical discourses. But given that social transparency is a wishful utopia, and that *Diskurs* is always latent, it seems that critical reason is in practice confined to the role of permanent opposition.

This problem is compounded by the observation in Part 1 that the distinction between lifeworld and system is purely analytic. Power and money are not really pure types detached from contexts of social reproduction, but rather are anchored in the lifeworld – markets and organizations presuppose sets of norms, habits and cultural practices which permit them to function. However, this anchoring of systemic media has contradictory effects on identities and the formation of social movements. First, colonization of the lifeworld provokes crises of socialization which threaten to destabilize systemic media and generate legitimation crises, since they undermine the very cultural practices within which states and markets are anchored. Secondly, however, socialization crises cause pathologies which give rise to withdrawal and disorientation, provoking defensive reactions with little emancipatory content. Thirdly, it was suggested in Chapter 4 that this process of anchoring means that the system and the lifeworld are interpenetrated in complex ways, such that markets and bureaucracies embody the material and cultural structures of the lifeworld (for example, gender divisions) whilst in turn systemic regulation segments the lifeworld by reinforcing, eroding or creating new divisions.

If this is so, then colonization has already structured the process through which social movements are formed and cultural learning is stored. Melucci (1989) and others have persuasively argued that diffuse and anti-hierarchical social movements, the 'nomads of the present', might constitute laboratories of experience and learning, but this still leaves open the question of how such social currents are incorporated within organizational forms where they can challenge the existing order. Further, the tendency in both Habermas and new social movement literature to (illegitimately) separate the politics of identity from more strategic goals leaves the crucial question of social movement impact relatively unexamined. Even if Habermasian theory specifies the conditions for critical politics, and theoretically distinguishes defensive from emancipatory *movements*, it is not entirely clear in what circumstances an emancipatory *outcome* is more, or less, likely.

Working through this thesis in detail and specifying the social environments in which movements arise requires more specific analysis. In particular it involves examining the ways in which the transformation of economic, cultural and state systems creates conditions conducive to particular outcomes. Habermas follows the thrust of classical sociology in conceiving the interface between system and lifeworld at the level of the nation-state, but, as Chapter 5 illustrates, this is becoming marginalized by the interplay of global and local socio-economic forces. This is an important development since the nation-state has in the past been the focus of much collective social action (struggles for rights, national independence, welfare provision, political-class organization, etc.). In peripheral social formations in particular, the state has had a central role as an agent of modernization, for example destroying traditional aristocratic landholding classes; has been a field of (often violent) contestation amongst local factional movements; and most important has been a vehicle of capital accumulation. In these senses the state in the periphery has been the organizational repository of adaptive defensive responses to both the global and local environments.

However, since the state has been an agent of accumulation, it has generated its own particular structures of interest and privilege. Where state allocation has to a greater or lesser extent replaced the market (notably in the state socialist countries, but in much of the peripheral world too) it has become over-burdened by problems of complexity and interest articulation arising from local and global systems of communication. Local state organizations are confronted by a contradiction (implicit in Habermas, 1976) between the contrary logics of power and money – both of which have advantages and disadvantages from the point of view of social regulation. Although the market gives rise to social conflicts structured by the wage relation, and therefore induces social crises, it also has the advantage of de-politicizing resource allocation by separating capital accumulation from the political form of the state. On the other hand, the juridical regulation of the market by the state has the social-evolutionary advantage of displacing economic conflicts from centre-stage, but in the process re-politicizes resource allocation. By rendering the mode of domination more perceptible, by partially or wholly replacing the invisible hand of the market by the visible hand of bureaucracy, statist or étatized societies are prone to wide-ranging legitimation crises.

Where, as in advanced capitalist societies, the state is bound by a democratic polity and powerful interests within civil society, the political terrain is likely to be marked by disputes over the extent or limits of state intervention *via-à-vis* the scope for private capital accumulation. However, things are quite different in peripheral formations where the state itself has often developed and owns productive resources, in the absence of a democratic polity or civil society. Here the state, in the context of increasing global and local complexity, is doubly burdened with the need to manage its extended reproduction whilst protecting its internal structures of élite privilege and patronage. If Habermas' characterization of the distinct logics of power and money are correct, then one might expect the peripheral state to respond to systemic problems by attempting to de-politicize rule, separating the institutions of political control from those of capital accumulation. Failing this, one would expect the state to enter profound legitimation crisis, which of course will have varying outcomes.

The more local economies are internationalized, and the more the state is over-burdened by steering and legitimation crises, the more likely is a kind of tactical retreat, an attempt to convert rule through the state into rule through the de-politicized mechanisms of the market. This adjustment, through which local states switch into plural economic and political structures, often involves the destruction of an old consensus in favour of new alliances, perhaps with the leadership of oppositional social movements. However, tactical retreat is an option only under certain circumstances and, since it involves a critical transition period, might be unsuccessful. It presupposes a relatively homogeneous élite (otherwise one faction like the military might disrupt the process) and the absence of mass opposition with radically divergent goals. The three cases through which this thesis is examined are selected partly because of their global importance, but also because they offer contrastive reactions to the underlying process. Throughout these three cases in Part 2, a general model of regulatory systems and lifeworld responses will be set against the peculiar features of each which gave rise to specific outcomes.

The collapse of state socialism offers a model closest to that of tactical retreat (or repressive modernization) where crises of the economic, political and socio-cultural sub-systems developed through social atomization and privatization. This systemic vacuum precluded the formation of social movements capable of articulating demands through institutional public spheres (with the exception of Solidarity, which is in many ways a special case). In Eastern Europe and the former USSR a consensus was held together by redistributive mechanisms underwritten by systems of regulation. When these arrangements became unviable, they gave way to the construction of a new consensus, not across the society as a whole, but between reform factions in the ruling parties and sections of the opposition amenable to marketization and privatization. The upshot of this could be that the social power of (some amongst) the nomenklatura, the former ruling élite, has not been abolished, but re-appears within the newly privatized economies. However, the absence of institutional public spheres and intermediate channels of interest articulation means that the stability of markets and democratic political structures remains uncertain.

The Iranian Revolution, however, illustrates a contrasting situation where the options of the *ancien régime* were limited by chronic legitimacy deficit, an acute bifurcation between state and society, and the existence of an alternative élite and social movement (whose existence was the result of a particular pattern of colonization). The collapse of the Pahlavi state, however, was followed by a more intensive consolidation of state power organized through mass terror and authoritarian populism. Although Islamic 'fundamentalism' (an unsatisfactory term but one which will suffice for the moment) aims at the reconstitution of an Islamic law and polity, it actually represents an *étatist modernizing* movement. Now it might appear strange to describe Islamic fundamentalists as 'modernizers', since the image which is predominant in the West is the converse – of anti-modernists resurrecting medieval practices. But in order to understand this phenomenon it is necessary to separate the *content* of Islamic ideology, the Shar'ia, the Rule of the Jurists, or whatever, from the *form of rule*, which has clearly modern structures and purposes (bearing in mind that 'modern' in this context refers only to system-rationalization). In Chapter 7 it is suggested that Khomeini's followers were 'Islamic Jacobins' whose revolution destroyed the aristocratic power of the old order (like 1789 or 1917) whilst extending the scope of state intervention and ownership.

In South Africa, protracted legitimation crisis, the obsolescence of a racially segregated labour market, combined with mass-based opposition, have resulted in attempts to establish new regulatory institutions. Apartheid was a state-dominated mode of regulation and accumulation, adapted to semi-peripheral conditions and the interests of Afrikaner capital and labour. The extremely limited consensus upon which the apartheid state had been founded, between the National Party and Afrikaner business and labour, was dismantled from within, following the acute systemic crisis which gained ground from the mid-1970s. In its place Afrikaner technocrats attempted to construct a new consensus to include not only the English Whites, but also the Congress Alliance. This apparent capitulation, however, should not occlude the fact that in the post-apartheid state highly unequal social relationships will persist and will be reproduced through market mechanisms, that is, through more de-politicized forms than previously. The South African élite, however, is sharply divided, and the ANC has a vision of an alternative set of social arrangements. Thus the conditions are not conducive to tactical retreat and such efforts (the CODESA talks) have been undermined by the hidden war of the security forces against the ANC.

This, then, sets the scene for the discussion in Part 2, which begins with a closer examination of statism and globalization and elaborates Habermasian analysis in unfamiliar terrain. This will examine the ways in which social movement formation and impact are conditioned by patterns of lifeworld colonization. Whether social movements articulate more offensive, fluid and open postures, or whether they are constrained by defensiveness and closure, is likely to be affected by two related factors. The first is the extent to which the new consensus requires a loose coupling of interests which will be articulated through negotiation and compromise. The second is the extent to which communication channels within movements open public spheres through which identities can be critically and reflexively examined. It should become clear from this analysis of peripheral and semi-peripheral formations, however, that the project of modernity, far from being exhausted, has the potential to release further cultural and organizational innovations and problems.

5

Legitimation in Peripheral States

Part 1 proposed an interpretation of Critical Theory which situated social movements within processes of social regulation, cultural transmission and resistance. According to this model, systemic crises release cultural reserves of cognitive and moral learning which are then selectively incorporated into the dynamics of development. This stabilization is accomplished through social conflicts which are resolved – in differing degrees of permanence – by a consensus which provides the basis for institutionalizing new forms of regulation around the state. However, like the welfare state compromise which followed the Second World War in most western countries, this settlement itself becomes the focus of new articulations of protest and crises. Within this context collective social action will form around two types of identities – those which are reactively defensive of endangered ways of life, and those grounded in fluid and plural conceptions of the personal and collective self. The latter, however, are premised on the development of a communicative public sphere through which identities and traditions are reflexively examined, and where this has been constricted, collective social action will tend to have a defensive character. What type of movement orientations develop, and how successfully they mobilize potential constituents, will depend on the amount of rationalization that these social infrastructures have undergone. This in turn will be structured by the pattern of systemic colonization. This is the model presented so far, which in this part will be elaborated with reference to global contexts, and this chapter sets the scene for further analysis by developing a model of the peripheral state in the vortex of the global system.

On a global scale collective social action has been organized around local states, which are subject to crisis-logics arising from internal and external pressures. This chapter first outlines the ways in which states outside the organic core regions (North America, Western Europe, Australia and New Zealand) have established bases of consensus through the extension of patronage via state structures. Secondly, it indicates how this impacts upon modes of social learning and patterns of collective action. Of course specific cases have different histories, levels of development and relationships with their global environments. The intention in developing an abstract model of regulation is to examine how Habermasian analysis might (or might not) elucidate particular manifestations of crisis and collective action within the context of the global system, and identify common dynamics and structures in apparently diverse societies, without violating their specific features.

Indeed, as the Introduction to Part 2 indicates, there is a *prima facie* similarity amongst social formations peripheral to the capitalist core states, including both Eastern European socialism and post-colonial societies, namely that they have, to different degrees, been étatist societies. At a general level, this is explicable in terms of the developmental problems confronted by the peripheral state, as a formally organized domain of strategic action. First, local states confronted a post-war global economy where, in the absence of national industrial capital capable of competing with organic core regions, they became engines of capital accumulation (as the mercantile state had in early modern Europe). This involves gathering resources, building industrial plant, protecting industry and taming a labour force (through corporatist as well as repressive strategies). Secondly, this developmental programme at some point requires taking resources and people out of agriculture, to permit primitive accumulation, increase productivity and reduce the necessary costs of labour (for example, by providing cheap food). According to Barrington Moore, 'The taming of the agrarian sector has been a decisive feature of the whole historical process of modernization' (1969: 429), which has involved restructuring agrarian social relations either through violent elimination of the traditional landed classes (as in Russia)[1] or by co-opting and subduing them (as in Britain). In the contemporary world, peripheral states approach this problem in a variety of ways, but whether small-holder production is maintained but with more squeezed out of it, or whether servile labour is aggregated on large units as with collectivization, the extraction of agricultural surplus requires strong political controls. Thirdly, however, whereas the state in the western capitalist transition was powerful, in peripheral societies, lacking a firm basis in local classes, it was too weak to resist colonial penetration (Turner, 1984: 172). Here, then, the pursuit of modernizing strategies carries risks of social upheaval, which the state attempts to reduce through trading off authoritarian, single-party rule against the creation of privileged sectors, in ways which will be illustrated here.

Indeed, the majority of non-core states, across a wide spectrum of ideological positions (state socialist, nationalist, Islamic, or even monarchic), have been ruled by single parties (or the military) and have extended state economies.[2] How effectively Habermasian state theory might address this situation is a matter of dispute, since central to Habermas' understanding of the state are concepts of legitimacy and consensus, which are related to the expansion of communicative structures of the lifeworld. Yet peripheral societies have adapted to a global environment in which they are structurally disadvantaged, and have sustained local capital accumulation through coercion combined with only sparse and fragile bases of consensus. States which lack popular loyalty find it difficult to institute within themselves political divisions since

insufficient mutual ground between opposing factions threatens to undermine the whole structure. Therefore, a more common tendency amongst
peripheral states has been mass mobilization around symbolic themes of
nation-building, anti-imperialism or specific national traditions, as well as
substantive legitimation through patronage, all balanced with repression
and the policing of opposition.

Legitimation and the Peripheral State

It was seen in Chapter 1 how, despite its concern with the authoritarian
state, earlier Critical Theory did not develop a differentiated state theory.
Rather, it tended to follow the orthodox Marxist analysis of the time,
which assumed that the centralized authoritarian state met the organizational demands of monopoly capital (although there were disagreements
as to its long-term stability). Adorno's totalitarian drift hypothesis did not
distinguish sufficiently between what was happening in the advanced
capitalist core – where capitalism moved to an intensive, state-regulated
mode of accumulation – and the peripheral regions of Central, Southern
and Eastern Europe which were dominated by the *Führerprinzip*. Thus,
despite being aware of the differences between 'totalitarian' and 'democratic' state capitalism, at a deep level of analysis they collapsed fascism,
Stalinism, the New Deal and the welfare state into a single movement
which was symptomatic of the end of Enlightenment. From a global stand-
point, however, the state was not the result of a single drift towards total
administration, but took different forms shaped by core–periphery relationships. Indeed, the authoritarian state was, by and large, found not in
areas where capitalism was most developed, but, on the contrary, in the
less developed peripheral regions of Eastern and Southern Europe.

Although Habermas has made a more detailed examination of the
functions and crisis tendencies of the modern state in western societies,
even this kind of rudimentary global analysis is largely absent from his
account, which concentrates on inter-system boundaries within the western
nation-state.[3] Where Habermas does extend his scope beyond Western
Europe, he tends as Arnason (1991) argues, to regard modernity as an
undifferentiated process – a kind of single tree with divergent branches.
For example, in discussion with Andrew Arato, Habermas (1982b)
suggests that the 'bureaucratic-socialist' line of development is a *variant* of
the basic structure of modernity. Thus for Habermas the primacy of money
is characteristic of the capitalist path, whereas the primacy of administrative power is dominant in the étatization of economy and culture in the
East.

In a mixed economy, the state responds to 'market failure', that is, it
intervenes to provide essential resources which the market cannot supply
effectively (especially welfare); protects infant industries; controls private
monopoly power; and cross-subsidizes to protect employment (Brett,
1988: 55). Through social welfare or labour protection the modern state

acts as a potential counterbalance to the trajectory of capital. This is because whilst the capitalist state still protects the private interests of capital, it is required by its own legitimating claims to represent the general interest, and by the adversarial nature of democratic politics to rule through consensus, or at least the appearance of consensus. As Sciulli (1992: 35) argues, 'purported "conflicts" and "struggles" within existing western democracies are essentially policy debates' in which the political institutions of rule are broadly accepted as legitimate.[4]

On the contrary, Arnason (1990, 1991) argues, 'the state' has quite different meanings for the core as opposed to the periphery[5] in at least four ways. First, Habermas accounts for the modern state in terms of 'juridifi- cation', but in peripheral formations the state has often had the freedom to engage in norm-free *raison d'état*, subject to no democratic principles. Secondly, the one-party state abolishes or attempts to abolish the public sphere in which legitimacy questions can arise, whilst broadening channels of participation through the recruitment into the patronage networks of the Party itself. Thus it might be more appropriate to speak of its relationship with the lifeworld in terms of ideological mobilization, social mobility and acquiescence than in terms of 'legitimacy'. Thirdly, the one-party state is not a field of contestation for competing political parties, but a highly extended entity which owns productive resources, mass media and other channels of communication; and mobilizes and 'modernizes' society through diktat. Finally, conditions of 'combined and uneven' development in the periphery give rise to explosive collisions between imperialist expansion and a non-capitalist environment, an 'ambivalent modernity', evidenced by traditionalistic movements such as nationalism, religious revivals, or ethnic communalism.

However, these differences between western and peripheral forms of the state should not be over-drawn, since even the authoritarian state requires legitimation, as David Beetham suggests, 'not so much to function, or even to survive over a period of time, but to achieve those purposes that depend upon the support of its population, and to maintain its political system intact in the face of serious policy failure' (1991: 118). The dramatic collapse of military and administrative apparatuses during the past two decades – Greece (1974), Portugal (1974), Spain (1976), Iran (1979), and then the former socialist states – demonstrates the importance of legit- imacy to the effectiveness and continuity of a system of rule. Moreover, although the legitimacy *conditions* of welfare capitalism, which Habermas analyses, differ from those of the authoritarian state, the same legitimacy *problem* might obtain in both. That is, the erosion by money and political power of traditional modes of justifying authority obliges the state to generate new forms of co-ordination and regulation to insulate the identity of the system from opposition social movements. Thus the difference between welfare capitalism and peripheral forms of the state might amount to this – the relative affluence of the core nations combined with the strength of social democratic labour organizations permitted a degree of class compromise within a democratic polity which was generally not tenable elsewhere. In the non-core nations the identity of the mode of accumulation – and especially the integration of the local economy and polity into global capitalism – would have been threatened by mass democratization, but this did not mean that local states were exempt from the need to generate some degree of consensus and support (even in terroristic dictatorships).

It should be kept in mind that this refers to the minimal conditions of legitimacy – that orders from the central authority are recognized as binding amongst those who have to execute them, combined with the creation of sufficient popular acquiescence and incorporation to forestall the emergence of mass opposition (examples of which are provided in the following three chapters). To these ends, specific forms of consensus generation are likely to be consolidated within the strategic learning mechanisms of étatist structures. A common though obviously not universal pattern of non-elective regulation is seen in structures of state socialism, and many nationalist-populist regimes in post-independence Africa and Asia (for example, the Iranian Republic, the Ba'ath parties of Syria or Iraq, Egypt after the Free Officers' coup, Kemalite Turkey, or even the conservative rule of the Kenya African National Union). The Soviet experience provided a kind of paradigm for peripheral development in at least three ways. First, command economies offer the potential for rapid modernization and disciplining vast strata of the population in early stages of development. Secondly, the Soviet-type state has higher internal stability (at least in the medium term) by concentrating political, economic and military power in the party-state apparatus. Thirdly, it offers the model of a mobilizing, heroic ideology of self-sacrifice, a 'secular religion and dedicated way of life' (Wiles, 1982: 359) for harnessing labour inputs to development projects (Zaslavsky, 1985).

Under the banner of nation-building state power is centralized, but also widens the base of political participation through the institutions of the party and employees of the enlarged state organs. The one-party state widens the base of participation partly through mass mobilization – in literacy or other educative campaigns, meetings and committees in villages or suburbs, but especially through recruitment to positions in the bureaucratic hierarchy (as Weber noted in his discussion of 'plebiscitary democracy') (Alavi, 1972; Clapham, 1989). However, as Weber further noted, although this type of domination might enhance the formal rationalization of economic activity, for example by increasing agricultural productivity, its interest in legitimacy in the absence of formal procedures can erode efficiency by over-extending state structures. In the socialist states, for example, social security, income maintenance, housing subsidies, culture and health, allocated on the basis of what Weber called substantive rationality, served to establish a limited legitimation basis (Konrad & Szelenyi, 1979; Markus, 1982).[6] Likewise, Callaghy and Wilson (1988: 179–80) and Standbrook (1988) argue that Third World state enterprises were more successful at achieving goals of legitimacy and integration than they were at generating economic performance. However, this brings with it a distinct set of crisis tendencies related partly to the size of the unproductive state sector and partly to the effects of state colonization of the lifeworld.

Habermas comments that through state ownership of most of the means of production and institutionalized one-party rule, 'the administrative action system gains . . . autonomy in relation to the economic system' and crises then arise from self-blocking mechanisms in planning, where rational action orientations come into contradiction with unintended systemic effects. Crisis tendencies are worked through not only in the sub-system in which they arise, but also in the complementary action system into which they can be shifted, thus policy oscillates between orienting economic programmes towards investment and towards consumption (Habermas, 1989b: 384).

This offers the beginning of a theory of crisis tendencies within étatist societies which are burdened by 'an over-extended administered public sphere' (Habermas, 1989b: 386). It has been noted already that the anchoring of steering media of power in social reproduction carries risks consequent on politicizing everyday life. Thus once repression is mitigated, the likelihood of mass political action is increased in statist societies, compared with its potential in developed capitalism. Where conflicts appear that have a class character, such as Solidarity, or recent miners' strikes in the Donbass region of the ex-Soviet Union, this thesis suggests that they are unlikely to be restricted to economic demands, but rather will become generalized struggles addressing the mode of domination itself. However, this focus on internal dynamics needs to be balanced with reference to the global environment from which crisis tendencies arise and which local states have limited capacities to control. That is, states were prone to crises of systemic regulation arising from their particular modes of consensus-generation which in turn were adaptive responses to the local and global environment. Let us examine these relationships in more detail.

Regulation in the Global Context

The post-revolutionary or post-colonial state forms which have been referred to above were responses to a particular configuration of global and local relationships structured by the dominance of international capital. For much of the twentieth century, and especially since 1945, populations outside of the industrially developed regions of the world have confronted the structural effects of colonialism and post-colonial dependency.[7] Theorists such as André Gunder Frank, Samir Amin and Fernando Cardoso have argued that the history of capitalist development has been characterized by the permanent transfer of value from underdeveloped to developed sectors of the global economy, as capital sought cheaper commodity markets. Amin, for example, argues that the accumulation of international value explains the double polarization of capital, which involves unequal distribution of income on a global scale, and heightened inequality within the periphery. Value is transferred from non-commodity sectors (household production) to non-capitalist commodity sectors (for example, smallholders) to capitalist production (for example, agribusiness), through a variety of channels both within and between the North and South, all of which is 'made opaque by the price structure' (Amin, 1989: 122).[8]

In the post-colonial period, states outside the industrialized core have confronted a range of problems in dealing with the global environment, which they have been largely unable to resolve.[9] At an economic level these have involved problems of controlling outflows of capital through transnational corporations, and of sustaining economic growth whilst balancing the costs of imported energy and manufactured goods against foreign currency earnings from exports. They have further involved coping with global fluctuations in commodity prices and the trade barriers erected by purchaser cartels such as the EC, and latterly managing the problems of foreign debt. In response to these structural inequalities an array of relationships with the global environment have evolved. These have ranged through autarkic 'delinking' from the global system (Albania, Burma); the creation of parallel quasi-international structures with their own transnational division of labour to promote economic growth through import substitution (for example, COMECON); relative delinking through a large state sector and partial state ownership of the local subsidiaries of transnational companies (for example, India or Turkey); to highly internationalized economies, with extensive direct foreign ownership but still interpenetrated with parastatals (for example, Kenya).

Trimberger suggests that the state has a high degree of autonomy in these matters, since 'control of the governing apparatus is a source of power independent of that held by a class. State power, and coercive power in particular, is the instrument of those in control, and what is important is whether they are personally committed to the present organization of the economy' (1978: 7). Constraints posed by the global environment, however, have tended to limit the possible range of variation in organizational forms.

None the less, the state is an independent source of power, and diverts resources into the construction of minimal consensus through extensive networks of clientelism. This has extended to the creation of classes themselves: for example the creation of the rural small-holding sector in post-colonial East Africa through the parcellization of the former settler estates; or bureaucratically ascribed classes whose privileges and income are dependent on the administrative system. In other words, the state does not maximize social utility subject only to resource and technological constraints, but is a vehicle of accumulation and through economic policies seeks to maximize its own utility (incomes, perquisites and power) not necessarily the welfare of its citizens (Lal, 1987). If, as is now the case, the social regulation of clientelistic states becomes more difficult to sustain in a changing global order, one would expect the state to attempt to secure its social domination through other channels.

Political Clientelism

Habermas' reading of Weber is rather selective, and tends to concentrate on the dichotomy between traditional society regulated by the sacred, and modern society regulated by power and money. However, political clientelism in post-colonial states has prompted the suggestion that this is a distinct social form, with its specific history and organization. This is sometimes termed 'neo-patrimonialism', because of its similarities with pre-modern bureaucratic social organization. The Weberian concept of 'bureaucratic patrimonialism' contrasted feudal societies, which were decentralized through fiefdoms and land tenure, with highly centralized bureaucracies connected through payments for service (that is, benefices or prebends), such as the Ottoman Empire (Turner, 1981: 245). In bureaucratic patrimonial societies there was no clear distinction between the centre and periphery, a relatively low symbolic and institutional division of labour, and narrow status association (Eisenstadt, 1980). This was a pre-modern form of social organization, where authority was ascribed to the person rather than to the office-holder, although personal authority was anchored in the social and political order through retainers whose loyalty to the sovereign was mediated by an oath of loyalty or by kinship. Weber (1978: II, 1014) argued that patrimonialism was characterized by an undeveloped market, a small entrepreneurial middle class and an undifferentiated bureaucracy. However, once its accumulation base shifted from tribute to profit-centred monopolism or taxation, this would signal the beginning of its decline, as local élites gained sufficient power to extract fiefdoms from the sovereign. Moreover, patrimonial administration 'is alien to and distrustful of capitalist development, which revolutionizes the given social conditions' (1978: II, 1108–19).

However, contrary to both Weberian and classical Marxist expectations, political clientelism has thus far demonstrated a capacity for flexibility and survival within party-political structures (Lemarchand, 1981; Mouzelis, 1985). A number of writers have suggested that in parts of the developing world, especially Africa and Asia, lineage networks and reciprocal clientelistic ties have been integrated into the local state where they re-assert themselves in new forms, adapted to the global capitalist environment. Here the political administrative system – often ruled autocratically – is pervaded by personal subordination, bribes and nepotism, and the use of public powers to achieve private goals (Clapham, 1982: 67). 'Neo-patrimonialism' refers particularly to the enrichment of a familial élite (like the Mobutos, Pahlavis, Ceauşescus, Brezhnevs or Zhivkovs) based upon clientelistic distribution of resources. Under personal dictatorship or one-

party rule, the neo-patrimonial state is particularist, in that mass organizations are not institutions of an independent civil society, but channel
demands from subordinate and clientelist groups. Ben Turok, following
Nzongola-Natalaja (1987: 85), describes Zaïre as a 'kleptocracy' stratified
by regionalism, 'marked by a high degree of patronage from the Presi-
dency. It is dedicated to self-serving activities, prestige projects, luxury and
consumption' (Turok, 1987: 50). Whilst Zaïre might represent an extreme
example, the pattern is replicated elsewhere. In Kenya, for example, under
the guise of a parliamentary system, the ruling Kenya National African
Union (KANU) came under the increasingly personalized rule of President
Moi during the 1980s. The 1986 Constitution of Kenya Amendment Act
abolished the last remnants of an independent judiciary or civil society, in
defence of which the Attorney-General said 'anybody who thinks he can
hold office without the pleasure of the President is day-dreaming', when
responding to criticism from the National Council of Churches in Kenya
(*Weekly Review*, Nairobi, 28 November 1986). Further, the 1992 elections
in Kenya might indicate the capacity for political patronage to survive in
multi-party structures (albeit in a more decentralized and weaker form). In
December 1991, following eighteen months of campaigning by the Forum
for the Restoration of Democracy (FORD), which was backed by diploma-
tic pressure from the USA and EC, KANU agreed to hold multi-party
elections in the following year. The results of the December 1992 elections
have been controversial, with President Moi and KANU's narrow victory
accompanied by accusations from opposition parties of intimidation and
vote-rigging.[10] Moreover, support for parties and presidential candidates
was distributed along regional and ethnic divisions, perhaps reflecting
more localized networks of clientelism, a conclusion strengthened by
reports of patronage, mafias and 'godfathers' amongst both KANU and the
new political parties (*Weekly Review*, Nairobi, 18 October 1991).

Thus political clientelism has provided a basis for both extending state
control over resource allocation and creating dependent constituencies.
Where one-party states (like Kenya) permit multi-candidate elections,
contenders for office will attempt to secure support by demonstrating their
closeness to the centres of power, especially the President, and hence their
ability to secure aid and investment from the centre. Meanwhile officials in
the bureaucracy will devise means of allocating resources which strengthen
their ties with particular locales. Applying this concept to state socialism in
Poland, Tarkowski claims that

> [p]atrons can be found everywhere, at all levels of the hierarchical structure in
> the economy, political and administrative spheres. . . . The most common
> relationship is based on personal ties with the community as a whole. The basis
> of the relationship may be the fact that the patron was born there . . . or used to
> work there. (1981: 185)

It should be emphasized, however, that *neo*-patrimonialism is not merely a
carry-over from traditional society, but is a functional response to economic and political insecurity, which is incorporated into the service of

accumulation within the state, and in turn is bolstered by international connections. Export earnings provide taxes for the administration through levies on transnational corporations, or through state trading companies. A non-convertible currency further increases the state's control of capital exports, since local producers sell to state marketing boards and are paid in local currency, whilst the state re-sells commodities in foreign exchange.

The concept of the neo-patrimonial state has augmented earlier attempts to theorize what Hamsa Alavi (1972) called the 'over-developed post-colonial state' which the post-independence or post-revolutionary élite inherits from departing colonialists. Already geared to extracting a surplus from subordinated indigenous classes, the over-extended state generates sufficient revenue to expand a bureaucracy. Similarly, Henry Bernstein (1981) argues that the post-colonial state lacks any indigenous class base, and antagonistically confronts the mass of producers, from whom it extracts a surplus through taxation and state enterprises, thus creating a bureaucratic-financial class. Although much productive capital is owned by transnational corporations, during the 1970s 'parastatal' ventures were launched, combining local, state and transnational capital. Moreover, the expansion of a salariat of bureaucratic employees is an attempt by the bureaucratic bourgeoisie to create a patronage-dependent social basis (Alavi, 1972).

Insofar as political clientelism channels resources in ways which protect pre-modern social structures, it constitutes a barrier to the formation of communicative public spheres. Craig Charney (1987), for example, argues that the preservation of domestic production and an undifferentiated economy perpetuates the powerlessness of women in rural households along with ideologies of hierarchy, rank and reciprocity. In Third World urban areas too, where 50 per cent of the population works in the informal sector, without protection, insurance, etc., their access to livings is regulated through lineage ties, whilst in the formal sector, patronage regulates political mobilization along traditional patron–client lines.[11] Bangura (1987) describes how the system of patronage recruitment, in the absence of employment labour bureaux, and with an over-supply of urban labour, enabled the management of Nigerian vehicle assembly plants to defeat strikes in the late 1970s.[12] At the same time, the partial reproduction of wage-labour through domestic relations (family small-holdings) reduces costs for the capitalist sector. Where the majority of the population (in Kenya, for example, 80 per cent) are engaged in small-holder production, and many urban workers are migrant, the survival of a small-holding sector will also sustain an individuated rather than collective class consciousness, which is conducive to clientelism.

These structures have frequently survived independence, especially where capitalization of agriculture or plantation economies were not viable,[13] and Third World states have sought to expand commodity production by integrating small-holders into the market economy. In this way, pre-capitalist social relations integrated into circuits of capital, through production of cash crops, can preserve rather than destroy traditional structures. Bernstein (1977, 1979) writes of the 'simple commodity squeeze', where industrial consumers of agricultural commodities promote small-holder production through contracts, a low-risk form of investment, since the household farm supplies labour and inputs. Similarly, Vergopoulos (1978) and Cliffe (1977) argue that through unequal exchange and exchange of quasi-equivalents,[14] capital secures cheap reproduction costs of its labour force, which especially involves the subordination of women's labour (Bujra, 1990; Meillassoux, 1972). In Kenya, limited cash cropping has tended to produce a group of rich peasants, rather than commercial farmers, and the tendency towards proletarianization, which had begun during the colonial period, was arrested by the local state, because of its political implications, through policies designed to support small-holder production (Alavi, 1982; Currie & Ray, 1987).

In other words, the creation of contract-dependent small-holders occurs primarily as a result of attempts to resolve legitimation problems of the state, and not simply because it can be adapted to the interests of global capital. As Michaelina von Freyhold (1987) argues, these 'survivals are the product of tenacious struggles' for preservation, and the dispossession of small-holders would destabilize governments which already have weak legitimacy-bases. Further, decisions as to where to expand cash-crop production provide state development agencies with further patronage resources. Of course, small-holder contracting arrangements might be beneficial to capital as well, especially where they reduce the reproduction costs of wage-labour by subordinating women to super-exploitation on non-viable small-holdings. Moreover, rural credit and indebtedness ties small-holders to the land and to the requirements of agribusiness (in order to service previous loans). Extension schemes, however, are one facet of a more general pattern of indebtedness which reinforces patron–client networks since peasants at all levels borrow money for urgent outlays, for production, social obligations and emergencies (Beckman, 1988).

The notion of the neo-patrimonial state has been challenged, however, especially by dependency theorists – who argue, like Colin Leys (1976) and Bjorn Beckman (1981), first, that the concept is misleading since it exaggerates the role of the state in relation to the private sector, and, secondly, that the local class/state configuration is less important than the fact that transnational capitalism is always hegemonic. The local state-bourgeoisie can develop productive resources only when technology and management skills are provided by transnational corporations, in return for which the local state delivers a low-wage, low-tax, low-regulation, economic environment, with repression of popular and trade union movements. Likewise, Amin (1991: 328) argues that, far from being 'the last vestige of an alleged precapitalist past', industrialization has modernized dictatorship and substituted fascistic violence for the old oligarchic and patriarchal systems. To some extent this is valid, but the peculiarity of neo-patrimonial clientelism is precisely that it has attempted to modernize pre-capitalist structures within global systems of capital accumulation without undermining the fragile supports of the state itself. Where this has involved sustaining rather than obliterating pre-capitalist forms the latter have been given new leases of life. Further, as Turner (1981: 281) claims, dependency analysis has tended to neglect the internal structure of post-colonial societies, and, as Joshua Forrest (1987) argues, it is precisely these domestic configurations which will account for local social struggles and political fractions within the global context.

Even so, to attempt to theorize diverse societies within a single category is to skate on thin ice, and at best the notion of neo-patrimonialism identifies a tendency within more complex state-society configurations. In these terms, clientelism is a flexible and modern adaptation of pre-modern social relations within the structure of dependent states which through the extension of their own administrative and allocation systems create minimal conditions of consensus. It refers to two types of relationship between the state and society – one in which pre-modern forms (like small-holder production) are preserved partly in order to increase the legitimacy-base of the state; and another where the state structures themselves create new channels of clientelism, patronage and participation and bureaucratic-ally ascribed classes.[15] However, clientelistic relations, whether between state agencies and segments of society, or within society, are normatively regulated in that they are based on the recognition of mutually (if asymmetrical) obligations (Habermas, 1989b: 276). They are therefore subject to erosion through strategic calculations and increasing complexity of demands on social regulation. Under pressure, clientelism is likely to give way either to mediatized co-ordination, or to what Sahlins calls 'negative exchange', the attempt to get something for nothing (Lemarchand, 1981: 15), which in turn presages collective action.

Political clientelism is subject to the invasive pressures of market rationality and is prone to crises of legitimation in at least two ways, which in turn have an effect on patterns of social movement formation. First, the support-bases with which the state constructs consensus might be extremely narrow. For example, in response to labour unrest the 1924 National–Labour Party Pact Government in South Africa subsidized Afrikaner business whilst protecting White labour through the colour bar (which was later developed into full-blown apartheid). Confronted by a permanent legitimation crisis, outside the privileged sectors of White labour and capital later Nationalist Governments attempted to extend networks of patronage through the so-called 'homelands' (where one-party mini-states such as the rule of Inkatha in KwaZulu constructed their own networks of clientelism). This pattern of ethnic and regional discrimination (which was institutionalized to an exceptionally explicit degree in South Africa) is a common characteristic of political clientelism, and threatens to explode into inter-regional conflicts or civil war when the centre is weakened as a result of internal or external pressures. This might account for the tendency for post-independence states to fragment or at least for violent fractures to appear along ethnic and sub-national lines, a process which is presently being replicated across Eastern Europe and the ex-Soviet Union.

Secondly, political clientelism is subject to recurrent fiscal crises (Lal, 1987; Turner 1981: 248) and an over-loading of its steering capacity through a proliferation of objectives. Since the central allocation mechanisms themselves absorb increasing proportions of the national product, étatist societies need either to be highly productive or to sustain flows of revenue (aid, loans or profitable export commodities) sufficient for redistribution along clientelistic networks. These problems in turn promote what Tarkowski (1981: 187) calls 'speculation with regulations', where a parallel economy develops and is based on mutual obligations and family ties at local levels in the bureaucracy, which reduces the predictability of behaviour and weakens steering media from within. It will be seen in discussions of state socialism in particular how parallel societies first mimic the system of central allocation through informal networks, creating a kind of system of local fiefdoms, and undermine bureaucratic structures whilst remaining dependent on them. Later, when the redistributive mechanisms of the official society have become sufficiently weak and over-burdened, the parallel society itself begins to take over from the state and a relocation of power, along with widespread social dislocation, ensues. The growth of a parallel economy, which is a direct consequence of the revenue crisis of the over-extended state, leads, as Lal (1987) puts it, to a 'very unMarxian withering away of the State', since funds are siphoned away from the official economy, and the state's tax and production bases are eroded, which further exacerbates the fiscal crisis. However, in addition to these internally driven systemic crises, the global context is changing in ways which further reveal the weakness of the neo-patrimonial state in relation to global powers and institutions.[16]

Crisis of the Dependent State

Clientelism, then, represents a form of steering anchored in lifeworld structures which are subject to erosion, once the global networks of support wear thin, something which began to happen during the 1970s. The success of the post-war period rested on two pillars (Lipietz, 1989). First, a model of development based upon mechanization and a particular organization of labour, Taylorism, established itself in the capitalist core and made for very rapid productivity gains. Secondly, these were partly distributed to the wage-earning population through a tight network of collective agreements and the institutions of the welfare state. This model, sometimes called 'Fordism', was thus primed by the growth of domestic consumption. International trade also grew, though at a considerably slower pace, so that the ratio of exports to domestic production amongst OECD nations declined to reach an all-time low in the 1960s, although the system was preserved for a time through the global dominance of the USA which compelled all countries to recognize the dollar as the universal means of exchange (Lipietz, 1989).

Towards the end of the 1960s this order came apart as the Taylorist organization of labour was confronted by renewed trade union activism amongst industrial workers, previously non-unionized sectors of low-waged women and migrant workers and increasingly amongst professionals (Aronowitz, 1981; Arrighi et al., 1989; Arrighi, 1991). The long-term recession combined with trade unionism in the metropolis meant that restoring the profitability of capitalism depended on a number of strategies. One involved the diffusion of capital into smaller, decentralized units, whilst new technologies of miniaturization reduced, first, the value of means of production; secondly, the skills required to operate machinery; and, thirdly, the number of workers in each location of production. Moreover, transnational capital became flexible and diversified, such that its links with 'parent' companies or countries became tenuous. Scott Lash and John Urry describe the spatial disorganization of the 'polycentric' firm, whose 'subsidies operate more independently, and a multidivisional organization pattern emerges. . . . The attachment to any single economy becomes more tentative as capital expands (and contracts) on a global basis' (Lash & Urry, 1988: 89–90). This in turn pointed to a strategy of increasing the mobility of capital which was moved into more peripheral locations that had not been affected by rising labour costs or had benefited from the higher prices of primary products (Arrighi, 1991).

Moreover, transnational companies deployed their productive apparatus across continents to boost productivity through economies of scale, and subcontracted production to a number of Third World countries in an effort to restore profitability; over the next decade these became the 'newly industrializing countries'. This turn to the periphery had three consequences in particular. First, world trade began to grow faster than each country's internal market, and the regulation of growth in both demand and supply increasingly eluded national governments. Secondly, the increasing competition of the Pacific Rim and of Western Europe *vis-à-vis* the USA meant that the latter lost its post-war advantage in relative income within the organic core regions, and the US share of world trade fell from 44 per cent in 1945 to below 20 per cent by 1990 (Jencks, 1991). Thus US global hegemony began to give way to the emergent tri-polar division of regional centres around the USA, Western Europe and Japan. Thirdly, the 1970s saw a massive flow of capital towards low- and middle-income states and 'practically unlimited credit lines for productive or unproductive investments as well as joint ventures and other forms of assistance in setting up production facilities' (Arrighi, 1991). Moreover, this expansion in global credit included the communist states, who moved in quickly to fund consumer expansion (and thereby offset mounting domestic dissatisfaction) by assuming financial obligations that were among the heaviest in the world (Zloch-Christy, 1987: 174).

The oil price hike in 1973 and the second rise in 1979 placed further demands on national economies to increase their international competition, since each was compelled either to pay for oil through increasing exports, or to sink into foreign debt. Meanwhile the earlier liberality of finance capital came home to roost as the scale of Third World indebtedness ($1000 billion in 1989) mounted during the 1980s, combined with the Federal Reserve debt ($155 billion in 1987). Then international creditors raised interest rates, but also began to tighten further the structural adjustment demanded as conditions for extending or restructuring loans to debtor governments. The Cancun Conference in 1981 resolved to use foreign aid to bolster the private sector in developing countries, and the World Bank's Berg Report further signalled the shift towards neo-classical economic models which directly attacked the public sector in less developed countries (LDCs). The latter argued that 'it is now widely evident that the public sector [in LDCs] is over-extended, given the present scarcities of financial resources, skilled manpower and organizational capacity' (World Bank, 1981: 5).

During the 1980s loan restructuring packages increasingly insisted on incentives to export and increase foreign investment combined with privatization of state industries and austerity cuts in public services. Between 1980 and 1986, 57 per cent of IMF structural adjustment packages required the removal of import quotas, 70 per cent the reform of the budget (cuts in 'non-productive' services of health and education) and 73 per cent the cutting of subsidies and price increases (Clark, 1991: 196). According to Ankie Hoogvelt, the IMF's conditionality rules, and the World Bank's structural adjustment contracts, 'have amounted to a degree of economic intervention in debtor countries which matches, perhaps even exceeds, the direct administration of bygone colonial governments' (1990).

It is a matter of dispute how far actual, as opposed to promised, divestiture of state enterprises has proceeded in LDCs and clearly the process has encountered problems, such as lack of interested buyers (Cook & Kirkpatrick, 1988; Young, 1991). However, whether or not there has yet been extensive privatization of state enterprises, structural adjustment packages have tended to reduce the scope for substantive legitimation within low- and middle-income countries. First, often extensive reductions in the numbers of public employees have alienated the professional middle class (the 'salariat') and closed off avenues of social mobility for graduates, a process which has in the past fomented oppositional sentiments.[17] Secondly, producer prices for export commodities have fallen, sometimes by a third relative to world prices, as the state retains a larger proportion of agricultural revenues to pay off debts (Clark, 1991: 186). Thirdly, austerity programmes bring cuts in social welfare, such as the Hungarian stabilization programme of 1977–8, which cut investment to improve the convertible-currency trade balance (Batt, 1991). Indeed economic policies amongst low- and middle-income states showed considerable uniformity during the 1970s and 1980s, largely irrespective of the politics of the local élite. Polish communists Gomułka, Gierek and General Jaruzelski, as well as Solidarity's Mazowiecki and Balcerowicz, all implemented the same anti-popular deflationary policies. Again, in Argentina, President Perón, the Junta generals and Presidents Alfonsin and Menem implemented one austerity package after another (Frank, 1991).

On the one hand, then, economic globalization and the off-loading of crisis tendencies from core regions on to the periphery has reduced the scope of local states to generate consensus through redistribution and patronage. Yet on the other hand, it has prepared the way for an uncoupling of the state from former consensual arrangements and prepared the way for new ones. Lal (1987) points out that where local states have become converts to neo-classical economics, this is partly because privatization of the public sector is a means of regaining control over economies which have become over-extended (and a similar case could be made for the former socialist states). Further, IMF and World Bank requirements that governments underwrite loans to public or private enterprises have the effect of opening a new avenue of accumulation. With global financial de-regulation, some debt conversion packages make it possible for residents of debtor countries to buy their national debt in secondary markets at discounted prices (often with fraudulently amassed assets) which are then re-sold to central banks in debtor countries as equity investments in privatized state companies (Hoogvelt, 1990). Through this 'round-tripping', former state-bureaucratic capital becomes finance capital, something which is further illustrated in the appearance of 'nomen-klatura capitalists' in Eastern Europe.

What happens next is of considerable importance. Either way, the erosion of bureaucratic systems of allocation is likely to undermine the centralized state – two supra-national states (the USSR and Yugoslavia) have already collapsed and further ethnic or sub-national differentiation in the periphery is highly probable. If privatized revenues are diverted into finance and consumption, rather than productive capital, then clientelist networks are likely to be sustained through local mafia-style organizations which, because of their illegality, will block the formation of critical publics or formal institutions. Moscow mayor Gavrill Popov, for example, justifies his expropriation of public property, declaring that 'a revolution is now occurring, and in a revolution laws no longer have any meaning, so I am not going to abide by any set of laws, either union or republican ones' (Medvedev, 1991). On the other hand, placing asset conversion on a legal footing, and constructing new popular alliances through public spheres, would extend the possibility for democratic control of markets and power. Without the latter it is difficult to imagine how the new democracies will stabilize rational forms of conflict resolution or protect themselves against the growth of populist authoritarianism. However, which type of exit route from the crisis of the peripheral state is taken could be crucially affected by the relative strength of social movements and their symbiosis with emergent social powers.

System Vacuum and New Identities

These relationships between local and global processes are presented in Figure 5.1, where the peripheral state is at the centre of a vortex of global and internal pressures, which together form the environment within which social identities are formed. Dual pressures from indebtedness and worsening terms of trade threaten the revenue necessary to sustain flows of patronage, with consequent tendencies towards disintegration of state regulation. This diminution of regulation combined with worsening con-

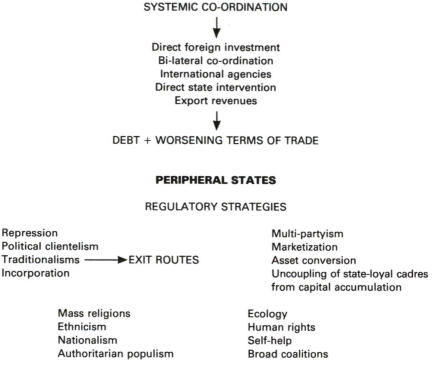

Figure 5.1 *Regulatory strategies and exit routes*

ditions of life (as core crisis tendencies are displaced to the periphery) releases diffuse social movements which enter the crisis process in various ways, and prompt the stabilization of evolutionary problem-solutions. Confronted with systemic crisis, non-core states hesitantly look for exit routes from problems of over-extension – through asset conversion and disengagement of the state from direct economic intervention, combined with the search for legal forms of rule through a multi-party pluralistic polity. These exit routes might change direction, however, depending on the intervention of mass-based social movements, in ways which will be examined in the following three chapters.

It is argued here that systemic crises release innovative social movements from the lifeworld which struggle for institutionalization into dominant forms of modernity. Indeed, the crisis of the peripheral state has been accompanied by a variety of oppositional movements from below, including labour unrest, human rights and democracy, grassroots organizations of mutual aid, and poor-people's religions such as Shi'ite Islam, the Algerian *Front islamique du slaut* (FIS) or liberation theology in Latin America. Amongst the diverse protest movements which were released amidst the collapse of communism – ecology, anti-militarism, minority rights, youth culture or independent trade unions – national identity and autonomy often provided an organizing focus. In this context, movements such as the Uniate Church in Belarus (formerly Belorussia) resurfaced after decades of suppression, illustrating the capacity of the lifeworld to store repressed affiliations and meanings.

It might be argued that these surface in response to systemic collapse because, as Anthony Smith (1991) says, they were already rooted in folklore, customs, myths, and symbols which stand opposed to the 'memoryless nature of any cosmopolitan culture created today'. Underlying this account is the view that in times of crisis and uncertainty people fall back on familiar, local and primordial associations – hence the new democracies are re-living bygone histories which have never been publicly worked over but have remained frozen within the lifeworld and covertly transmitted with all their earlier intensity. This could be described as a Rip van Winkle hypothesis – after decades of 'sleep' a people awake to resume affiliations and grievances that were apparently long forgotten. Commenting on the political scene in post-communist Hungary, for example, Ivan and Szonja Szelenyi report that 'astonishingly, as the curtain was raised, the audience was confronted with a still life: the "act" that was interrupted forty years ago with the transition to socialism seemed to have resumed, as if nothing had happened in between' (Szelenyi & Szelenyi, 1991).

Engaging as this metaphor might be, things are surely more complex since the lifeworlds within which social movements took shape had not been preserved in some kind of pristine isolation, but had rather been shaped and infused by dominant forms of systemic intrusion. The various forms of integration which regulated clientelistic states have created new structures of communication and socialization, both through the official channels of participation, and in the diffuse informal mechanisms and parallel societies which fed off the state bureaucracy. In Poland, for example, Jerzy Hausner and Andrzej Wojtyna argue that people are increasingly assuming the attitude of defensiveness and conservatism which 'is obviously not a result of the current transformation, though [this] does engender uncertainty . . . and entails a fall in . . . standards of living. The root of these attitudes is above all the mechanism of social integration and interest representation characteristic of the former system', especially the corporatist way of thinking (Hausner & Wojtyna, 1991: 84). Similarly, with reference to the resurgence of racism throughout Europe, Balibar (1991) refers to a 'power vacuum' and 'identity panic' engendered by the crisis of states whose existence was feared, but whose disappearance is feared even more. The national and racist conflicts that this ferments are not, he suggests, a return of ancient antagonisms, but relate to relatively recent juridical forms of identity created by the state itself and which correspond to divisions within the labour market (for example between 'indigenous' and 'guest' workers).

Moreover, the Rip van Winkle hypothesis does not explain why narrowly focused, xenophobic or exclusive movements appear at the same time as those advancing human rights or ecology. Nor does it explain why in the present religious renaissance in Africa and Eastern Europe it is not only the traditional forms which are being invigorated but also new sects such as dispensationalism (Gifford, 1991). Religion, nation, ethnicity in themselves do not explain anything, but rather need to be explained, in terms of class, state and power (Doornbos 1991). Why should the global crisis of Fordist integration generate variegated combinations of democratic and nationalist movements in the former communist states, Islamic revivalism in Iran and elsewhere, and the ANC in South Africa? A differentiating theory of social movements might begin by examining the specific ways in which the global system impacts on peripheral social relations, which have themselves undergone varying degrees of rationalization and pluralization. With reference to religious revivalism, Wuthnow (1980, 1983) argues that revitalization movements are attempts by collectivities to restore or reconstruct patterns of life rapidly disrupted or threatened by the effects of the global economy. However, this is not an automatic response, but will appear when the world economy separates local élites from the global system which increases the mobilization chances for popular movements. Here disparate local customs and social structures combine in variegated ways depending upon the specific forms of dislocation, and the structures available for mobilization. Apparently opposing value systems, such as Bolshevism and nationalism, or Calvinism and Tridentineism, arise on the same mobilization base, because both address questions of collective identity in the context of systemic vacuum.

An advantage of this approach is that it permits the identification of a universal process (globalization) with different local effects which will be dependent on the type of communicative and solidaristic structures which have evolved. However, it lacks an overview of the trajectory of evolutionary development or new learning potentials released by different types of social movements or carrier strata. An adequate theory of systemic crisis and collective action needs to account for the interactions between the selection of identities from amongst multiple possibilities, and for the ways in which some of these get locked into processes of social regulation. The destabilization of dominant networks of social regulation occasioned by global restructuring offers potentials for the formation of more fluid and decentred communication, but these in turn are dependent on the interaction of the system and lifeworld in the global context.

Notes

1. This is not to say that it was accomplished effectively even in its own terms. Citing evidence that the Soviet state actually subsidized agriculture during the 1930s, Seldon (1983) argues that 'the case . . . that imposed collectivization is an indispensable measure for rapid industrialization can no longer withstand scrutiny'.

2. In most developing countries the share of public sector investment was over 25 per cent of fixed gross capital investment during the 1980s, and in many cases (e.g. Egypt, Iran, Tunisia or Zambia) was over 60 per cent (Cook & Kirkpatrick, 1988: 5). In Soviet states, of course, it was much higher.

3. Habermas is hardly alone in this, since the nation-state is the historical reality behind the sociological concept of 'society', although one might have expected Habermas to reconsider this stance in view of the importance of global systems of communication for his interlocutor, Niklas Luhmann.

4. British politics during the 1980s illustrates how even a radically restructuring capitalist state, engaged in dismantling the post-war welfare consensus, runs up against limitations when its legitimacy is seriously called into question. As Robin Blackburn (1991) comments, 'the menacing groundswell of popular restiveness, aggravated by a faltering economy and the deeply unpopular poll tax' resulted in Margaret Thatcher being dumped in an 'extraordinarily unsentimental' way.

5. Arnason addresses state socialist societies and Third World étatism within a common framework, which might be valid in several ways – partly because the Soviet systems provided a model of development for post-colonial societies, and partly because the post-communist world exhibits a number of problems comparable with those of the Third World (such as foreign debt, a weak productive base, chronic shortages, a crumbling infrastructure). But the comparison should not be over-stretched, since European socialist states achieved high levels of industrialization, energy production, urbanization, literacy and complex social welfare systems.

6. Weber described substantive rationality as 'the provisioning of given groups of persons with goods . . . under some criterion of ultimate values, which are often geared to social justice' (1978: I, 85).

7. Dependent states are often mono-economies, in which all or most foreign exchange is dependent on a single commodity. For example, Nigeria is 92 per cent dependent on oil exports; the Gambia 91 per cent on groundnuts; Mauritania 82 per cent on iron; Uganda 82 per cent on coffee; Morocco 46 per cent on phosphates; and Zaïre 41 per cent on copper (Freedman & Molteno, 1982: 36–7). This means that all other economic life fluctuates with the pricing structure of the main export. In the world recession of the 1970s, the value of Morocco's phosphate exports fell by nearly half, between 1974 and 1977 its trade deficit grew ten times, from 852 to 8542 dirhams, and its debt service ratio (the percentage of export earnings spent on foreign debt) rose from 5.3 to 14.5. Between 1980 and 1988, most major

agricultural export crops depreciated, whilst the prices of manufactures appreciated by an average of 25 per cent (Hoogvelt, 1990).

8. For example, women's domestic labour in Third World small-holdings produces use-values on the farm, and subsidizes household members, whose labour is in turn appropriated by local and transnational capital, reducing input costs in the metropolis and creating global circuits of unequal exchange. A central thrust of dependency theory has been to argue pace modernization theory (e.g. Rostow, Eisenstadt or Lerner) that the conditions for capitalist development which pertained in core countries can never be replicated in the periphery precisely because continued growth in the former depends on the under-development of the latter. For a review of dependency theory in the context of Critical Theory, see Leonard (1990: Chapter 4).

9. Two exceptions to this would be the oil-producing states which established the only Third World producer cartel yet to be effective; and the Pacific Rim nations (South Korea, Taiwan, Hong Kong, Singapore) which benefited from lying on a fault line in the Cold War and were encouraged by the USA to sustain export-oriented economic growth, but still with high levels of state protection. Further, two of these being city-states are atypical of peripheral regions, and South Korea's economic performance is less dramatic than is sometimes suggested – by 1988 its per capita GDP was 20.2 per cent of the average for the organic core regions, whilst Japan's was 117.9 per cent (Arrighi, 1991).

10. Moi was re-elected with 1.9 million votes (35%), his nearest rival, Kenneth Matiba getting 1.3 million (24%). But KANU won only 77 seats out of 149 (the remainder being distributed roughly evenly between the opposition parties: Ford-Kenya, Ford-Asili and the Democratic Party).

11. Dependence on the informal economy tends to involve reliance on clientelist networks. Contracts for out-workers, who are provided with instruments of production by a firm, or producers who rent the means of production, for example, are awarded largely through contacts (Gerry & Birkbeck, 1983).

12. He does point out that patronage 'works both ways' in that mass dismissals would undercut the social base of patronage, and threaten to spread social unrest into the local town.

13. Land ownership was often a major factor in independence struggles (e.g. the Mau Mau's 'land-hunger' in Kenya) with the result that post-independence governments sought legitimacy by breaking up some estates and selling land parcels to local farmers (often on a lineage-clientelistic basis). Also, where marginal, semi-arid land was being bought into service, this did not lend itself to plantation cultivation, and contracts through which agribusiness transnationals agreed to purchase cash crops from small-holders (with perhaps one or two hectares) reduced risks and costs for the company.

14. Quasi-equivalent, because the price which small-holders receive for commodities like tea, coffee or tobacco is determined not on an open market but (often) by the monopoly purchasing power of the transnational company or state marketing board. Producer prices therefore conceal an unequal exchange of labour for cash, and a mechanism through which value is accumulated not by the producer, but by the state and transnational agribusiness (see, e.g., Cowen & Kinyanjui, 1977).

15. For example, Zaslavsky (1982) argues that the Soviet system defined two 'classes' on collective farms – 'farm workers' (13 per cent of *kolkhozniks*), who were issued with internal passports and were paid about 30 per cent more than 'collective farmers', who until 1974 had no right of mobility.

16. Andrzej Walicki (1991) argues that a mistake made by the Polish opposition during the 1980s was to regard the Jaruzelski government as powerful when in fact it was weak, and 'had rejected, silently but consciously, its Communist identity'. The brutality of peripheral states in the face of opposition is a symptom of this weakness, just as the diminution of terroristic rule (e.g. in the Soviet states after 1953) indicates an ability to rule through minimal consensus.

17. Joseph Ben-David (1962–3) has suggested that in societies with a small middle class, in which intellectuals represent a relatively large group, where there is an autocratic élite, but where education is regarded as a channel of mobility, students and intellectuals assume 'increasingly important parts in the revolutionary movements'.

6

The Crisis of State Socialism

This chapter provides an analysis of bureaucratic socialism[1] as a complex system of crisis management, and offers a framework for understanding the relationship between its collapse and current social struggles. The first part outlines the principle of organization of state socialism. This circumscribes the range of possible variation consistent with the continued identity of the system, and co-ordinates two dimensions: capacities for systemic steering and the scope for the deployment of cognitive and moral learning. Further, regulatory strategies protect the identity of the system through co-optation, crisis management or the displacement of conflicts to social locations where they present least threat (such as the privatization of public issues). This enables complex social systems to tolerate relatively high levels of internal conflict and crisis potential without disintegrating (as was the case with the Soviet-type systems for many decades). However, steering problems have crisis effects if they cannot be solved within the range of variation defined by the principle of organization. An overloading of systemic problems exacerbate what Offe (1976) calls 'crises of crisis management', where social integration is threatened as previously displaced crisis tendencies break into newly emerging public spheres, releasing new learning potentials, which compete for stabilization.

Habermas argued that the 'bureaucratic-socialist' line of development was a *variant* of the basic structure of modernity, where the primacy of money, characteristic of the capitalist path, had been substituted by the primacy of administrative power. Capitalist modernization requires (as for Weber) formal separation between the household and economy, differentiation between the economic and administrative systems, wage labour and a formal-legal state. Habermas contrasts this with bureaucratic socialism where the administrative system gains priority over the economy and political public sphere through state-controlled means of production and one-party rule (Habermas, 1982b: 282).[2] However, whereas Weber (1978: 1402) believed that the 'rational' rule of state bureaucracy would be 'unbreakable', for Habermas both forms of modernity generate contradictions, at the root of which is resistance to colonization of the lifeworld. That is, institutions which have lost the spell-binding power of the sacred cannot ultimately be consolidated on the basis of repressive legitimation.

Although this sets out a general conceptual framework for addressing bureaucratic-socialist societies, it does not provide much detailed analysis of their dynamic nor, what is now crucially significant, possible outcomes of their crisis tendencies. It was noted earlier that Habermas has not developed a sufficiently nuanced theory of crisis management to account for two divergent tendencies. First, as Habermas suggests, crisis management tends to implode under the weight of its own complexity by generating new sites of resistance. Secondly, however, crisis management has the capacity to neutralize oppositional movements through complex strategies of crisis displacement. This analysis of the systemic vacuum in post-socialist societies attempts to illustrate both these points. Habermas tends to write as if societies had a single system-identity (liberal capitalism, late capitalism, etc.), but complex societies display various and conflicting goal-functions, and it is 'meaningless to discuss conditions of equilibrium for the system as a whole if conditions for maintaining some goal functions preclude maintenance of others' (Cancian, 1964: 118). Further, a crisis of one sub-system, even the collapse of certain social institutions, might none the less contribute to the equilibrium of another goal function. For example, the steering media of money and power are separate subsystems with potentially contradictory consequences. A crisis in bureaucratic allocation might arise from the over-extension of the state, as noted in Chapter 5, which has come under pressure from internal complexity combined with a hostile global economic environment. A collapse of state regulation might in turn generate crises in institutional supports of the socio-cultural sub-system. However, when a set of institutional, economic and political arrangements has become unviable these crises might occasion sufficient scope for adjustment to keep the core of the system in place. None the less, the stabilization of a new principle of organization requires the resolution of the crisis in a way that permits the release of new learning potentials which increase its range of variation. Otherwise the outcome will remain unstable and, in the midst of protracted social disorganization, prone to authoritarian 'solutions'. One of the problems of implementing neo-liberal strategies is that disengagement in certain areas of the economy leads sooner or later to increased interference in others (Jessop, 1990: 363). In this context, the crucial dilemma posed by social and economic restructuring in post-socialist societies is whether the critical potential of the lifeworld will be closed off within another authoritarian regime of regulation.

System Identity and Regulation

The collapse of state socialism serves as a paradigm of crisis in peripheral regulatory systems. In the context of Russian history, Stalinism could be understood as a wave in a long cycle of modernization through revolution from above, beginning with the Petrine reforms (1682–1725) and continuing through the nineteenth century, each of which attempted to redress Russian underdevelopment through enhancing the centralized power of the state (Szamuely, 1988: 136; White et al., 1984: 85).[3] The extension of the system to Eastern Europe created what Zaslavsky (1985) viewed as a closed 'world system', with its own centre/periphery, largely insulated from the capitalist system through parallel international institutions (for example, the Council of Mutual Economic Assistance [CMEA] or Warsaw Pact) closed borders, state monopoly of foreign trade and inconvertible currency.[4] Further, the system was multi-layered, with centre/periphery relations within the Soviet Union, and between it and Eastern Europe. Since these core/periphery relations were regulated predominantly by bureaucratic power rather than money, management required extended and self-reflexive monitoring of policies with reference to the goals of the system, which was a feature of Soviet rule especially in the post-Stalinist period.[5]

Soviet modernization was to be achieved initially through intensification of heavy industrial production and collective consumption, combined with the heroic goal of achieving a *higher* stage of modernity than capitalism. The autarkic path of development, which has been described as 'Fordism in one country' (Voskamp & Wittke, 1991), was a kind of parody of western productivism which fetishized output and technological development whilst acknowledging no human or ecological costs (Feher et al., 1984). Andrew Arato (1982: 203) defined the principle of organization of Soviet-type systems as an 'industrial redistributive command economy', which dominated the economic and normative-cultural spheres. Bureaucratic planning subordinated questions of profitability to administrative decisions about production and deployment of resources, within a highly centralized system geared to military-industrial investment rather than personal consumption goods.[6] However, neither Arato nor Habermas defines the cognitive-moral dimension of the principle of organization. During the Stalinist period, and to some extent subsequently, 'the amalgam of bureaucratic discipline and charismatic correctness' (Jowitt, 1983), along with the cult of personality, precluded the development of post-conventional normative structures in public life. Rather, unquestioned execution of the orders of the Party, underwritten by terror and mass mobilization, presupposed a conventional orientation to 'doing one's duty'.[7]

Bureaucratic domination, moreover, was exercised through the mechanism of élite recruitment known as the nomenklatura system, which created a mode of domination and social regulation specific to state socialist societies. The Party list, drawn up by the Organburo and ratified by the Central Committee, controlled appointments to all significant positions, including nominally 'elective' ones (Rigby, 1988). In Hungary, for example, by 1949 over 90 per cent of newly appointed high-level bureaucrats were from the Party list (Hankiss, 1990: 45) and similar proportions are reported in other state socialist societies (for example, Majkowski, 1985). Arch Getty (1985) describes how during the purges of the 1930s Stalin attempted to undermine the powers of the local nomenklatura, but ultimately without success. Once consolidated after Stalin's death into a system of permanent tenure, the nomenklatura appropriated surplus product though privileges and, increasingly, political corruption (Jowitt, 1983).

This was a mode of accumulation and regulation distinct from western capitalism. As a discrete privileged stratum within a bureaucratic hierarchy, the nomenklatura possessed common collective interests and entered into structurally antagonistic relations with direct producers (Nove, 1975; Szelenyi, 1979).[8] The exceptional comprehensiveness of the system converted its occupants into a distinct social category defined by common behavioural, attitudinal and organizational features. Most important though, it was not from ownership of private property, that is, economic power, that the state domination of the nomenklatura arose. Rather, its power to appropriate an economic surplus through the planning mechanisms was derived from the possession of state power, allocated in the form of bureaucratic 'fiefdoms'. For this reason, state socialism has sometimes been described as a kind of 'socialist feudalism' (Voslensky, 1984: 70).

However, the consolidation of state bureaucratic power into a social structure capable of reproducing itself occurred gradually. Whereas the Stalinist practice of opposing the NKVD (Narodny Kommissariat Vnutrennikh Del, People's Commissariat for Internal Affairs) to the Party apparat left cadres vulnerable to purges, Khrushchev and Brezhnev's generation of leaders ended revolutions from above (Feher & Arato, 1989) and the nomenklatura consolidated into cadre patrons overseeing what Jowitt (1983) describes as 'political capitalism'.[9] The latter takes place within administrative hierarchy (rather than the market); involves created predictability rather than market relations; and its primary agent is the fiscal corporation, rather than the entrepreneur. Although wage-labour became universal, the value form was not operative in a system of artificial pricing, where exchanges between enterprises (as well as trade within the CMEA) often occurred through credits and requisition.

Further, the planning system avoided economic crisis tendencies which characterize capitalism, since it protected against over-production and competition, and mobilized immense human, material and technical resources (25 per cent of all scientists used to work in the USSR). Feher et al. (1984) regarded this pursuit of productivist goals as ends in themselves (*Zwecke der Produktion*) as irrational, which it was from the point of view of the lifeworld. However, from a systemic perspective the only restraints on production are those set by the extent and technical composition of resources, rather than by a structure of demand. As Feher et al. (1984: 236) argue, needs were channelled into pre-figured forms, and the system was brutally enforced, producing both excess and scarcity to an unparalleled extent.[10] Productivism consisted of fast industrial growth, import substitution, a high percentage of accumulated GDP, restriction of consumption in favour of capital goods production, and great spurts to close the technology gap with the West (for example, the Stakhanovite movement). Further, the system involved complex bureaucratic structures, with dual systems of authority, one running from the Central Committee through the Party apparatus, shadowing the other, the administrative hierarchy of planning boards and ministries, down to single enterprises or villages (Lovenduski & Woodall, 1987: 93).

These complex systems of vertical and horizontal differentiation imposed huge regulatory demands in order to achieve the goals set by the planning apparatus (Boella, 1979). It was suggested in Chapter 5 that the regulation problem is how to secure minimal conditions of legitimation (that is, at least one part of the population acknowledges rule as exemplary and binding and the other part does not confront the existing social order with the image of an alternative one as equally exemplary). In this context, Arato usefully theorizes Soviet states in terms of systemic regulation, arguing that de-politicization and liberalization were regulative processes aimed at protecting the central principle of organization: 'But it is not consciously directed by a social agency, whether the latter be a "class", an "order" or even the party élite itself' (1982: 205).

Similarly, Zaslavsky pointed to the recuperative power of Soviet systems, which 'usually manage to develop institutions, mechanisms and policies to neutralize and suppress any internal challenge. . . . Periodic explosions in some Eastern European countries do not undermine the overall stability of the Soviet bloc which remains largely immune to local crises' (1985). Again, Ulam (1985) wrote that 'despite all those crises – mass terror, famines, catastrophic defeats in the first phase of the Second World War, a single one of which would have brought down any other regime – the Soviet system has not only survived, but grown in strength'. In retrospect, it might appear that Zaslavsky, Ulam and others, who argued that post-Stalinism meant more rather than less efficient control (for example, Rupnik, 1988), simply got it wrong. Yet Soviet-type systems *did* display self-reflexive strategies of crisis management, and understanding why these failed and with what consequences illuminates the general theory of system–lifeworld exchanges.

As mass mobilization campaigns faded to give way to mass de-politicization (Hankiss, 1990), and terror for the most part became a 'memory' rather than lived reality (Lovas & Anderson, 1982), systemic equilibrium depended increasingly on strategies of crisis management. These attempted to increase the range of variation permitted by the principle of organization, fluctuating between co-opting and repressing dissent. Kecskemeti (1969), for example, described how the New Course in Poland and Hungary in the early 1950s was a reaction to problems of collectivization and central planning combined with an awareness amongst sections of the élite of the extent of popular resentment at the regime.[11] The 1960s and 1970s saw the beginning of attempts to build a new consensus based on increased personal consumption and welfare (Evans, 1986). Linda Cook (1992) describes the Brezhnev period as founded on a new 'tacit social contract' between the state and workers, which has also been described as 'corporatist'. A 'new mode of interest intermediation

. . . sought to minimize conflict and maximize productivity by incorporating dominant economic and political interests directly into the policy process, while cultivating the support of the masses through an expanding welfare state' (Bunce 1983). Similarly, Zaslavsky writes of an 'organized consensus' based on recruitment of skilled workers to the closed cities (where residence was restricted to scientific and highly skilled cadres), and the accumulation of power and patronage by leaders in the republics (Zaslavsky 1982). The importance of national integration through patronage is also taken up by Graham Smith (1991), who writes of a centre–periphery corporatism within the Soviet Union, in which the autonomy of local élites was exchanged for loyalty to Moscow, and local governments could retain revenue for distribution along clientelist networks.[12]

Central to corporatist strategies was what Szelenyi, Hegedus, Toscis and others have called the 'redistributive economy' (Figure 6.1). This was essentially a system of state-regulated collective consumption, which guaranteed full employment, basic needs and social welfare. In the absence of generalized market systems, however, the redistributive economies generated complex bureaucratic rules of allocation which against a background of chronic scarcity permitted informal negotiation amongst sectoral interests. Privileged access to resources such as housing was dependent upon occupation, patronage and informal networks within the planning bureaucracies, which in turn generated favoured clientele sectors. For example, the nomenklatura and intelligentsia were over-represented in better-quality state housing whilst manual workers were highly represented in poorer state housing and the self-build sector (for example, Andrusz, 1990; Dangschat, 1987; Musil, 1987; Szelenyi, 1983; Tosics, 1988). Whilst the creation of privileged sectors might have generated loyalty and dependence on the redistributive mechanisms, the coalescence of sectoral interests (heavy industry, the mass public, specialists or consumer lobbies)

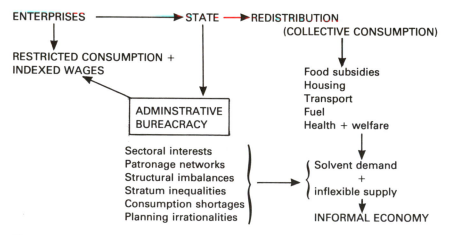

Figure 6.1   *The redistributive economy*

created conditions for fiscal crisis (Campbell, 1992). Planners faced the dilemma of either promoting stability through transfers of resources to key groups, and thereby undercutting growth, or risking instability by depriving the redistributive system of resources, and investing instead in capital goods (Bunce, 1983).

However, as Habermas suggests, there were inherent systemic limitations to the planning mechanisms. Faced with over-extension and scarcities of distributive goods, officials developed coping mechanisms in the form of clientelist networks and horizontally integrated relationships which spanned all levels, from local councils to the Politburo (Baker 1982: 44). These defensive reactions, rational enough in a chronic shortage economy (Kornai, 1986), themselves exacerbated shortages and dysfunctions. Enterprises hoarded capital equipment against the possibility of future shortages; local party secretaries colluded with factory managers to procure materials or falsify data; enterprises relied on 'storming' at the end of the planning cycle to fulfil monthly quotas.[13] Informal networks were consolidated into a system of exchanges which paralleled the official economy, based on patrimonial protection through mutual security and political corruption (Feher, 1982: 66; Jowitt, 1983).

Moreover, informal bureaucratic exchanges were replicated by more extensive social networks of the 'second' or 'parallel' society which offset shortages and planning deficiencies through mutual assistance, reciprocal labour exchanges, barter of scarce commodities, and, eventually, petty commodity production. Davies (1988) describes how increased prices combined with scarcity of welfare resources were absorbed by local communities through the 'self-management of austerity', which was dependent on the deployment of women as unpaid carers and low-wage workers.[14] Thus the division of labour between the 'command economy' and 'second economy' was 'much more than functional, it [was] an ingenious, not fully conscious, not fully accidental arrangement that sustains and reflects the invidious distinction . . . between the privileged exclusivity of the cadre stratum, demesne, and style of life on the one hand, and the dependent, privatized situation of the politically excluded on the other' (Jowitt, 1983). Again, Sampson (1985–6) describes the informal sector as a 'de-bureaucratized' social space, characterized by relationships of mutual obligation and patronage, which not only survived well within 'the interstices of bureaucratic organization' but also to some extent assisted the latter to function. These informal connections were proto-spheres of social organization, symbiotic with mechanisms of social regulation, which were to be crucially important in structuring later developments.

Contradictions of Regulation

A tentative hypothesis could thus be proposed to account for the collapse of Soviet-type systems. Habermas believes that systemic regulation by the state creates an especially high risk of legitimacy loss because, unlike the market, state redistributive economies re-politicize social relationships. Power has 'no sign system equivalent to money'; it cannot be 'deposited', and whereas expansion in money supply (credit) 'heightens the internal complexity of the system, super-imposition of power is a mechanism that de-differentiates system. Unlike markets, power needs legitimation to anchor in the lifeworld' (Habermas, 1989b: 267). Rather than reducing complexity, the intrusion of bureaucratic steering into the lifeworld increased regulatory demands and provided a visible focus for resistance. This might explain why economic disputes (such as strikes) could very easily turn political and call the rule of the Party into question, as occurred with Solidarity or the Donbass and Kuzbass miners' strikes in 1989–90 (Friedgut & Siegelbaum, 1990). As David Ost argues, 'since the state is the sole employer, all social conflicts are directed at the state, not against other classes' (1991).[15] Again, Piccone (1990) claims that the 'collapse of "really existing socialism" translated into politics the abysmal economic performance of bureaucratic regimes', and Bunce (1983) makes a similar point.

If this is so, then it might account too for the evolution of strategies of post-Stalinist regulation. First, the regulation or elimination of public spheres in which critical argumentation could be articulated offset the re-politicizing effects of the redistributive mechanisms, through repression, co-optation, secrecy or technicization (converting political questions into matters of technical efficiency). However, in the period of organized consensus, the Party emphasized co-optive strategies, in the form of 'constructive criticism', persuasion and compromise, especially at local levels, such as work-place representation (Lovenduski & Woodall, 1987: 429).[16] Yet there was a counter-logic built into these strategies since legitimation was no longer grounded in the charismatic-heroic Party ideology, but rather in an instrumental exchange of loyalty for social security, underwritten by informal clientelist networks. From this it followed, first, that organized consensus would hold together only so long as the state could finance the redistributive economy; and, secondly that as instrumental norms replaced organizational charisma, the rationale for the leading role of the Party would sooner or later be called into question. In the event, the latter appeared as a crisis of confidence amongst factions within the Party itself, who saw an exit from fiscal crisis in terms of abandoning political capitalism, with its heavy regulatory cost, in favour of more marketized, and hence less visible, forms of social regulation in the framework of a legal state. Let us examine these shifts in more detail.

During the 1970s and 1980s, endogenous problems of regulation complexity combined with exogenous pressures of the arms race and linkage with the global economy. The presence of long-range systemic problems in the Soviet economy had become apparent in the 1960s. For example, much national product growth resulted from oil and gas production which involved high capital investment and transportation costs. Since 1945 each 1 per cent increase in growth had required a 1.4 per cent increase in investment and a 1.2 per cent increase in raw materials supply (Guber,

1985). Moreover, as the geographical integration of the USSR weakened with population dispersal, logistical problems accumulated – coal from Siberia increased in cost two times with every 1500 km transport (which was why nuclear reactors were situated in the more populous western USSR) (Walker, 1988: 70). Moreover, imported technology and the increasing pressure of competing with western military systems highlighted the poor differential productivity of the USSR, which ran at about 70 per cent of US industry, and was 3.3 times higher in energy consumption (Shlapentokh, 1988). Meanwhile, in the mid-1970s, Soviet-type states continued to develop 'Fordism in one country', at precisely the time when these organizational principles were giving way in the West to flexible specialization and expansion in the tertiary and finance sectors (Voskamp & Wittke, 1991).[17]

These endogenous systemic difficulties were compounded by exogenous problems of debt and the failure of *détente* in the early 1980s, which was followed by the USSR's decision to maintain parity with the USA in nuclear weapons. Increasing proportions of foreign currency earnings from oil and gas exports were being used to pay for grain imports, heavily subsidized trade between the Soviet republics and the CMEA (Bunce, 1983) and imports of western technology. This coincided with the recession in the global economy, which, awash with petrodollars, found the prospect of lending to stable, centrally planned economies attractive. During the 1970s, East–West economic transactions had become highly asymmetrical, characterized by accumulating debts and trade imbalances, such that by 1985–6 the USSR's foreign debt stood at $24 billion (Carlo, 1989) and the CMEA as a whole, at $93 billion (Zloch-Christy, 1987: 49).

It was in response to these system-problems that the Gorbachev team launched the programme of restructuring in the late 1980s. Priorities were to eliminate external pressure by ending the Cold War, reducing subsidies to Eastern Europe and increasing the productivity of agriculture and industry. *Perestroika* attempted to both address the systemic problems, which the Brezhnev period had largely failed to do, through creating conditions for the anchoring of the state in the lifeworld, whilst protecting the integrity of the system. Hauslohner (1989) describes the programme in terms of three objectives. First, there was to be a reduction in dependence on the redistributive economy – rising real incomes would be set against fewer entitlements and price increases for basic consumer goods, there would be meritocratic distribution and a rise in inequality. Secondly, there was to be a re-allocation of economic security – with better protection through child payments and pensions, but an end to guaranteed social security and full employment. Thirdly, there was to be a shift in political rights and personal liberties, with a wider participation-base (for example, work-place democratization) and personal freedoms, addressing norms of personal responsibility, self-discipline and the legal state.

Thus the Gorbachev reforms raised the question of whether this was merely another wave of systemic regulation, or whether the core identity and security of the corporate ruling group was affected. Feher, Heller, Markus and Arato claimed the former, arguing that the Gorbachev period amounted to no more than changes in personnel in the Politburo and bureaucracy; cultural and human rights (but without a legal-rational foundation); 'micro-democracy', for example, in local soviets or the work-place (but leaving administrative structures unchanged); and economic reforms in the direction of limited legalization of private enterprise and co-operatives. They argue that these failed because they were too limited, whereas radical reform, transferring power from the nomenklatura to civil society, would have called into question the power and privilege of the corporate ruling group. Gorbachev's aim, according to this view, was to enlarge the range of variation of the principle of organization (more efficient resource management, and increased receptiveness to popular participation) without undermining its goal-function.

However, an analytical problem arises here if one supposes that there was a single systemic goal-function underlying regulatory practices. On the one hand, the Gorbachev reforms were more radical than Feher et al. supposed, in that they represented an assault on Brezhnevite corporatism. The Gorbachev team was composed of younger cadres whose career mobility had been blocked by the consolidation of the nomenklatura system and they defined their reform project in opposition to the 'years of stagnation'. When in 1984 Tatyana Zaslavskaya (a sociologist at Novosi-birsk and later a Gorbachev adviser) attacked the rigidity of the planning system, corruption, inflexible work practices and the 'inhibition of market forces', she identified middle-ranking bureaucrats, planners and enterprise managers as the most likely opponents of reform, since they would defend their privileges.[18] This division of the political terrain became the theme of the reform movement after 1985 when Gorbachev and Yeltsin repeatedly attacked the Brezhnev leadership as an 'inert stratum of careerists with a party card' (for example at the XXVIIth Congress of the CPSU). Indeed, their strategy was to open up potential conflicts as a means of shaking the inertia of the bureaucracy and perhaps dissipating opposition by dividing it (Hauslohner, 1989).

On the other hand, the Gorbachev team were in no sense outsiders, but had risen via the usual career channels of the Party, and through Andropov had had close links with the KGB. *Perestroika* was an attempt to implement strategies that had evolved, but not been dominant, amongst the Party intelligentsia during the 1960s and 1970s. Although the hesitant Kosygin and Aganbegyan/Liberman reforms ran aground after 1968, other experiments, often in specific enterprises, continued through the 1970s (as they did in the GDR and Hungary).[19] But alongside specific experiments in enterprise autonomy and financial accountability, a debate continued amongst economists and sociologists through the 1970s, for example in *Deng'i i Kredit* (Money and Credit), over means of increasing productive efficiency. They developed strategies for reducing the inflexibility of

Gosplan, but also challenged many assumptions of the redistributive economy. In December 1980, for example, these debates spilled into the public domain with a piece in *Pravda* by Gavrill Popov (economist at Moscow University and again later a member of the new team) which advocated wages cuts, work incentives and planned unemployment. Similarly in Eastern Europe in the mid-1980s, younger members of the Party intelligentsia regarded increased marketization and democratic pluralism as crisis-solutions.[20]

In short, the abstract goal-function of increasing efficiency and offsetting the fiscal crisis overrode the substantive goals of protecting Brezhnevite corporatism. However, *perestroika* failed to prevent systemic crisis because it presupposed greater scope for variation than the principle of organization would permit. Structural reforms required not only an opening up of communication through debate (to expose inefficiencies) but also the building of a new social contract which would withstand the dislocations and disruptions consequent on the restructuring.[21] At the same time, however, foreign debt and loan conditionality imposed by western lenders resulted in reduced resources for the redistributive economy (Batt, 1991: 13; Bunce, 1983).[22] This weakened the legitimation resources of the planning mechanism and forced ever-heavier dependence on informal adaptive strategies. Yet the more the socialist economy relied on an informal and semi-legal sector to satisfy consumer demand, the less legitimacy the system had, since moonlighting and illegalities became institutionalized (Kornai, 1986). Although for a time the privatization of public issues acted as a regulatory strategy, to reduce pressure on the redistributive economy, the growing importance of the parallel economy, along with the beginnings of a new civil society (political clubs, *samizdat*, local protest, etc.), increasingly subverted the state sector.

The crisis appeared first in Eastern Europe (and especially Poland) for several reasons. Systemic problems were especially acute because of limited import substitution capacities, dependence on energy and raw material imports, and heavy indebtedness; whilst communist institutions, widely regarded as representatives of foreign occupation, were weakly anchored in the lifeworld, creating a 'permanent legitimation crisis' (Heller, 1982). The upshot of this was that in Eastern Europe the bifurcation between the state and socio-cultural life occurred earlier and more sharply than in the USSR. Crisis management in Poland, for example, had been weak throughout the communist period, partly because the failure of early collectivization programmes meant that the state's control over the means of production was never complete.[23] Partly too, of course, it had been weak because the church's historical role in defining the Polish nation meant that it had deep links with the socio-cultural subsystem, with the result that the Communist Party confronted a religiously based mass movement of workers – a process without parallel elsewhere in the bloc (Ascherson, 1987; Wieriorka, 1984).

System Identity and Social Movements

Habermas (1990) suggests that the problem faced by post-socialist societies is one of 'overcoming distance', of replicating institutions of advanced capitalist economies, rather than of constructing something historically novel. Perhaps this has not been sufficiently acknowledged on the western Left by those who either invested utopian hopes in the brief explosions of popular protest which accompanied the abdication of communist parties, or view with dismay faltering efforts to construct market economies (as though repressive statism was a system worth defending). Post-socialism needs to create conditions for a new principle of organization which will expand and stabilize productive techniques, the articulation and negotiation of interests, abstract impersonal relationships, differentiation of cultural value spheres and democratic pluralism. However, unless Habermas now wishes to forget his 'two-sided' concept of modernity, overcoming distance presumably is a matter not simply of 'catching up' with the West, but of recapitulating dilemmas faced by capitalist societies over the regulation of markets and bureaucracies. How these are resolved in the East, though, is likely to be conditioned by the effects of prior lifeworld colonization, combined with the exogenous problems which fuelled the crisis in the first place. If pursued in the form of 'shock therapy', which is popular amongst new élites in post-socialism, these societies will further encounter obstacles springing from efforts to implant social institutions (especially markets) into settings where they are socially disembodied, having no anchoring in the lifeworld.

Hausner and Nielsen (1992) have argued that the 'protracted death agony of socialism' led to a systemic vacuum. This notion contains the idea that not only did the previous system disintegrate but the disintegration occurred in such a way that new social forces, which could have created new systemic structures, failed to emerge. Innovation came not so much from a challenge to the Party from *outside* as from *within* the Party and planning bureaucracy itself. The old-guard leadership, such as Honecker, Zhivkov, Ceauşescu or Kádár, were removed by internal Party coups, which were generally followed by appeals for mass support and attempts to locate new legitimacy resources (such as the efforts of Hungarian leaders Pozsgay and Nemeth to claim the mantle of Imre Nagy and the 1956 uprising). However, these last-ditch attempts to mobilize whatever residual loyalty might have been available in socio-cultural systems were short-lived. The institutions of the bureaucratic state were not anchored in the lifeworld, and failures of the redistributive system, queues, inflation, shortages and general decay of the infrastructure indicated that there was no mileage left in the corporatist strategy, and reformist leaderships either detached themselves from the Party, or gave way to post-communist governments.

One feature of the systemic vacuum in post-socialism is the absence of mass-based organized social movements capable of channelling interests through institutional public spheres. The revolutions of 1989–90 reflected the atrophy of the redistributive economy and political subsystem such that political élites capitulated, in most cases extremely quickly. With the exception of Poland, the bursts of mass action were relatively brief, like Moscow after the attempted coup, the breach of the Berlin Wall, the fighting in Bucharest, or the Lantern Theatres in Prague, and the crowds were largely spectators to an unfolding drama. In Hungary, for example, Imre Pozsgay, leader of the ruling Hungarian Socialist Workers' Party, assisted with the establishment of an opposition forum (the Hungarian Democratic Forum) with which it could negotiate a transition to democratic pluralism. Even so, in some cases elements of the former communist party retained power under new names (the former Soviet republics, except the Baltic states; Romania; Slovakia; and Bulgaria). Elsewhere the Party apparat was replaced by an opposition coalition (as in the Czech Republic, Hungary or Poland), although this did not preclude the preservation of nomenklatura influence at lower levels of administration (in Hungary, for example, the cadres of the ruling MDF coalition came largely from the middle-level apparat: Glenny, 1990: 83).[24]

The apparent tenacity of the former ruling group has prompted a number of writers to suggest that there was a 'Grand Coalition' between the intellectual opposition and sections of the nomenklatura who understood that the existing system had exhausted its reserves of legitimacy (Hankiss, 1990: 250). Whether or not there existed the degree of collusion between the opposition leaders and reform communists that Grand Coalition theories suggest, it is true that the closer oppositional movements came to power-sharing or a negotiated transition, the more earlier visions of social re-organization were revised to accommodate market ideologies. In part this was attributable to the power of the global system to set the agenda in peripheral states, especially where it can use the levers of aid and debt rescheduling (Ost, 1991). In Hungary, for example, János Kis' Alliance of Free Democrats (currently the major opposition party) emerged out of the dissident, intellectual and socialist subculture of the Kádár era to fight the 1990 elections on a programme of swift and radical marketization. In Solidarity, too, earlier, alternative conceptions of social organization – of work-place politics and radical democratization – were subordinated to an acceptance of national capitalism and privatization following fragmentation of the worker–intellectual coalition (Staniszkis, 1989; Wolnicki, 1989).[25] By the time Solidarity resurfaced in 1989 it had largely dropped earlier commitments to self-managed socialism, and its leadership shared Jaruszelski's commitment to privatization (Fields, 1991). Similarly the more diverse counter-cultural movements that attended the crisis of bureaucratic socialism, such as ecological protest or local political initiatives, largely dissipated after the fall of communism.[26]

On one level, then, the disintegration of the Soviet system was attended by an increasing isomorphism between new carrier strata in the social protest movements and the market-oriented nomenklatura. Various path-

ologies might arise, however, from another revolution from above, this
time in the form of rapid marketization prior to the evolution of social
supports. Further, the systemic vacuum created by crisis in the political
subsystem prepared the way for the nomenklatura to convert administrative power into capital within a market economy. 'Spontaneous privatization' enables former managers to become owners of productive
resources in a situation where economic restructuring is subject to little
regulation (Hausner & Wojtyna 1991; Kowalik, 1991; Levitas & Strzalkowski, 1990; Mandel, 1991). This is not a uniform process, and it takes at
least two forms – the legal purchase of state enterprises by former
managers (whose investment capital might well have been accumulated
through *blat* i.e. corruption) and the acquisition of state property by virtue
of current position and privileges. It is not yet clear whether this represents
the formation of a grande bourgeoisie, as Hankiss (1990), or Staniszkis
(1989) suggest, or whether state assets are being appropriated mainly for
consumption (Levitas & Strzalkowski, 1990).[27] However, it was noted
above that when a set of institutional, economic and political arrangements
have become unviable, crises or an absence of institutional regulation,
might offer sufficient scope for adjustment to keep the core of the system
in place. This illegal divestiture of state property preserves the social
power of the nomenklatura, which can no longer be guaranteed within
the redistributive economy, but without stabilizing a new principle of
organization.[28]

Spontaneous privatization is dependent on the organizational culture of
the former system in that illicit asset conversion presupposes informal
social networks and the culture of illegality which emerged within the
parallel society. For example, in Leningrad, 250,000 foreign currency
roubles were moved from the Soviet Executive Committee's account into
Lentok (a private firm) as joint-enterprise capital. On instructions from the
mayor, the account was then moved to the Russian Ballet fund in
Switzerland. Amongst the small entrepreneurs backing Lentok, who
supplied the enterprise with buildings and state funds for capitalization,
one-fifth were administrative bodies. Moreover, members of Soviet executives were frequently setting up small firms (*Izvestia*, 10.10.90). Again,

> Moscow markets are completely monopolized by the 'mafia' structure of a single
> market which makes thousands of roubles a day. The 'mafia' is a growing fusion
> of the bureaucracy, economic administrators, and 'affairists' of the private
> sector, who create shortages through monopoly structures, and illicitly transfer
> state resources and funds into private hands. (*Komsomolskaya Pravda*,
> 12.12.90)

As public funds are converted into share capital and the directors become
shareholders, three groups of major property owners are emerging: former
managers, ministry officials,[29] and the Soviets, who turn capital over to
private companies and become executives. (*Komsomolskaya Pravda*,
6.2.91).[30] David Mandel (1991) argues that the conversion of state assets
into private capital involves collusion between administrators and the

shadow (*tenevaya*) economy, consequent on the weakening of central control (*Rashidovshchina*). Joint ventures are set up for sale abroad, or to the private sector, a process which the Law on Co-operatives has facilitated. Whereas exchanges within the state sector are non-monetary, sub-contracting work to co-operatives turns non-cash credits into cash. 'Joint venture construction' companies, or agricultural co-operatives, can make profits of 4000 per cent by importing and selling computers rather than building or producing food. Mandel concludes that 'transition to the market' involves the formation of monopolies through which public wealth is illicitly transferred into private capital.[31] Again, in relation to Poland, Zbigniew Dresler (1991: 18) refers to the 'self-enfranchisement of the nomenklatura' as factory directors serving on commissions preparing for privatization were first appointed as liquidators, and subsequently took top positions in enterprises taking over the assets of state firms.

The process of spontaneous privatization combined with systemic vacuum hampers the formation of institutions of civil society and the stabilization of new moral-cognitive learning capacities. Divestiture of state assets, the absence of effective taxation systems, and continuing balance of payments deficits sustain the fiscal crisis of the state (since revenue-bases are declining faster than expenditure). Further, nomen-klatura privatization presupposes a weak framework of civil law combined with repression of institutional public spheres through which competing interests might be articulated, and thus blocks the stabilization of a new principle of organization. Unless the new economic structures are brought within a binding framework of legislation which provides for formal interest articulation and negotiation, then the likelihood of a 'populist-authoritarian scenario' (Zon, 1992) will increase. This would involve state-regulated marketization and protection from the world market, heavy restrictions on trade unions, a weak bourgeoisie and nationalist ideology (perhaps supported by the army) with a high probability of conflicts with neighbouring countries over borders and the treatment of minorities.

Ost argues that such an authoritarian reversion is unlikely, since 'no significant political tendency is pushing in this direction and no Western government . . . is ready to countenance it' (1991). Szelenyi and Szelenyi (1991), however, argue that there is a social democratic constituency in Hungary and elsewhere which is represented by neither the nationalist-populist nor the centre-Right parties (evinced by the low turn-out in both of the 1990 elections). Thus a social democratic party could mobilize support for a transition managed within a framework of legality – mixed ownership combined with a plural public sphere. Failing this, however, 'it is possible that a right-wing force could rise to power . . . further to the right than Anatall's regime . . . [and] fill the gap that the potential centre-left parties failed to occupy in the last election' (Szelenyi & Szelenyi, 1991). Whether a mode of regulation can be stabilized which permits the formation of more emancipatory possibilities, deploying new learning capacities, will depend upon the outcome of struggles around the definition and delimitation of the public and private not only at the level of the state, but also within micro-public spheres located within social movements.

The populist-authoritarian scenario would in some ways reproduce the form of peripheral étatism within an adjusted regulatory mechanism which sustains the conventional cognitive structures of the old order. Lack of control over markets is a major obstacle to the expansion of new learning potentials, since this has opened the way for 'mafias' to benefit from the culture of illegality and perpetuate risk-free appropriation of former state property. In the socio-cultural sub-system, this process is encouraged by an attachment to the organizational culture of the former system. Zon (1992) argues that (in Poland, Hungary and Czechoslovakia) there are no mechanisms for conflict-resolution, and there is no revitalization of civil society. On the contrary, apathy and dependence on former structures of allocation seem to be widespread. Hausner & Wojtyna similarly point to the predominance of vertical structures along a subordination–domination axis, whilst 'mechanisms of interest representation develop in a spontaneous and uncontrolled manner, with a heavy leaning towards traditional corporatist structures' (1991: 89).

In the socio-cultural sub-system, rapid marketization and deflation threaten the security of the self as effectively as communist rule ever did and impede the development of critical and self-reflexive communication structures in which traditional boundaries are subjected to argumentative doubt. The systemic vacuum following an unregulated collapse of social supports dislocates social integration in ways which predispose towards populist, nationalist and authoritarian politics. Unemployment, rapid inflation, acute shortages and hardships, what Habermas describes as a 'crisis at the level of expressive sociation', (see Chapter 3 in this volume) result in the destabilization of collective identities. The issue of social protection against the effects of privatization is being taken up (amongst others) by populist-authoritarian groups and the former ruling parties.[32] In relation to the former Soviet Union, David Mandel (1988) and Kagarlitsky (1988, 1990) argue that attempts to implement the economic liberalism advocated by Shmelev and Popov (and now Yeltsin) will have catastrophic consequences. Social disruption forces people back on to the informal lifeworld coping responses which developed during the state socialist period. Since this 'atomization and egotism of small groups' (Tarkowska & Tarkowski, 1991) is premised upon mutual obligations, familial and personal connections, it also tends to reinforce ascribed status and group loyalties, rather than decentred 'risk-bearing personalities'. An evident manifestation of this is nationalism and ethnic exclusivity, which, combined with inter-state conflict, can result in the kind of 'ethnic cleansing' seen in Bosnia-Herzegovina.

Moreover, a resolution of the systemic crisis which presupposes ascribed rather than fluid identities, combined with continued reliance on informal networks to offset the fiscal problems of the state, has critical implications for definition of the boundaries of the public and private. It was noted above that the second economy was dependent upon the intensified exploitation of women's domestic labour. Now the stabilization of a new mode of regulation threatens to further institutionalize the subordinate position of women. For example, the Czech Association for Independent Social Analysis made it clear that economic restructuring would reinforce the patriarchal authority of male 'breadwinners' by reducing women's employment whilst increasing their dependence on men. 'It will be a question', the report concludes, 'of an essential change in the way the household forms its income – and here the emphasis should be placed on higher remuneration for higher work performance and higher work results of the breadwinner' (Boguszak et al., 1990: 16). For women unemployment should be compensated for by a 'revival of a long-term tradition of social contacts on the basis of hobby, civic, local and other associational activities, as well as a change in the manner in which people use their leisure'. As privatization extends to the provision of social services, it can only intensify women's exploitation, against the background of increased gender segregation in the labour market (Molyneux, 1990).

Critical Theory and State Socialism

In summary, then, the problems of post-socialism provide the basis for a more elaborated model of crisis and its aftermath than Habermas develops. At a general level this was a crisis of peripheral étatism, which originated in both global and internal crisis tendencies (Figure 6.2). From

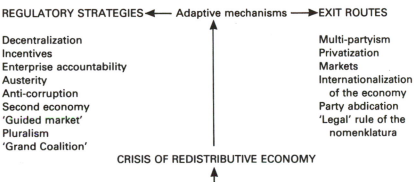

Figure 6.2 *Regulatory strategies and exit routes*

the global environment, an accelerating arms race which was increasingly technologically driven, along with growing foreign indebtedness, exacerbated the systemic dysfunctions of the Soviet planning mechanisms. From the endogenous system, the redistributive economy became difficult to sustain as it was over-burdened by increasing complexity and steering problems. Under these pressures the Party planning bureaucracies themselves developed successive attempts at technocratic adjustment which eventually led towards an abandonment of the redistributive economy altogether. Such a major change, however, was not possible within the existing principle of organization, and required the construction of new constituencies favouring reform, which were built across sections of the Party and the leadership of opposition movements. This in turn involved a gradual uncoupling of the Party from the structures of economic power as well as a collapse in central systems of regulation. At the same time the state economy – more specifically the enterprise-based nomenklatura – had already become highly interpenetrated with the informal economy and the culture of illegality. This in turn had functioned as a crisis displacement mechanism, along with a privatization of public issues into quasi-familial realms through which resources were allocated in structures parallel to the official economy. When the diverse social networks from the parallel society burst into the public realm, the chronic systemic crisis became a crisis of social integration, releasing alternative social potentials and problem-solutions. However, despite the initial appearance of social movements (for example, pacifist, ecological, nationalist or self-management), the protracted atrophy of the system which was premised on mass de-politicization left a weak civil society which offered few resources for mobilizing and articulating interests. Thus the collapse of social integration which appears pathological from the stand-point of the life-world might be quite functional for primitive accumulation and the establishment of new property relations. However, it has been suggested that this outcome presupposes the restriction rather than expansion of cognitive-moral learning capacities, and a reinforcement of ascribed identity of nationality and gender. At an abstract level, conflicts over appropriation of the transition involve the problem of whether the parallel society and new political forms can be linked up in ways which permit the scrutiny of identities and expansion of plural social organization; or, on the other hand, whether repressive socialization will be consolidated into the closure of learning capacities within an authoritarian privatized regime.

Notes

1. Soviet-type systems represented something of a terminological enigma, partly because the dominant categories of western sociology had been developed with reference to capitalist societies. Hence a plethora of concepts appeared at different times, such as 'totalitarian', 'state capitalist', 'actually existing socialism', 'bureaucratic socialism', 'bureaucratic collectivism' or 'neo-patrimonialism'. The descriptive terms 'Soviet-type systems' and 'state socialism' are used here interchangeably.

2. He now, however, writes of the post-socialist societies 'overcoming distance' (1990) with the West, which implies a more uni-dimensional concept of modernity than he suggests elsewhere – this is refered to in the third section below.

3. Étatism was a deeply-rooted historical response to Russia's peripheral status which was reflected in the authoritarian egalitarianism of intelligentsia social movements like the Populists and the Bolsheviks. Later nineteenth-century populists, such as Tkachev's Russian Jacobins, were precursors of Leninist authoritarian revolutionary modernization (a link which was acknowledged by early Bolshevik historians of the Revolution, such as Pokrovsky [1924]).

4. Zaslavsky underestimated the extent to which, even by 1985, the Eastern bloc had been linked up with the wider global system, especially through convertible currency debt.

5. It will be seen that innovations in crisis management were a feature of the Brezhnev period (1964–81) despite its widespread image (in the West and in the USSR under Gorbachev) as being 'years of stagnation'.

6. Analyses of bureaucratic domination in the Soviet Union were influenced by awareness of the independent power of administration in both capitalist and socialist societies. Weber's general observations on bureaucratization, and his prescient warnings about the 'dictatorship of the public official' under socialism, were clearly influential. So also were Burnham (1962), Lauret, (1940) and Rizzi, (1985), whose concept of 'bureaucratic collectivism' was adopted by Trotsky.

7. This period has often been described as 'totalitarian' (e.g. according to Friedrich and Brzezinski's six-point syndrome) and the later period as post-totalitarian, in which the diminution of terror, the de-politicization of everyday life, combined with attempts to secure a mantle of rationality and legality, actually rendered the systems more secure than under Stalinism (Feher, 1986; Havel, 1988; Rupnik, 1988). Neither concept is very helpful since they are ideal-types of a form of rule, rather than dynamic analyses. The features these writers identified as 'post-totalitarian' are perhaps better described as systemic management strategies, which (unwittingly) prepared for the disillusion of the system.

8. There is disagreement as to whether they constituted a social class: Djilas (1957), Rakovski/Kis (1978) and Konrad & Szelenyi (1979) arguing that they did, Feher et al. (1984) claiming that they did not, since they were defined by relations to neither property nor the market.

9. Indeed, Khrushchev's decline between 1958 and 1964 was the result of his behaving in an increasingly arbitrary manner and ignoring his patronage commitments with the Central Committee (Hill, 1988).

10. Feher et al's provocative study *Dictatorship Over Needs* (1984) will not be considered at length here partly because it has been overtaken by events. But two points are still worth making: first, that although they argue persuasively that the Soviet system represented a distinctive form of domination, their emphasis on its goal-function does not give sufficient weight to structural factors nor to the role of the Party itself in initiating the change of the system; secondly, they have no framework within which to account for the formation of inner contradictions, oppositional movements and the eventual demise of the system. Their notion of a 'permanent legitimation crisis' cannot account for the specific timing of the fall.

11. The New Course (backed by Stalin's successor, Malenkov) called for liberalization of the economy and increased freedom of cultural expression. In Hungary and Poland between 1953 and 1955 intellectuals, journalists, members of the Politburo and increasingly workers and students were able to make advances against the Stalinists, until of course the potential of reforms to spill over into wider social protest became apparent, which ended in the Hungarian catastrophe of 1956. In Poland, too, the initial hopes invested in Gomułka for decentralized self-management were to be disappointed.

12. The Soviet policy of building locally recruited bureaucracies in the republics was to backfire once the availability of resources from the centre diminished, since local apparatuses were regional centres of resistance to Moscow and often backed independence movements (Kagarlitsky, 1990: 60–1).

13. Storming refers to accelerated production to meet planning targets. For example, 'We never use a screwdriver in the last week', said a worker at a Lithuanian television factory, 'We

hammer the screws in. We slam solder the connections, cannibalize parts from other TVs . . . and the management is pressing us to work faster' (Walker, 1988: 42).

14. Elson (1988) points out that the 'success' of informal economies, small-holder production or reciprocal labour exchanges in state socialism was always dependent on women's labour, in a context of patriarchal relations, generally combined with first-economy employment.

15. During their 1990 strike, the Workers' Democratic Movement of Vorkuta (northern Russia) declared that radical reform of the system, not just of one industry, was required.

16. For example, Pickvance (1992) reports that a protest over the Ajka flue-ash factory (Hungary) was used by the management and the local party to demand additional resources from the ministry.

17. Despite economic reforms, the systems were still attempting to give priority to growth of the capital sector at the end of the 1980s. In Bulgaria, Czechoslovakia, the GDR, Hungary and Poland the proportion of National Material Product re-invested ran at between 26 (Poland) and 34 per cent (Bulgaria) compared with an average of 20 per cent for Western Europe. (Zon, 1992).

18. The text is published in English as 'The Novosibirsk Report' (Zaslavskaya, 1984).

19. For example, at the Tula Chemical Plant the wage fund was frozen in 1967 and the plant was given a five-year target plus financial autonomy. Over the first five years, average wages had increased by 45 per cent, although 1300 workers (one-third of the work-force) had been made redundant. Over ten years output rose by 170 per cent and productivity by 240 per cent, and the share of wages as a proportion of production costs fell from 14 to 5 per cent. Such schemes were extended to 1000 enterprises in the 1970s and by 1980 all heavy industry was self-sufficient and responsible for its debts (Walker, 1988: 41).

20. This observation is based on interviews conducted by the author with members of the Research Bureau of the Hungarian Socialist Workers' Party in October 1985 and September 1988, and in the Research Bureau of the Marxism-Leninism Institute in Sofia, September 1988.

21. Similar processes took place in other ruling parties. In autumn 1988 the Research Bureau of the Bulgarian Communist Party held a meeting at Varna, at which the author was present, where wide-ranging reform models were discussed, including workers' self-management, privatization, indicative planning and price reform.

22. As early as 1977–8 Hungary was obliged to introduce a 'stabilization programme' of austerity, in order to secure foreign exchange credits (Batt, 1991).

23. As elsewhere in the socialist bloc, the Polish Government instigated a 'campaign against the *kulaks*' in 1945, confiscating all arable land in excess of 50 hectares, but the majority of land was owned by peasant farmers (the average holding was 5.4 hectares). In 1956, following massive peasant resistance, collectivization was abandoned, and Gomułka increased credits to private farmers whilst state land was leased (1 million hectares between 1957 and 1960) (Lovenduski & Woodall, 1987: 87; Majkowski, 1985).

24. The case of the former GDR was different in some respects, because of its absorption into the FRG, which was followed by a purge of administrators and officials connected with the former system.

25. Divergent tendencies in Solidarity came to a head with the split in the Sjem between Walesa supporters and the liberal-Left faction around Mazowiecki and Michnik, and again in the dilemma posed by the trade union over Balcerowicz's programme of radical economic reforms, which met with grass-root opposition amongst workers during 1990–1.

26. Such as the campaign against the proposed Nagyarmaros dam across the Danube; Eco-Glasnost (Independent Committee for Environmental Protection in Bulgaria); the Latvian Environmental Protection Club; or the Estonian Green Movement. Ecological protest could develop into national independence movements, however, like the Estonian Heritage Movement, whose protest against Moscow's plan to indiscriminately mine phosphate snowballed into an independence struggle.

27. Levitas and Strzalkowski ask: 'Why . . . should one make the long-term investment in domestic skilled labour and technology, if through a combination of a little industrial

collusion and some personal connections one can re-write tax legislation, export credits and bank policies? Or . . . why not simply sell off your newly-acquired state factory . . . and live off the interest one can earn in a Swiss bank?' (1990).

28. The Czech sociologist Ivo Možný (1992) has argued that by the 1980s the nomenklatura had become established, but because their power derived from bureaucratic position rather than ownership, they could not transfer property through inheritance. To facilitate inter-generational reproduction of their social position, they permitted the political guarantees of public ownership to disintegrate.

29. Such as the erstwhile USSR Ministry of Gas, which has become Gazprom Co.; or the Ministry of Construction in the north west, which is now Severo-Zapad (NW) Construction Co.

30. The Moscow River Borough Soviet Executive Committee used municipal best stock to found Energia Interbank Associated and became its executives.

31. *Pravda* conducted a campaign through 1990–1 to expose links between the shadow economy and the top bureaucracy, which was part of the rationale for the August 1991 attempted coup. Article 10 of Yanayev's State of Emergency proclamation (18 August 1991) stated: 'The holding of a permanent position in the structures of power and administration is to be considered incompatible with participation in entrepreneurial activity.' This, perhaps cynically, articulated a popular demand for regulation of the privatization process.

32. In the 1991 Russian Presidential elections, for example, the previously unknown Zhirinovski of the 'Liberal Democrats' stood on an openly chauvinistic and antisemitic platform and won 7.9 per cent of the votes (12–13 per cent in Rostov, Stavropol and Krasnodar) (*Sovetskaya Rossia*, 30.7.91).

7

Islamic Jacobins

The analysis of crisis in Soviet-type societies showed how a regulatory system imploded creating a systemic vacuum, the outcome of which will depend upon which types of presently weak social movements gain control over the transition process. Unable to sustain terroristic organizational charisma, the system developed into repressive corporatism which eventually became overloaded with regulatory demands. However, the world system impacts in different ways on local structures, and the crisis which brought about the Iranian Revolution, despite sharing some features with the crisis of state socialism, had a different outcome. Here the long-term legitimacy-deficit of the Pahlavi state created conditions for the growth of an authoritarian religious mass movement, the outcome of which was to consolidate, rather than diminish, the power of the state. Even if the Islamic Republic in due course succumbs to the kind of legitimation crises described above, the success of 'Islamic fundamentalism' (which has in some respects replaced Marxism as a combative ideology of Third World liberation) indicates that the statist solution to problems of dependency has not yet exhausted itself.[1] Indeed, the ability of the Islamic Republic to recapitulate a form of rule based on terroristic charisma, in many ways an organizational feature of early rather than late modernity, suggests that the global system permits the co-existence of parallel temporal realities, rather than imposing a homogeneous socio-cultural form on the whole system. Even so, the global system might be effective at containment, which might account for Iran's relative lack of success in 'exporting' Islamic Revolution, even amongst its potential constituency in the Middle and Near East.

There were features specific to Iranian society which created structures conducive to the neo-revivalist 'solution' to the crisis of the state. These features were the result of an historical inability of the state to secure legitimacy, combined with the existence of an alternative élite with access to what could loosely be described as 'traditionalistic' social networks. However, this does not imply the view which has informed much sociological analysis in this area, namely the 'Great Dichotomy' between occidental and oriental societies. This attempts to explain divergent patterns of development with reference to fundamental differences of economy and culture, and to some extent appears within both Marxist analysis of Asiatic modes of production and the Weberian concept of oriental patrimonialism. Attempting to explain the absence of autonomous capitalist development in Islamic nations, Weber, for example, argued, first, that the structure of oriental patrimonialism meant that investment in land was unsafe, which led to investment in *waqfs*, unproductive charitable religious foundations, which in turn resulted in the decline of the money economy. Secondly, Islam itself, as the religion of a warrior class, insisted on loyalty to ritual, and lacked a 'tragic conception of sin'. Thus, unlike Christianity, a salvation religion, Islam blocked the transposition of cultural rationalization into spheres of practical action. Thirdly, despite the co-existence of secular and religious law in the Near East, Islamic law lacked a formal legal tradition because of the hiatus between the Shar'ia (rational-substantive revealed law) and Qadi law (sacred rulings of jurists) which could be bridged only by *fatwas*, or legal opinions. This created a lack of predictability, especially in Persian Shi'ah Islam, where in the absence of the Sunna,[2] *fatwas* generated 'greater irrationality' than elsewhere in the Islamic world, and interfered with the secular legal system (Weber, 1978: II, 818ff.). Developing this line of analysis, many sociologists, who are discussed in the first section below, have explained Islamic revivalism in terms of the rebellion of traditional society against modernization, for which superficial support might be sought in the contrast between pre-revolutionary 'modernization' in Iran and 'traditionalistic' religious opposition.[3]

Such accounts have been criticized by writers who explain the underdevelopment of the Near East in terms of European colonialism which subordinated local economies and polities to the needs of core development (for example, Abrahamian, 1982; Amin, 1989; Halliday, 1979; Turner, 1981, 1984; Zubaida, 1989). Weberian approaches have further been criticized as 'essentialist', in assuming that social evolution corresponds to quasi-genetic codes inherent within cultural development, rather than dependency and contradictions of uneven and combined development. According to the latter position, it is global capitalism that 'fossilizes and insulates pre-capitalist modes' in the periphery (Wallerstein, 1980). On the other hand, Cheryl Benard and Zalmay Khalilzad (1984: 9–10) argue that world systems approaches over-emphasize the determining influence of the core and cannot account for autonomous mobilization amongst people in the periphery.[4] Analysis should therefore address the mutual interaction of core structure impact with local cultures and social structures.

The notion of arrested development might, from a Habermasian perspective, be extended to the development of cultural and communicative spheres. It is true that Habermas' theory is mainly concerned with debates over western modernity and leaves unanswered the implicit question of how to theorize the effects of modernization in societies which cannot recapitulate the developmental stages of the West.[5] However, he too objects to phenotypical explanations of modernization (or its absence) (1989b: 286)[6] and identifies in the medium of speech a universal capacity for rationalization.[7] Indeed, one of the advantages of his admittedly abstract concept of social evolution is its ability to cut through debates about traditionalism and modernization in two ways. First, far from representing a model for emulation by other societies, the particular form taken by modernization in the West is distorted and incomplete, as a result of the over-extension of systems of strategic action into areas of socio-cultural reproduction. Secondly, the theory of communicative action stipulates the necessary condition for an emancipatory social organization in terms of post-conventional ethics (outlined in Chapter 3) which are implicit in everyday communication (whether acknowledged or not) and therefore independent of particular cultural traditions. Complex and differentiated societies, which can no longer be integrated through the spell-binding power of the sacred, confront the problem of negotiating multiple interests and identities which can be successfully accomplished *only* through post-conventional formal procedures. However, in western society, this rational and emancipatory potential is suppressed (or arrested) by the extension of capitalism and bureaucratic organization in ways which give rise to pathologies. These arise where there is a scarcity of the kinds of meaning and personality development which the expansion of complex systems of action require. Then, 'disturbances in the symbolic reproduction of the lifeworld . . . identity-threatening crises or pathologies' result (Habermas, 1989b: 305). This is because areas of life that primarily fulfil functions of cultural reproduction, social integration, socialization and mutual understanding cannot be replaced by media – symbolic relations cannot be 'bought' and 'collected' like labour and taxes. Pathologies result from the disintegration of community, rupture of tradition, and loss of meaning as a consequence of which individuals preserve their identity 'only by means of defensive strategies that are detrimental to participating in social interaction on a realistic basis' (Habermas, 1989b: 141).

Since Habermas places the dislocation of traditional social relations at the centre of his theory, it might be of value in understanding the impact of colonialism on non-western forms of state and society. For this it would be necessary to show that an initial process of rationalization and pluralization was arrested by the intervention of global systems of power and money (even if mediated by local structures). It would then be necessary to show how the institutional forms which emerged sustained traditionalistic socio-cultural relations with consequences for patterns of social movement formation. If social movements, as has been suggested, embody proto-typical forms of new social organization, then the ways in which they construct identities and appropriate traditions are likely to affect outcomes of systemic crises. However, Habermas tends to discuss pathological socialization in terms of privatization, withdrawal, loss of meaning, etc., but to become social forces with effects on historical outcomes, these processes need to be mobilized and enter the public domain. It is suggested that this might happen where an alternative élite, excluded from the state and adversely affected by the impact of the global system, has a mobilization-base in traditionalistic social networks. This is not a sufficient condition for the success of neo-revivalism, however, since such mobiliz-ation requires in addition a general social crisis. This chapter examines the evidence for such a model, with reference to social movement formation in Iran. It will be argued that although a number of studies confirm the drift of Habermas' claims about social disorganization, their explanatory power would be enhanced through developing a more systemic concept of the relationship between re-traditionalization and the state. The remainder of this chapter will explore the ramifications of such a framework.

'Fundamentalism' as Eclectic Modernism

Islam has served as a resource-base for anti-colonial movements since the early nineteenth century – in the Algerian uprisings in 1832 through to the War of Independence (1954–62); the First Afghan War (1842); the Indian Mutiny (1857); the Mahdi uprising in Sudan (1881–98); and the long history of Iranian resistance. However, one should beware of regarding Islamic traditionalism as a continuous motif, a kind of permanent oppo-sition to modernity. Defensive, and generally authoritarian, social move-ments, which display what Habermas calls 'the melancholic longing for irretrievable pasts', are in many respects post-traditional and presuppose modern forms of the state.

Many studies would confirm Habermas' view that traditionalizing social movements are reactions to the impact of modernity on traditional lifeworlds. For example, Watt (1988) claims that the ulama[8] continued to affirm a traditional world-view and became a locus of reaction to moderniz-ing influences. Geertz (1968) argued that traditional world-views gave a feeling of confidence and that Mahdism was an 'emotional' reaction to the West. Badie (1986), following Weber, contrasts the cultural differentiation of the Occident with oriental 'religious totalitarianism' consequent on 'neo-prebendalism', and Kelidar (1981) refers to Khomeini's thought as 'untouched by modernization'. Similarly, Vatikiotis (1981) and Carré (1983) regarded the secular political order as peculiar to the West, with Vatikiotis characterizing the Middle East after the Iranian Revolution as 'caught in a great dilemma, one between tradition and modernity, between an Islamic value system and a positivist doctrine of modernity' (1981: 15). Silvers (1984) writes of neo-revivalism as 'unself-consciousness traditional-ism', arising from rural resistance to government planning, and entering the towns via rural migrants, who become self-employed in the bazaar sector. Vieille (1984) has a variant thesis, but argues that the cultural specificity is not Islamic but Mediterranean, and that modernization strategies have failed as a result of having been forced on pre-modern peoples (such as compulsory unveiling under Reza Shah in Iran). Faced with modernization failure, the state turns to an 'ideology of authenticity' (a term also used by Vatikiotis [1981] and Arjomand [1984]) in which a traditional and exclusively male public domain is reconstituted.

Other writers, however, emphasize how traditional values are re-created by carrier strata experiencing anomie and social disorganization (drawing on explanations of 'totalitarian mass movements' such as fascism and communism). Fischer (1982) describes the petite bourgeoisie (including intellectuals) along with the lumpenproletariat as groups most susceptible to the experience of social strain, having a predilection for authoritarian nationalism. Beneath the vocabularies of the past, the 'traditionalizing non-traditional ideologies', is 'the world of ademocratic mass politics', and 'the structural problems of mass society'. (A comparable account is found in Gellner, 1983.) Arjomand (1984) argues that Islam is a 'fully religious' movement organized around 'authenticity', a revolt against modernity, and, again, the relevant social agents are the petite bourgeoisie, the dispossessed, such as Shi'ite clergy under the Pahlavi regime, middle peasants in Algeria, and intellectuals. Both Fischer and Arjomand refer to the 'intellectual proletariat', unemployed graduates produced by an over-developed education system, whose support for ademocratic politics is understood as 'status preservationism'. Not unlike Ben-David (1962–3), Anderson (1988: 127) argues that whilst education expanded under colonial administration, graduates remained excluded from power. Thus global imperialism could be countered by vernacular-based movements constructed by intellectuals who remained a potential focus of radical opposition within the new regimes. Moreover, the military officer core, 'intellectuals in uniform', became public politicians whose educational socialization and independent power-base meant that their loyalties were not necessarily to the local bourgeoisie (Hourani, 1968; Khalid, 1978).

Tehranian (1980) refers to social atomization, the centralization of authority, and homogenization of culture; and Esposito (1983) argues that colonialism provokes an 'identity crisis', in response to which religion becomes the focus of anti-colonial movements, the early phase of which was 'modernizing', whilst the later phase is Islamist. Bourdieu (1979a) writes of 'affective quasi-systematization' consequent on the destruction of agrarian relations which are experienced by workers without a sophisti-cated understanding of the operation of the global system, and who therefore call upon traditional notions of social solidarity, communal aid and patron–client relations. The drift of this analysis is further shared by Abrahamian (1982) and Benard and Khalilzad (1984).

The emphasis in these accounts is slightly different – one group viewing tradition as a continuous counter-weight to modernization, another emphasizing the impact of social disorganization on the re-creation of traditional social values and networks. Whilst elements of these analyses are probably valid, they present two types of problems. First, Zubaida (1989) argues that explanations in terms of anomie and petit-bourgeois rebellion are inadequate, since they explain equally well the support enjoyed by the (Marxist) *Mujahedin-i Khalq* and the Islamic Republic Party, both of which drew support from alienated intellectuals (a view shared by Abrahamian, 1982: 481). Indeed, cultural resistance theories would need to explain why the secular Communist Party (*Tudah*) was able to mobilize the urban working class (especially oil workers) in 1946, but had very little impact in 1978–9. Secondly, the implication (which is not shared equally by the above writers) that Islamic resistance is a traditionalistic survival from pre-colonial times obscures the degree of adaptation to which traditional meanings are subjected. Revolutionary Islam involves *ijtihad* (the independent judgement of jurists based on the Qur'an) and the politicized reinterpretation of religious symbols, such as the martyrdom of Husayn in AD 680.[9]

Likewise, the term 'fundamentalism', which evokes orientalist images of the irrational and dangerous East,[10] is problematic for at least three reasons. First, it is used to denote a range of political and religious positions, which variously include eighteenth-century Wahhabism in the Arabian Peninsula,[11] the Muslim Brotherhoods in Egypt and Syria,[12] the Algerian FIS[13] and Iranian political concepts such as Khomeini's doctrine of *wilayat al-faqih* (Guardianship of the Jurists) or Ali Shariati's notion of Islam as a popular mass movement.

Secondly, 'fundamentalism' actually blends the modern with the traditional in novel discursive combinations, such as Shariati's combination of Marxism, sociology and dissident Islamic thought in *Red Shi'ism* (1979). Drawing on Fanon, Qutb and western sociology, Shariati claims that Shi'ism represents a de-legitimating tradition which justifies revolution against oppressive rule. Similarly, Khomeini claimed that the Iranian Revolution opposed all societies where the *mostakbirin* (arrogant) rule over the *mustaz'afin* (deprived), and supported Third World liberation movements (Watt, 1988: 98).[14] Khomeini further broke with Shi'ah orthodoxy by accepting the title of 'Imam' in 1970 (a term previously reserved for the occulted Mahdi). Thus Nikki Keddie concludes that

> It is common to speak of Khomaini as a 'traditionalist' or a 'fundamentalist' – the latter appelation is true within certain limits – but the former is misleading. In maintaining that ulama knowing Muslim law should rule directly, Khomaini was stating neither what is found in the Qoran nor in early Shi'ism, nor what is said in the treatises of . . . postoccultation Shi'ism, nor even a position expressed by religious leaders . . . since 1890. (1981: 30)[15]

Shariati's politics, too, were anti-traditionalist in many respects, such as his attacks on the ulama, his synthesis of Islam and western revolutionary thought, and his invocation of *mujaddid* (renewal based on rational deduction). He used the language of class, contradiction and dialectic, criticized the traditional ulama as 'the timeless ones', yet his messianism insists on the divine necessity of Shi'ah revelation as the foundation of practice and the unquestioned binding of norms and the law through *tawhid*, the doctrine of the oneness of God. As a faith of protest, Shariati's Shi'ism cannot accept a separation between religious and political spheres, which is quietistic, but rather requires the life of a partisan – to act 'as if the Mahdi (messiah) indeed lived in the world' (Akhavi, 1980: 154).[16] In this context, Fazlur Rahman (1982: 137) identifies what he calls 'postmodernist fundamentalism' – the self-conscious thematizing of issues that most distance neo-revivalism from 'western values', namely the demand for a ban on interest and on contraception, the exclusion of women from public life, and the collection of *zakat*, Islamic purity taxes.

Thirdly, writers who emphasize the 'traditionalistic' nature of Islamic revivalism overlook its most important facet (at least in the Iranian case), namely that it is a populist and statist doctrine which derives its rationale from the capacity of the modern state to regulate socio-cultural life (Abrahamian, 1991). Indeed, much commentary on 'fundamentalism' suggests a version of the dormant traditionalism (or 'Rip van Winkle') thesis noted in Chapter 5 above, where pre-modern world-views threaten to awake and take their revenge on modernity. On the contrary, it will be argued that 'fundamentalism' is better understood as an étatist, modernizing, authoritarian social movement, originating in the legitimacy and mobilization problems of the peripheral state. These problems involve the attempt to anchor state regulation and accumulation within the lifeworld whilst closing off self-reflective public spheres where legitimation questions might be posed. As a modernist movement Islamicism, insists that there is no distinction between the political and religious in Islam, and uses modern vocabularies of nation and popular sovereignty, conceiving of 'the people' as a political force.[17] Further, the political structure of the Islamic Republic is modern, and aspects are reminiscent of French and Russian revolutionary states (Zubaida, 1989: 143); moreover, as Sivan (1990) stresses, 'fundamentalism' is a viable political programme only in the context of a modern authoritarian state – since in a plural democracy religious observance would become a matter of personal preference.

The World System and Islamic Movements

This line of argument can be developed with reference to the formation of religious mass protest in Iran and its relationship with the arrested development of both the state and the formation of post-conventional public spheres, especially with the failure of the Constitutional Revolution (1905–12). Nineteenth- and early twentieth-century social protest indicated the capacity of the lifeworld to generate autonomous rationalization potential, prefiguring a route to modernity different from that actually taken. However, this was arrested by the combined effects of colonization by the global and local systems of power and money.

Nineteenth-century Persia displayed features of both prebendalism, where state lands seized by conquest were allocated as military benefices to the holder, who collected land tax, and feudalism, based on hereditary entitlement (Turner, 1984: 164). However, the former predominated, in local and horizontal social networks of lineage which the Qajar state[18] was unable to overcome sufficiently to establish a viable centralized administration (Abrahamian, 1982: 39). The Qajars could not break the power either of local Khans, or, despite early attempts to confiscate their property, of the ulama, who consolidated the *waqfs* from which they derived income and *zakat*. Combined with property in Ottoman Iraq, the ulama thus had a social base independent of the Qajars (Hiro, 1989: 143; Zubaida, 1989: 33) which was to be crucial to their subsequent role in Iranian politics.

However, these decentralized and localized power-bases offered a poor defence against colonial domination (Keddie, 1980: 131; Turner, 1984: 164). Indeed, Turner argues that whilst Weber was correct to identify patrimonialism and military-sultanism as obstacles to the development of a money economy, their main significance was that decentralization and internal conflicts weakened the Islamic polity in the face of colonial penetration. Iran's proximity to India and Russia meant that the British were interested in maintaining a neutral buffer against Russian expansion on the north-western frontier. A series of invasions, such as the Persian-Russian War (1828), the Herat expedition (1855) and the Anglo-Iranian War (1856), were followed by commercial concessions, which offered monopolies to foreign powers (especially Russia and Britain) to the detriment of local merchants. The Treaty of Turkomanchai (1828), for example, limited tariffs on Russian goods to 5 per cent (which was subsequently extended to other countries). However, the more heavily dependent the Persian state became on the sale of trade concessions, the more difficult it became either to resist further penetration or to handle demands for local political participation or protection from foreign competition. Meanwhile, early attempts at modernization ran aground, faced with resistance from the court, whose revenues were reduced to finance military reorganization; from local Khans who were losing their tax-base; and from the bazaar merchants (*bazaari*)[19] adversely affected by foreign competition. Dependent on foreign revenues, the state inadvertently stimulated religious social protest through which theological concerns were transposed into social and political issues.

By the late nineteenth century the Qajars were touting concessions for sale around European capitals as a means of rasing revenue and offsetting rapid inflation. For example, in 1872 a concession was sold to Baron Reuter, a British citizen, for £40,000 and 60 per cent of profits from an exclusive right to finance a state bank, farm out customs, exploit all minerals, build all roads, canals, railways and telegraphic communications (Abrahamian, 1982: 55). However, the practice began to generate resistance, some of which was supported by the Russians who were losing out to western powers, and the Reuter concession was withdrawn, although the Imperial Bank and telegraphic communications remained in British ownership.

The consequence of foreign penetration was that Iranian producers were linked up with the global system; thus between 1800 and 1914 Iranian trade increased by twelve times, but .the balance of trade was increasingly unfavourable as the price of Iranian raw materials fell relative to imported manufactured goods.[20] Further, inflation (600 per cent between 1850 and 1900) and devaluation of Persian currency weakened the competitiveness of the local bazaars, decreased state revenues and prompted merchants to invest in land rather than industry (Abrahamian, 1982: 33–49; Turner, 1984: 172). Class and regional conflicts were exacerbated by the combined and uneven effects of linkage with the world economy – expansion of trade increased the power of the merchants who were integrated into Qajar patronage networks and of large landlords who benefited from land consolidation, whilst state taxes increasingly fell on peasants, small artisans and the *waqfs*.

This polarization created a rift between the state, on the one hand, and native merchants and the ulama, on the other. The bazaars coalesced into a cross-national middle class, and protests over the Tobacco Concession (1891–2) illustrated both the existence of nation-wide organization amongst *bazaari*, and the linkage between popular and religious resistance.[21] Indeed, nineteenth-century religious resistance was transposing ethical and other-worldly concerns into social and political demands as theological discourse became a vehicle for addressing the social and intellectual problems posed by foreign domination, and the lack of effective response from Qajar rulers (Watt, 1988: 46).[22] Movements such as Shaikhism or Babism, and modernizers such as al-Afghani or Rashid Rida, deployed traditionalist imagery both to challenge the West and to express frustration with antiquated structures (Keddie, 1980).

Indeed, this 'traditionalism', was actually the vehicle through which aspects of traditional authority were questioned. This social protest was initially defensive of endangered ways of life, although it was informed by concepts of social justice, and later demonstrated a capacity for offensive orientations. Shaikhism was an eighteenth-century mystical movement which refused to accept temporal state power as binding, whilst insisting on an allegorical rather than literal interpretation of beliefs such as the resurrection of the dead, the Prophet's Ascension, or the occulted Imam (Bayat-Philipp, 1981). Shaikhism found its most radical expression in Babism, when Sayyed Ali Mohammad (1821–50) proclaimed himself *bab* (gate) to Divine Truth, and an essentially religious dispute broke out of the mosques into the madrasas (religious colleges) to became a popular movement. Babism called for social reforms (including the legalization of money lending and legal protection for merchants), women's equality (encouraging women preachers and poets to unveil) and regarded revelation as progressively unfolding through social stages in the evolution of humanity, rather than having been definitively related by the Prophet. Supporters of this heretical movement tended to be *bazaari* and intellectuals, and attacked the ulama for worldly corruption and abuse of *ijtihad*. Ali Mohammad was involved in nationalist uprisings and was executed in 1850, after which there followed sporadic anti-western and anti-Qajar insurrections, and the radical Azal faction went underground, to resurface in later conflicts (Bayat-Philipp, 1981: 47).

Whilst Shaikhism and Babism were pre-modern movements, they indicated an incipient potential for rationalization, since they transposed religious-ethical concepts into worldly activity (resistance to the Shah and to western domination) whilst re-addressing the validity basis of traditional authority. These tendencies were further developed by the Persian pan-Islamic activist Jamal al-Din ('al-Afghani'), who called on Muslims to resist colonialism whilst emphasizing the social and political potential of Islam to a greater extent than did Shaikhis and Babis.[23] Although al-Afghani used the traditional language of *al salaf al salih* (the pious ancestors) to unite against domination by unbelievers, he also insisted on *ijtihad*, that each believer had the right and responsibility to interpret the Qur'an and Sunna for themselves (Keddie, 1980). In this sense the subsequent Salfiyyah movement not only challenged the ulama's hegemony over Qur'anic interpretation but implicitly opened the way for further rationalization of the world-view by acknowledging that validity-claims be submitted to individual conscience and argumentative scrutiny.[24]

These social forces coalesced to end Qajar rule in the Constitutional Revolution (1905–12), which illustrated the potential for autonomous social and political rationalization. The temporary dislocation in the global environment following the 1905 Russian Revolution and Russo-Japanese War, combined with economic crisis, increased tariffs on merchants and further sales of concessions to create the conditions for mass uprising (Issawi, 1978). Further, mass organization was possible since the *bazaari* had become a national middle class; frustrated with failed modernization under the Qajars, the intelligentsia supported constitutionalism, national-ism and secularism; whilst the Shah's intention to diffuse resentments through liberalization released social protests which, in the absence of a national army, the Qajars had little ability to control (Keddie, 1980: 67). The Constitutional Revolution abolished feudal land-holdings, regularized taxes and established a national banking system, within the framework of a constitutional government and a Bill of Rights. (Abrahamian, 1982: 80; Keddie, 1980: 68).

However, the Constitution acceded to the demands of the ulama to retain jurisdiction over religious law, proscribe heretical movements and restrict Cabinet posts to Muslims. Whereas earlier mass religious protest, like the Babis, had challenged both the state and the rights of the ulama, the Constitutional Revolution illustrated that the ulama had retained hegemony over popular protest (hegemony based largely on their ability to mobilize the mosques and madrasas, combined with close ties with the *bazaari*). As a competing élite, they provided religious legitimation for the uprising (for example, comparing the Shah to Yazid, a strategy Khomeini was to follow seventy years later) but were essentially defensive, combin-ing the grievances of the *bazaari* with protection of religious property and *zakat*. Disputes arose with radical constitutionalists over the religious veto on legislation, the separation of secular and religious law, and women's representation. This was a portent for future developments, since in a post-traditional society the ulama faced the prospect of contending for status (and hence, of course, for the preservation of privileges) within an increasingly formal-rational discursive field competing with secular nationalists, constitutional liberals, Marxists, socialists and feminists.[25] The insistence of conservative ulama (the Wise Mujtahtedin) on constitutionally defined authority was an attempt to establish privileged access to the state (substantive rationality) against pluralization of the political system, which might in due course have initiated a process of secularization.

Had it not been defeated by civil war, the military coup of Colonel Reza Khan (later Reza Shah) and the Anglo-Russian invasion in 1910, the Constitutional Revolution might still have stabilized secular rule and a plural polity. Thus it does seem plausible to claim that an initial process of rationalization and pluralization was arrested by the effects of the global system. However, this suppressed potential did not disappear, but rather was manifested in subsequent liberal or socialist movements, which were to come to the fore again in the conflicts surrounding Muhammad Mossadeq's National Front Government (1951–3).[26] It was seen above that many writers stress forced secularization under the Pahlavis as the principal cause of the traditionalistic backlash. Although the attempts to separate religion from the state, expand and modernize the education system, and prohibit public displays of religiosity[27] alienated the ulama, it will be argued that this was not necessarily the decisive factor. Of more significance perhaps was the Shah's conservative holding procedure, to construct centralized state capitalism without an independent civil society, which precluded an alliance with secular forces. Relying on the triple pillars of the army, court patronage (especially from oil revenues which financed the Pahlavi Foundation) and a centralized bureaucracy, the Shah 'failed to secure social foundations for his institutions [and] . . . ruled without the support of an organized political party' (Abrahamian, 1982: 149). It was not so much the programme of 'modernization', then, which generated the backlash, but, on the contrary, the suppression of the secular opposition which left the field open to religious forces with a mobilization base in the mosques, seminaries and bazaars. In this sense politicized Islam was not so much the antithesis of the Pahlavi state as its mirror image, in that both substituted coercive statism for plurality and rational consensus.

The Invasive State

How did these institutional forms sustain traditionalistic socio-cultural relations and with what consequences? The defeat of the Constitutional Revolution and the subsequent process of authoritarian modernization under Reza Shah involved an over-extension of bureaucratic and commodified systems of action, which blocked the further development of the secular protest movements. Mid-twentieth-century Iran to some extent shared the legitimation problems of other post-colonial Middle Eastern states, which during the 1950s and 1960s experienced mass mobilization led by military élites, which created pervasive bureaucracies, mass production factories and an official culture. These were invasive of the lifeworld in that they redrew the boundaries of state and civil society, weakening voluntary associations and institutions, education, welfare and economic activity, and popular culture. Regimes such as those in Egypt or Algeria developed minimal legitimacy through an ideology of combative anti-imperialism combined with a military cult of order and ruthlessness, the use of the security apparatus, and a monopoly over mass communications.[28] They subsequently had to contend with what Sivan (1990) calls the 'revenge of civil society' – the appearance of Islamicist opposition (the Brotherhoods, Da'wa or FIS) which was grounded in the very structures of social solidarity which the authoritarian-populist states had attempted to marginalize.

However, the Pahlavi state, which survived in 1953 only because of the CIA coup which removed Mossadeq, had an even greater legitimacy-deficit in that it could not claim the mantle of an anti-colonial war of independence. Its response was to attempt further secularization from above, aimed at consolidating central authority through artificial organiz-ations of mass participation, whilst isolating opposition from any genuine channels of consensus formation. The effect of this political underdevelop-ment was to off-load opposition into an incipient alternative society, whilst blocking channels of communication between the political system and interest groups such as the *bazaari* and ulama. The ramifications of this can be illustrated with reference to the Pahlavi regime's programme of socio-economic modernization in the 'White Revolution' and the one-party state.

It has been seen in Chapter 5 that the peripheral state is generally caught in a dilemma, between expanding its participation-base, which limits scope for accumulation, and dysfunctional repression, which leaves it further susceptible to systemic crisis. This dilemma is often resolved through political clientelism and the expansion of an unproductive state sector. The Pahlavi state tied up large proportions of revenue (largely from oil, which rose from $13 billion to $38 billion between 1973 and 1977) in the military and state bureaucracy.[29] The latter employed half of all urban employees and provided privileged benefits of medical insurance, unemployment insurance, student loans, pensions and low-income housing. Further, the bureaucracy replaced local magnates in the countryside, regulated agricul-tural prices, water distribution, migratory routes and state co-operatives (1.7 million members). The principal avenue of this clientelism was the Pahlavi Foundation. Officially a charity sponsored by the Shah, the Foundation was used as conduit for his personal investment (of around $40 million per year) and through loans to entrepreneurs, investments in infrastructure, capitalization and agricultural reform, exercised economic control and funded royal ventures (such as the Bank Omran). The Foundation had multi-billion dollar assets in banks and investment com-panies, insurance, property, leisure complexes, industrial holdings, the automobile industry, publishing and agribusiness (Graham, 1978: 214–17).

The peripheral state might attempt to increase its capacity to act through further rationalization of its productive base and broadening avenues of participation. Rather than call parliamentary elections in January 1963, the Shah called a referendum on the White Revolution (1963–72) which initiated a further wave of modernization from above.[30] Its effects illustrated, however, that system rationalization that has weak anchoring in the socio-cultural sub-system, and leaves intact pre-modern social structures, is likely to be counter-productive. Despite the break up of large-scale ownership, absentee landlords retained economic power (Turner, 1984: 181) and the extent of unviable holdings (65 per cent under 5 hectares) meant that the original aim of creating a class of independent small-holders was frustrated (Abrahamian, 1982: 429). Its effects were to expand mechanization, increase the size but not the prosperity of small landowners, encourage urban migration by increasing the numbers of landless labourers, and extend credit and money relations in the country-side, all of which exacerbated social conflict, whilst the avenues of its articulation were being closed off (Mahdavy, 1964).[31]

Further, the White Revolution undermined the traditional power and patronage of rural élites, whilst in new urban shanty towns, recently dispossessed migrants who had been previously indifferent to religious observance, 'used religion as a substitute for their lost communities, oriented social life around the mosque, and accepted with zeal the teachings of the local mulla' (Abrahamian, 1982: 535).[32] In November 1962 the ulama demonstrated their potential for counter-mobilization in protests following the Local Council Election Bill (to enfranchise women) and in March and June 1963 in protests against the White Revolution, when Khomeini's arrest was followed by days of fighting at seminaries, in which hundreds were killed.

The introduction of one-party rule in 1975 was a further attempt both to protect the state against mounting civil disturbance, and to broaden its regulatory and participatory capacities (for example, by recruiting some ex-*Tudah* cadres). The *Rastakhiz* (Resurgence) Party was used in three main ways. First, as a parallel watchdog organization of the administration and popular police force (like mass organizations in Soviet systems). For example, in the anti-profiteering and prices campaign in the summer of 1975 students were recruited to check shop prices, humiliate merchants and break up supermarkets which were over-charging. Secondly, *Rastakhiz* channelled and de-politicized public debate, strengthening the Shah's traditional authority in the face of social and economic modernization (Kamrava, 1990: 20). Thirdly, it orchestrated debate in Parliament through two 'wings', which organized two systems of clientelism under the contenders for premiership: Hushang Ansari (Finance Minister), leader of the 'constructive liberals', and Jamshid Amouzegar (Interior Minister), leader of the 'progressive liberals'. The former emphasized rapid economic growth and industrialization, and the latter decentralization, social welfare and broader participation (Graham, 1978: 135).

However, Habermas has argued that the over-extension of power is ultimately self-defeating since it enhances the potential for resistance from the socio-cultural sub-system. The last years of the Shah might illustrate this. *Rastakhiz* (assisted by SAVAK[33]) had three major repercussions. First, state control over the salaried middle class, the urban working class and rural producers was intensified. Secondly, for the first time in modern Iranian history, the state systematically penetrated the bazaars and the religious establishment. The party opened branches in the bazaars, forced donations from small businesses, dissolved the traditional guilds, which were replaced with party-controlled Chambers of Guilds, and set up state corporations in competition with local merchants (Abrahamian, 1982: 443–4). *Rastakhiz* restricted religious publishing by the Waqf Organization, and began auditing accounts of seminaries. Thirdly, by closing off alternative avenues of protest the one-party state polarized civil society into the communication structures of the state and the mosque networks dominated by the radical ulama.

On the one hand, there were the state-controlled electronic and print media which were prevented from dealing with anything controversial (Tehranian, 1980). Rather, they were used 'to undermine both traditional and progressive values . . . [but,] eventually, the divisive stereotyping and distortions used to deepen mistrust and polarization . . . became a weapon in the hands of the victims' (Nafisi, 1982). On the other hand, religious ceremonies like Muharram plays had been tolerated because it was believed they channelled social frustration into harmless directions as a form of crisis displacement. However, the mosque network provided the means of disseminating information, food, fuel, clothing – it formed a social infrastructure which would subsequently be conducive to mobilization (Abrahamian, 1982: 535). This popular medium of communication, especially pamphleteering and eulogies for Husayn at Friday prayers, 'promoted the idea of Khomeini as leader of opposition to the Shah – to the exclusion of other leaders and movements – and they widely disseminated the idea of the "Islamic government" as the form of government which would replace the monarchy' (Bakhash, 1984: 144). Manipulating the pathos of the Karbala paradigm, Khomeini gave symbolic structures multiple uses and, in the absence of an alternative mass opposition, could define the discursive arena of debate. Khomeini's shrewd ability to gauge the popular mood accounts for his 'charisma', in that familiar meanings were condensed into new symbolic figures, which resonated with deeply felt understandings about the world. Khomeini effected an identity between the central Shi'ah myth of Husayn, and the people's struggle against the Shah. The more people suffered, both through economic hardship and at the hands of SAVAK and the military, the more the revolution was a metaphorical re-enactment of Husayn's martyrdom. The lamentations at Friday prayers constituted an identification with the people of Kufa who invited Husayn to lead them into revolt against the Caliph Yazid, and then left Husayn to be martyred. Thus culturally ingrained messianic ideals – of a just society, resistance to tyrants, struggle against overwhelming odds – were tacitly mobilized (Fischer, 1980b) in the interests of the alternative élite.

Hegemony and Mobilization

How did pathological socialization, the result of the Shah's repressive modernization, become a material force affecting the outcome of the crisis? Largely because the radical clergy were able to mobilize defensive social networks under the umbrella of a broader coalition. As with the collapse of state socialism, the implosion of bureaucratic structures of regulation released a plethora of social movements with potential to develop in emancipating or repressive directions. Like the fall of Haile Selassie (Ethiopia, 1974) and Ayub Kahn (Pakistan, 1964), the fall of the Shah was effected by a coalition of urban forces, including the ulama, the shanty towns, *bazaari* and students (Clapham, 1985: 81).[34] Indeed, it is unlikely that the revolution would have succeeded had the uprising remained confined to the ulama's traditional support base in the bazaar. By late 1977 a stalemate had been reached between the military and the protesters, which was broken by the strikes in textile mills, machine tool factories, automobile plants and oil fields, demanding a return to the Constitution of 1906–7 (Abrahamian, 1981). In December 1978 workers occupied plants in all industrial areas, doctors occupied hospitals, which became battle grounds with the army, prisons were broken open and SAVAK members lynched. The first wave of armed insurrection was accompanied by an upsurge of movements for autonomy as *shora* (councils) were formed in factories, schools, oil fields, universities, Tehran airport and the army. Peasants began to seize land, and form collectives, and in Turkaman-Sahra a Turkaman People's Political-Cultural Centre organized education, land distribution, trade unions, and published a paper, *Iel Goygi* (People's Power) (Azad, 1981). In April 1979, a month after the Shah's departure, the Kurdish Democratic Party was in open conflict with the state (Bakhash, 1985; Wright, 1989). Sannandaj was occupied by Kurdish rebels, who set up a Provisional Revolutionary Government, which lasted until June. Kurdistan became a 'magnetic pole for Iranian progressive forces' where dozens of leftist and nationalist groups formed. In July 1980, the *Fedayan-i Khalq* (People's Sacrifices, a Marxist guerilla organization) organized a Solidarity Conference in Tehran, in which all national minorities were represented, the only time such a meeting has been held in Iran (Malek, 1989). Why, then, were the competing SMOs, especially the modernist and left opposition, so ineffective?

Benard and Khalilzad (1984: 112–13) suggest three reasons why modernist groups such as the National Democratic Front, Liberation Movement or *Tudah* were unable to prevent the Islamic radicals gaining control of the revolution. First, they failed to establish a unified political organization; secondly, they were divided over strategy and attitude to the radical clerics; and, thirdly, secular leaders like President Bani-Sadr were intimidated by Khomeini's apparent popularity. However, the inability of the secular movements to prevent the formation of an Islamic Republic was further rooted in their inferior mobilization-base, which in turn reflects the conditions under which opposition movements evolved under the Pahlavi state. Whereas in the 1940s *Tudah* had been able to mobilize the urban working class, its position by 1978–9 had been weakened by repression, compared with Khomeini's ability to communicate through the mosques and religious associations. Meanwhile, that the *Mujahedin-i Khalq* and *Fedayan-i Khalq* resorted to terrorism indicated that they were far from being mass movements. Thus, 'what produced the Islamic form of the revolution was not Islamic revivalism so much as repression of other modes of political discourse' (Fischer, 1980b: 185).[35]

Moreover, the outcome illustrates the complex play of inter-élite competition for social mobilization and the role of defensive social movements enhancing the capacities of the state to act. In Chapter 5 it was suggested that religious revitalization movements are attempts by collectivities to restore or reconstruct patterns of life rapidly disrupted or threatened by the effects of the global economy. Wuthnow (1980, 1983) suggests that when the world economy separates local élites from the global system, the mobilization chances for popular movements are increased, and disparate local customs and social structures combine in variegated ways depending upon the specific forms of dislocation, and the structures available for mobilization. The Pahlavi regime did encounter problems of financing the over-extended bureaucracy out of oil revenues, which declined in real terms after 1977, and pressure from the Carter Administration to improve its human rights record, but these were short term and hardly signalled a separation from the world system. However, since the Constitutional Revolution, when the ulama won short-lived political authority, they constituted a counter-élite in alliance with the *bazaari* which *was* to some extent separated from the global economy. Indeed, Nafisi (1982: 200) concludes that 'the present clerical state in Iran is, to some extent, the result of a struggle within the power élite'.

Even so, dislocation of the lifeworld alone will not provide collective organizational capacities or autonomous resources for mass opposition. Rather, grievances are channelled through pre-existing social networks which have been subject to varying degrees of rationalization. By re-establishing voluntary associations (*jama'at*) based on age, gender, occupation, social position or residence, the ulama mobilized the institutions of the mosque within the political sphere. Mosque committees organized vigilante-style action to enforce fasting on Ramadan, abstinence from alcohol, 'modest' attire for women or the avoidance of licentious television. *Jama'at* provided funds for gender-segregated schools or buses for students, summer camps, co-operatives and welfare organizations, and enhanced the movement towards a parallel society through recruitment of judges, and pacts amongst members of the *jama'at* not to have recourse to state courts but to use imams as arbiters (Sivan, 1990).

Moreover, the White Revolution and the restrictions on religious organizations provided the impetus for counter-élite consolidation, and strengthened the hand of radicals *vis-à-vis* those who did not find a political role congenial (Green, 1980). Akhavi (1980: 24) points out that 'a very considerable number of ulama have abjured politics'; Ayatollah Burujirdi, for example (*marja'i taqlid*, the highest religious authority), 'maintained cool aloofness', and in 1949 led 2000 clerics into retreat at Qom. The ulama fluctuated between political involvement and withdrawal, whilst retaining their hegemony over a public sphere largely undifferentiated into secular value spheres.[36] Paradoxically, when the Pahlavi state entered legitimation crisis during the 1960s and 1970s, the earlier withdrawal from politics constituted the power-base which could be consolidated through the madrasas network of 90,000 talabehs (seminarians) nationwide, and between 12,000 and 15,000 at Qom alone (Tehranian, 1980).

The mosque network served as an embryonic administration for the *komitehs* and *pasdaran* (Revolutionary Guards). When, in January 1979, Shapur Bakhtiar formed a government after the Shah announced his departure, Khomeini, not yet in Iran, had an Islamic Revolutionary Council ready as a provisional government, although he continued to rule through the coalition whilst the Islamic Republic Party (IRP) was established to formalize control over social networks (Benard & Khalilzad, 1984: 106). During the Bazargan period, which ended with the seizure of the US embassy, the National Democratic Front, the *Fedayan-i Khalq* and the Islamic Republic Party fought to gain control of the instruments of government and communication. Conflict ensued for control of the streets, as millions marched in Tehran, half-a-million in Mashad, in support of Khomeini and an Islamic Republic, whilst the Left also demonstrated and Marxist papers warned Khomeini not to try to monopolize the revolution, in turn to be denounced by Khomeini as 'against Islamic law'. When Khomeini returned to Tehran in February 1979, the army withdrew support from Bakhtiar, and recognized the Khomeini-backed provisional government of Bazargan, against whom Khomeini organized in the Revolutionary Council.

During the period of dual power under the secular liberal Prime Minister, Mehdi Bakhtiar (January–November 1979) and Khomeini's Revolutionary Council, religious forces successfully established Islam as the umbrella language of moral protest (Nashat, 1980). Post-traditional issues were articulated through an apparently traditionalizing language. Thus within the coalition the discursive terrain was occupied increasingly with the 'battle of the Qur'an'. For example, as Khomeini was using the Qur'an to decry the role of women under the Pahlavi regime and extol women's mothering and domestic virtues in the Islamic Republic (Tabari & Yeganeh, 1982), Abholassan Bani-Sadr was referring to it in order to establish the 'natural and instinctive rights' of human beings in marital relations (Tabari & Yeganeh, 1982: 108–11). At the same time, the *Mujahedin-i Khalq* were arguing that the Qur'an supported equality for men and women, and that the Qur'anic prophets were the inspiration of social and political struggle at the time of the formation of social classes (Tabari & Yeganeh, 1982: 117). The opposition was forced on to the ideological terrain of Islamic Republicans partly because it was the latter who had control of the streets, where the Revolutionary Guards were organizing the mass Terror.

Ultimately the coalition between liberals, *Tudah* and Islamic radicals was undermined by the Terror. However, the Terror, as in the Jacobin Republic of Virtue, could become an effective instrument of policy because popular impulses were brought under rational and centralized control, fusing popular anger with the centralization of state power.[37] Ayatollah Khalqali's *komitehs*, initially only partially controlled by the Revolutionary Committee, executed thousands without trial, not only for crimes of the Pahlavi regime, but also for 'sexual crimes', political dissent or having contacts with Israel (Benard & Khalilzad, 1984; Fischer, 1980b; Hiro, 1989). In this context of intimidation, a referendum in March 1979 gave Khomeini overwhelming support for an (undefined) Islamic republic (which national minority and leftist groups boycotted). Resistance continued, for example the unemployed demonstrated in Tehran in October 1979 chanting 'death to this fascist regime', but the Terror, Khomeini's control of the streets, and the absence of a mass secular leftist movement secured his hold on the revolution. During 1979–80, the *shora* were either incorporated into a consultative capacity in the Islamic Republic (and run by the *pasdaran*, Revolutionary Guards empowered to execute or imprison opponents) or, like the entire leadership of the Turkaman People's Political-Cultural Centre, were gunned down by the IRP's 'black gangs' (Azad, 1981).

Revolutionary Populism

Once in power the ulama could not rule through a plural constitutional state because this would have reduced the programme of re-Islamization to one project amongst others, within a process of formal-rational negotiation. However, *étatiste* rule has, temporarily at least, given the state greater capacity for action than under the Pahlavis. The doctrine of *Vilayat-e Faqih* (Rule of the Jurist) ensures that the ulama are heavily represented at all levels of government, and goes far beyond the demand of the Constitutional Revolution for Wise Mujtahedin. Revolutionary Guards are placed at every level and intervene in government, local community and the armed forces. Again, there is a parallel with the Soviet Political Commissars in the 1920s and 1930s, or with the Red Guards in Chinese Cultural Revolution. The *pasdaran* maintain discipline in factories and other enterprises, and rival the regular forces, as did the politically constituted structures of fascism or communism. The neighbourhood committees constitute localized organs of the state exercising surveillance characteristic of plebicitary charismatic dictatorship. Further, like the nomenklatura system in Soviet states, the IRP appoints office-holders at all significant levels of policy-making (Benard & Khalilzad, 1984: 120).

The IRP has remained dependent on oil revenues (which declined by 16 per cent between 1980 and 1984 as a result of the destruction of oil fields in the war with Iraq) and attempts to construct legitimacy through mass mobilization (especially during the war) and a redistributive economy which trades off loyalty against collective consumption (Skocpol, 1982). Between 1979 and 1981 a system of wage controls and income tax changes benefited middle- and lower-middle income households (Behdad, 1989). The Pahlavi Foundation has been taken over by the IRP as the Mustazafin Foundation, and its ownership of the economy has been considerably extended with nationalizations of banks, insurance companies, aircraft production, shipping, automobiles, heavy industry, pharmaceuticals, warehousing and road haulage. By 1983, the Mustazafin Foundation owned 495 companies and was the largest employer after the civil service. It is the major avenue of redistribution, providing interest-free loans to small businesses and housing, having built 50,000 units between 1984 and 1985 (Hiro, 1989: 188), which have been allocated to active supporters of the IRP (Behdad, 1989).[38]

For Zubaida, the revolution was a seizure of the state apparatus which could be transformed to perform Islamic rather than secular functions without major alterations in its structural forms. The concept of *jamhouri* (Republic), he says, is held in common with the 'discursive products of the French Revolution' (Zubaida, 1989: 173). It has a written constitution, an elected president, a parliament (still called the Majlis) and a contradictory duality of sovereignties written into the Constitution (Bakhash, 1985). Further, the Majlis enjoys legislative power and is only occasionally restricted by the Council of Guardians. Similarly, Abrahamian stresses the 'modernity' of the Islamic Republic, pointing to the Constitution, the 'central structure of which was taken straight from the French Fifth Republic, founded on Montesquieu's separation of powers' (1991).

However, like these earlier modernist revolutions, the Islamic state embodies one, amongst other possible routes to modernity. It institutionalizes a heroic authoritarian modernity which, like the Pahlavi regime it replaces, gears capital accumulation to a deep and destructive penetration of the lifeworld. The Islamic Republic involves a radical de-differentiation of cultural value spheres and as such actually intensifies the statism of the Pahlavi period. The Cultural Revolution in September 1980 closed the universities, to be prepared for 'Islamization' of the curriculum, a process which was extended into the media, art, clothing (imposition of the *hijab*, Islamic dress) and family. In particular, despite the mass participation of women in the revolution, Khomeini ordered a review of the Family Protection Law and a return to the *chador* (the complete covering of women's bodies). By 1981, women were executed for prostitution, the legal age of marriage was lowered to 13, divorce and child custody laws favoured fathers, women were barred from many public offices, and schools were re-segregated. Nashat (1980) suggests that the Cultural Revolution was in direct response to feminist organizations' power-base in the universities. The reclaiming of the public space as exclusively male represents a defeat for Iranian feminism, which had already mounted a challenge to both the ulama and the patriarchal pseudo-emancipation under the last Shah (Az, 1981).

Summary

This chapter has been concerned to develop the explanatory model of the rise of Islamic Republicanism in terms of the effects of systemic coloniz-ation of the lifeworld. Several points have emerged from this discussion. The process of social movement formation is not an automatic response to colonization; rather, it is subject to complex interactions between strat-egies of crisis management and the defensive reactions of the lifeworld. A precondition for social movement formation is the existence of networks which serve in proto-typical ways as the precursors of new levels of social organization. These are released through systemic crisis, when otherwise privatized defences are channelled into collective action. The existence of a counter-élite with access to tightly coupled social networks and indepen-dent communication flows like the *jama'at* will not only reduce the likelihood of successful crisis management, but will also reduce the mobilization success of competing SMOs. However, authoritarian and defensive mass movements are carriers of the very étatist structures which they appear to struggle against, and therefore they do not release any new cognitive-moral learning capacities, even though they might enhance the state's capacity to regulate capital accumulation within the global context.

Notes

1. For example, Kelvin Dwyer reports a Moroccan professor who comments: 'Over . . . the last two decades a kind of secular, leftist ideology dominated the universities. But now there is an alternative in the form of Islamic ideology. . . . [however,] some people, behind a religious or metaphysical language, are really using a political language expressing political and social protest' (1991: 37).
2. 'The beaten track' – the collection of ethical and legal interpretations from the eighth to tenth centuries AD which form the basis of Sunni Islam.
3. Between 1973 and 1976, Iran's GDP had grown by over 50 per cent; per capita income had reached a Third World record of $2000; the urban population had doubled between 1956 and 1966; there were 100,000 university and 500,000 secondary school students; the educated middle class had doubled between 1956 and 1976 from 6 to 13 per cent of the population (25 per cent if merchants are included); and the number of industrial plants increased from under 1400 in 1953 to over 8000 in 1978 (Benard & Khalilzad, 1984: 12–13). Moreover, since the 1950s women had been entering professions such as law and medicine, and had won the franchise in 1963 in the teeth of opposition from the ulama at Qom, led by the Ayatollah

Khomeini. By 1978, there were two women Government Ministers, two Senators and nineteen Majles (Parliament) deputies.

4. This criticism is directed particularly at Wallerstein. Leslie Sklair's (1991) 'marginaliz-ation of domestic practices' hypothesis ('only those domestic . . . practices that do not threaten the global capitalist project are tolerated') might further exemplify this tendency to disempower everyone outside core élites. However, this fault is less common than they suggest and is not true of Turner or Zubaida who document the mutual interaction between Iranian society and global systems.

5. The question remained unanswered when Peter Dews asked Habermas what impli-cations his theory might have for the Third World, since he declined to answer (Habermas, 1986: 187).

6. This objection is made more in relation to Parsons than Weber, although it was seen in Chapter 3 that he criticizes Weber for offering no explanation of the differential socio-economic development of occidental and oriental societies.

7. Following the discussion in Chapter 3, rationalization refers to breaking the 'spell-binding power of the sacred', permitting differentiation of cultural value spheres, post-conventional ethics, and freeing the argumentative facility of language.

8. Religious scholars, who perform several functions: they judge at Shari'a courts, provide legal interpretations, administer the Mosques and preach (the Iranian ulama are known as Mullahs).

9. For Imamite Shi'ism (about 8 per cent of Muslims worldwide) the rightful successor to Muhammad as Imam (Spiritual Leader) was his cousin and son-in-law Ali, although his effective successor was Abu-Bakr. Hasan, son of Ali, made an ineffectual claim on the caliphate in 661 and then withdrew. The rightful successor was then his brother, Husayn, who claimed the caliphate but was killed along with his supporters at Karbala in 680, after refusing to surrender to the Caliph Yazid. The rightful imams after Husayn were his descendants through to the twelfth generation (AD 874), after which the imam went into 'occultation', and for Twelver Shi'ism the return of the 'hidden imam' as al-Mahdi (guided one) will usher in a messianic age. The death of Husayn serves as a model of resistance and martyrdom in contemporary Shi'ite writing, deployed, for example, by Ali Shariati and Khomeini.

10. For Edward Said (1985), the Orient has provided Europe with its deepest and most recurring images of the Other, a discourse of writers, poets, theorists, philosophers, etc., through which Orient was *made oriental* by constructing a fundamental difference between East and West, where the latter constructs an image of itself as civilized, against the barbaric East. In orientalist discourse history and progress were possible only in the West since oriental backwardness or fatalism precluded autonomous development, which 'forgets' that the European–Atlantic powers colonized the Islamic world. The 1991 Gulf War occasioned the re-construction of the Islamic Orient as irrational barbarism, contrasted with the 'civilized' New World Order.

11. Wahhabism (from Muhammad ibn Abdul-Wahab, 1703–87) was a reformation move-ment in the Arabian Peninsula which opposed changes in Islam since the first century, especially certain Sufi practices.

12. The Muslim Brotherhood (*al-Ikhwan al-Muslimun*) was founded in 1928 by Hasan al-Banna, whose ideas were later developed by Sayed Qotb. The latter's *Social Justice in Islam* (1970) developed the programme of subsequent 'fundamentalism' (Haddad, 1983) from an eclectic mixture of European fascism (statist and antisemitic) and Wahhabism. However, Qotb's claim is essentially anti-traditional, in that, for him, usurpations and betrayals began a mere thirty years after the Prophet, and all the regimes from the Caliphs Omar and Uthman to the Umayyad and Abbasid dynasties were 'non-Muslim'.

13. Based in impoverished urban areas, the *Front islamique du salut* emerged from the 1992 elections as the largest party, having already taken control of 55 per cent of 1500 local councils, and 66 per cent of the 48 regions in 1990. The FLN Government declared a state of emergency which nullified the elections.

14. Actually, Zubaida argues that after early Shi'ah rebellions it became largely quiescent,

so 'The [subsequent] history of orthodox Shi'ism . . . does not lend support to the claim that it challenges the legitimacy of the government' (1989: 29).

15. It could also be argued, as does Ferenc Feher, (1986) that Romantic anti-modernism (often linked with antisemitism) 'is fundamentally modern' in that the idea of the 'authentic man rescued from industrialization' is a construct of modern intellectuals. See also Chapter 1 above.

16. Further, Shariati's anti-feminism rather tarnishes his image amongst commentators like Zubaida, Turner or Abrahamian as a representative of 'progressive' political Islam. Islamic women, he wrote, should aspire to the image of Fatima (daughter of the Prophet who raised the Imam Husayn, the Shi'ah martyr and revolutionary hero), who combined the feminine virtues of 'modesty, education, courage, and patience' (Nashat, 1980).

17. Shariati, for example, re-interpreted the Qur'anic *al-nas* ('The People', as a collectivity, of 'the righteous' or of 'evildoers') to read 'the people' in the modern sense of popular sovereignty. Likewise, the Imam becomes a charismatic leader in the Weberian sense.

18. Established by Aqa Muhammad Khan Qajar in 1797 after seventy years of civil war which replaced the Safavid dynasty.

19. The *bazaari* were not homogeneous, including wholesalers, retailers, pedlars, craftsmen, porters, but were bound by collective identity and social networks (Zubaida, 1989: 74).

20. Imports of textiles, hardwares, glass, sugar, tea and spices increased in value between 1830 to 1900 from £2 million to £5 million, whilst the value of Iranian exports (wheat, rice, tobacco and carpets) increased from £2 million to £3.8 million.

21. This sold control of the tobacco industry to a British merchant, generating considerable local protest. Encouraged by a *fatwa* (religious opinion) prohibiting the use of tobacco, strikes in the growing region of Shiraz spread to a general Persian bazaar strike, which ended in the treaty's abolition.

22. The pattern for this had already been established from the end of the eighteenth century, when an initially theological dispute between orthodox jurisprudents (*fuqaha*) and mystics (*urafa*) became politicized as each side began to appeal to the masses (Bayat-Philipp, 1981).

23. In Egypt, his disciple Muhammad Abduh (1849–1905) and the Syrian Rashid Rida (1865–1935) founded the Salfiyyah movement to re-create classical doctrines, with the intention of effecting Islamic political, legal and intellectual reform. At the same time Qasim Amin's *The Liberation of Women* (1899) supported education for women, reform of divorce law, women's employment, and insisted on women's equal intellect (Hoffman-Ladd, 1987).

24. For example, al-Afghani argued that 'wherever it became established, this religion [Islam] tried to stifle science. . . . Religions, whatever names they are given, all resemble one another . . . [and] impose on man its faith and its belief, whereas philosophy frees him of it totally' Quoted by Keddie (1972: 193).

25. Such as the Patriotic Women's Society, which campaigned for laws to protect women, held literacy classes, published a journal and put on plays to raise public consciousness. The Society was suppressed and its offices burned with the contrivance of the police in 1927 (Abrahamian, 1982: 139).

26. Amidst waves of strikes, nationalist activism, and counter-mobilization amongst conservatives, the National Front Government attempted to nationalize the British-owned Anglo-Iranian Oil Company, provoking Anglo-American sanctions. Leading ulama like Ayatollahs Behbahani and Burujirdi hesitantly supported Mossadeq, but withdrew their endorsement when he moved closer to *Tudah*, which itself subsequently withdrew support and left the government vulnerable to the CIA-initiated coup which returned the Shah in 1953 (Abrahamian, 1982: 280; Hiro, 1989: 156).

27. Such as demonstrations on the Day of Sacrifice, flagellation in Muharram, or the 1928 Uniformity of Dress Law which proscribed the veil for women, and banned traditional dress for men (Abrahamian, 1982: 141; Fischer, 1980b: 40).

28. This could be precarious. Abdel-Malek (1968) points to the weak ideological formulations of the Egyptian officers after the 1952 coup, for whom national integration was to be based on a rudimentary ideology of unity, order, and work combined with an appeal to Islam

as the ideology of Third World revolution (which failed to satisfy *al-Ikhwan* (Muslim Brotherhood, see n.12, above), for whom it was still too secular). Similarly, the Algerian National Liberation Front's state bureaucratic socialism was hostile to independent religious organizations like the Islamic Superior Council, whilst courting them when necessary (Vatin, 1981).

29. Although GDP grew by 8 per cent between 1962 and 1970, 14 per cent between 1972 and 1973 and 30 per cent between 1973 and 1974, military expenditure took 32 per cent of the state budget, rising from $210,000 in 1963 to $543,000 in 1977.

30. In agriculture, the White Revolution was to extend cultivation through new irrigation schemes, deploy more efficient productive techniques and reduce agricultural unemployment (Keddie, 1980: 187). It was further to introduce profit-sharing, women's suffrage and mass literacy.

31. Keddie, however, questions whether the political effect of land reform was uniform, arguing that in addition to landless labourers it created 'a relatively satisfied class with a greater stake than ever before in existing relations' (1980: 198).

32. The *Iran Almanac, 1975*, likewise reports a rise in religious observance (measured by attendance at shrines) by a factor of nearly 130 between 1964 and 1974.

33. The Shah's secret police, who, along with the military, and again not unlike the security forces in Eastern Europe, were by the later 1970s amongst the few groups still loyal. SAVAK had used torture and assassination widely since the demonstrations against the White Revolution in the 1960s.

34. Only a few key details of the events of 1978–9 will be given here. A full chronology is provided by Nikazmerad (1980).

35. The Catholic Church in Poland found itself in a similar position in the 1970s, which meant that much of the rhetoric of Solidarity was expressed in a religious vocabulary. It was noted in Chapter 6 that there is now a struggle underway in Poland between traditionalizing religious movements and modernists although, unlike post-revolutionary Iran, this is still conducted within a formal-rational legal framework.

36. After Burujirdi's death in 1960, Ayatollah Khomeini became more prominent, but it was rumoured that Burujirdi had said 'Do not follow Ruhallah [Khomeini], lest you find yourselves knee-deep in blood' (Fischer, 1983). Some leading clerics, such as Ayatollah Shari'atmadari, who was placed under house arrest after the 1978 Revolution, continued to side with intellectual and liberal ideas against the traditionalists, defending the secular state and warning against 'religious despotism'.

37. In the Jacobin Terror, Robespierre and Montangne fused the resentment of the *sans-culottes* against price rises with bureaucratic impulses and used the Terror for their own purposes, as a weapon against popular forces (Moore, 1969: 101).

38. According to Sohrab Behdad (1989), however, 'with the normalization process which started in 1981, the redistributive trend was reversed'. Land redistribution, some of which occurred spontaneously during the revolution, was halted, as were expropriations of productive property, and wage differentials increased.

8

State, 'Race' and Regulation

In the previous three chapters, Habermasian theory has been used as a base from which to construct a theory of regulation, social crisis and social movement impact – a dimension largely absent from his theory. It has been suggested that realignment of the world order, combined with economic globalization, has weakened the resource bases of authoritarian states, whilst increasing the potential for internal conflict and social movement formation. Underlying this process is the general theory of communicative action, which claims that communicative socialization cannot be converted into steering media, and attempts to do so result in pathologies and resistance. Therefore, repressive forms of modernization will, first, require mechanisms of crisis displacement to offset these consequences, and, secondly eventually encounter the 'crisis of crisis management' noted in the last two chapters. The reason for this is that the over-extension of power creates levels of complexity which eventually become self-defeating. However, it is also clear from the foregoing discussion that the outcomes of these crises are unpredictable. On the one hand, they hold out the possibility for more pluralistic, democratic and rational institutional arrangements; on the other hand, core elements of the former system might regroup, so to speak, within an adjusted mode of regulation which provides for an increased range of variation. The latter is possible in part because social movement identities are structured by the contradictory effects of lifeworld colonization, which creates sites of resistance and proto-organizational forms but also preserves traditionalistic orientations and repressive dependence. The latter outcome is more probable where mechanisms of crisis displacement create social sites which have absorbed systemic contradictions and transmit pathological socialization which inhibits the formation of new public spheres. This thesis will be developed now with reference to the evolution and crisis of apartheid.

The regulatory model that this chapter develops is outlined in Figure 8.1. It is argued that apartheid was a system of 'labour repressive' regulation[1] which developed in response to the peripheral position of Afrikaner capital and farmers in the global economy; their weak competitive position *vis-à-vis* English capital; and consequent efforts to guarantee a supply of 'cheap' labour.[2] The latter was maintained through socio-spatial differentiation, the expropriation of land, a tight linkage between space and racial categories and a mechanism of crisis displacement. The core of the system, White South Africa, had an interventionist state and corporatist

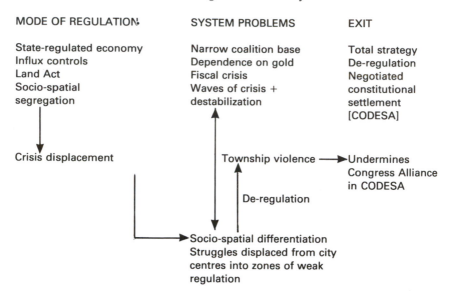

MODE OF REGULATION	SYSTEM PROBLEMS	EXIT

Figure 8.1 *Systemic crisis of apartheid*

integration of Afrikaner capital and labour – a class coalition which guaranteed uninterrupted rule of the National Party (NP) from 1948 onwards. However, from the outset, this was a weak coalition which confronted waves of mass resistance, to which it responded with repression, combined with adjustments in crisis displacement strategies. The latter, however, engendered a worsening fiscal crisis of the state and constituted new sites of struggle, especially in the townships where apartheid had created multiple layers of labour segmentation and local patronage.

However, more geared to primitive accumulation than to a complex division of labour, apartheid structures became self-defeating, and under De Klerk a new core coalition of the NP with South African capital initiated a tactical retreat from politicized regulation. As it is presently unfolding, this new settlement involves dismantling corporatist structures and replacing apartheid with market mechanisms which, unless attenuated, will consolidate the acute inequalities which arose under apartheid. However, this tactical retreat requires an agreement between the NP and major opposition movements, especially the ANC, which the CODESA[3] talks were designed to achieve. This transition is threatened, however, by violence arising from the very process of de-regulation which is necessary for a new settlement. Having displaced structural violence into the spatial territory of the townships, de-regulation releases the 'third force' (criminal gangs, local police, South African security forces, Inkatha and neo-fascist commandos) which threatens to undermine negotiations at a national level, whilst defining the nature of the post-apartheid state. This chapter first outlines the South African étatist model of regulation; then examines the formation of struggle and its relationship with crisis displacement; and finally examines the forces at work in the contemporary situation and prospects for the future.

Regulation and Dependent Development

Until the Second World War, South Africa's position in the world economy as a whole was essentially peripheral. It conformed to the classical pattern of a colonial economy, exporting raw materials, most importantly gold,[4] and importing consumer goods. Its manufacturing sector (which developed rapidly after 1948) was uncompetitive in global terms, remained dependent on gold exports to cover oil imports, and required high capital investment to output ratios (Milkman, 1979). The racially segregated labour market and state-managed capitalist development that occurred during the second half of the twentieth century fulfilled dual trajectories of protecting Afrikaner capital and labour against British capital (especially in mining[5]) whilst subduing organized African and Indian labour.[6] The basis of an étatist system had been established under the National–Labour Pact Government (1924–33), which, despite opposition from British capital, had politicized market relations through protectionist policies and created African labour reserve areas, the nucleus of later 'homelands', which reduced labour costs. To protect (largely Afrikaner) industries the Pact Government set up parastatal corporations and a system of state-regulated national bargaining through the Wage Act. A state-funded Land Bank supplied credit for rural capital, and the Agricultural Marketing Act (1937) created a single-channel marketing system in which central boards determined prices.

Most important, however, were the 1913 and 1926 Land Acts which began a process of massive land expropriation, creating landless African labour for European farms, mining and the local manufacturing sector. Thirteen per cent of total land was allocated to Africans, who constituted 70 per cent of the population, and on the remaining 87 per cent, designated 'White', Africans could neither own nor rent land, a policy that destroyed a class of African tenant farmers, who were converted into landless labourers. Lacking land to mortgage, those who remained could not borrow, the effect of which both increased the supply and lowered the costs of labour.[7] White South African agriculture subsequently produced 95 per cent of agricultural output, the remaining 5 per cent being produced by small-holdings and grazing cattle on communal land. This is illustrated by Lesotho, which early in the twentieth century had been the 'granary of the Orange Free State', but by mid-century had been converted into rural slums exporting labour and importing food (Lipton, 1986: 104).

This forcible uncoupling of system from lifeworld is characteristic of an early stage of capitalist development and becomes untenable as social movements institutionalize more plural forms of regulation, and as the system itself demands more scope for variation. However, in response to South Africa's peripheral status, combined with the relative weakness of Afrikaner capital and mounting class conflict, the NP attempted to freeze further development by encasing primitive accumulation within a comprehensive system of state-regulated capitalism after 1948.[8] This created what is sometimes called 'colonialism of a special type', with a European core region displaying features of an advanced capitalist society (although the local bourgeoisie was dependent on intimate links with the state) and a colonial 'non-white' periphery (Stadler, 1987: 22). As in other peripheral regions discussed above, state-dependent development absorbed risks of capital investment through a combination of state and foreign capital in a complex system of parastatals, such as the Industrial Finance Corporation, the Development Corporation (which facilitated mergers and economic rationalization), Afrikaner finance houses, or the Iron and Steel Corporation, through which the state owned 27 per cent of the assets of the top 138 companies.[9] Thus the institutions of apartheid (the Group Areas Act, Population Registration Act) were part of an extensive system of étatist regulation, reinforced by repression of opposition both within and outside the core, which guaranteed rule of the Nationalists effectively as a one party-state.[10] Further, through the Immorality Act, Mixed Marriages Act and tightening of the pass laws, the state effected an exceptional degree of juridification of the lifeworld, reflected in so-called 'petty apartheid' (segregated public areas, transport, park seats, toilets, etc.), as a system of institutionalized humiliation and state violence entered the deepest levels of the socio-cultural sphere.

The regulation of space through bureaucratic-racial categories was to be central to the dynamic, and later the crisis, of apartheid. Regulation of the labour supply was facilitated in racist controls such as the Pass Laws, the Group Areas Act and 'influx control', which were central pillars in the operation of apartheid. Control of migration was expressed in the doctrine that, as 'temporary sojourners', the African population was 'only temporarily resident in European areas . . . for as long as they offer their labour there in the labour market', after which time, it is expected that they will 'return to their . . . territory . . . where they fit in ethnically, even if they were not born or bred . . . ' there.[11] The doctrine further meant that townships were desolate wastelands, lacking shops, phones, entertainment or electricity. Influx and efflux control was designed to channel labour from the reserves into three streams: to white farms, mines and towns, and even if the system operated imperfectly, in the sense that the *verswarting* (blackening) of White spaces was never ultimately prevented, it none the less created a highly fragmented and rigid labour market (Lipton, 1986: 92). This resulted in often violent struggles over the occupation and control of space. For example, periodic resettlement, such as the destruction of Crossroads, has involved the violent eviction of whole townships declared 'illegal', and between 1960 and 1983 resulted in the forced removal of 3.5 million people, the largest in any country since the mass deportations under Hitler or Stalin (Cobbett & Nakedi, 1987; Smith, 1990: 48). The long-term consequence of this was to inscribe violent exchanges within the communicative structures of the lifeworld such that it became the 'normal' channel for resolving conflicts (Morris & Hindson, 1992).[12]

Like the systems of bureaucratic regulation discussed in Chapters 6 and 7, apartheid adapted to its environment with increasingly complex mechanisms of crisis management. Stadler (1987) argues that the South African state has vacillated between two models of control: Stallardism, allowing Africans to reside in urban areas so long as they were economically functional to Whites, and Godleyism, allowing Africans to enter towns subject only to registration.[13] Whereas Stallard sought to homogenize the African labour force and dampened the tendency towards stabilization, Godleyism permitted stabilization. Much of the resilience of the South African state, Stadler suggests, has been in its capacity to shift between the two forms of urban labour control, and hence the last decade or so has seen a shift in emphasis away from direct physical control over Black movement to control over housing, prompted by two political effects of Stallardism. First, by homogenizing the African urban population, subject to anomie, overcrowding and extreme exploitation, it allowed the ANC to develop on the basis of an alliance of classes; and, secondly, the de facto growth of an African urban population (in 'townships'), combined with the limited financial base of White municipalities, meant that local authorities had to increase charges for services, which were met with African rebellion. The upshot was wide-ranging reform of local government and revision of the influx controls (Stadler, 1987), the implications of which are discussed in the following section.

At the heart of the system was the socio-spatial differentiation of power which displaced struggles away from the core into more vulnerable zones in peripheries where land allocation and control was weak. Thus conflicts over marginal resources took place in the townships and Black residential areas, amidst chronic and violent confrontations. The basic model for this regulatory system was Verwoerdian apartheid instituted through the Bantu 'homelands' (Bantustans) in the Surplus Peoples Project. The 1959 Promotion of Bantu Self-Government Act defined ten 'nations',[14] four of which were later to become 'independent': Transkei, Bophuthatswana, Venda and Ciskei (TBVC). The coercion of 'surplus labour' into the 'homelands' was intended to diffuse Black political power, and reduce pressure on wages by displacing the reproduction costs of labour on to the homelands which would bear responsibility for housing, education and domestic work. Within these peripheral structures rule was devolved to local parties (such as Inkatha in KwaZulu) which engineered consent through patronage, corruption and coercion. Membership of the local ruling party was the quickest and safest way of acquiring housing, land, business rights, jobs, pensions and disability grants (Taylor, 1990). These were not nations in any sense of lived collective identities transmitted through lifeworlds, but 'imagined communities' (Adam, 1990) whose histories had been invented to sustain the apartheid ideologies (Marks & Trapido, 1990: 53). None the less once established they took on a material reality which was to be important for future developments. Thus the 'creation of independent homelands has succeeded in a far-reaching political-legal respect unrecognized by the left . . . by creating new citizenships, the white polity has disempowered any moral obligations towards these blacks' (Adam, 1984).

The thesis is therefore that crisis management relies on an over-extension of bureaucratic-repressive power into the lifeworld, but this is self-defeating because it serves to generate new loci of resistance. Further, modes of regulation appropriate for primitive accumulation might be unable to sustain complex social relations which erode ascriptive forms of status stratification (such as race) which are replaced by the encoding of inequalities into anonymous regulation via the market. Lipton, (1986) for example, argues that capitalist farmers and mine managers preferred 'stabilization', that is, permanent settlement of labourers, to migration from townships. More generally, she argues that capitalists have never been unanimously in favour of apartheid, and that the trend is now towards increasing opposition, because the balance of interest of capital since the 1960s has favoured abolition. This is because the early benefit for capital was the supply of cheap, unskilled African labour, but with the shift in the structure of capital from dependence on mining and agriculture, to greater dependence on manufacturing and services, the need for unskilled labour has diminished, whilst apartheid has become an obstacle to the creation of a mobile, competitive labour market (Lipton, 1986: 6–7).[15] This created an internal contradiction between capital and the state, which through the NP had created an apartheid-bureaucracy, resistant to reform. In addition there was pressure from international capital (the flight of finance capital in 1985), sanctions and boycotts that were affecting markets, especially for South African agricultural goods.[16]

However, it was seen in the discussion of Islamic neo-revivalism that a crucial question for Critical Theory is under what conditions resistance is mobilized and whether particularistic identities (based, for example, in consciousness of ethnic oppression) can hold together broader social movement coalitions. One way of approaching this is to examine the effects on social movement formation of regulatory strategies themselves. The two mechanisms of regulation referred to above, stabilization and patronage, were to have unintended consequences, especially when the core state attempted to offset fiscal problems by devolving financial responsibility to township councils. By the mid-1970s, lack of coherence and effective control were becoming evident, despite two decades of state repression. The suppression of African trade unions and the massive application of pass and influx control laws required further layers of control, as rising labour surpluses in the Bantustans threatened to overrun the regulatory institutions. The African working class, which had been given no institutionalized normative basis for participation, began to resist as strikes spread across the major industrial centres (with 60,000 Black workers on strike in 1973) and urban revolts swept the townships, attacking state institutions like police stations, schools and pass offices. Let us look at these crisis tendencies in more detail.

Impact of Regulation on Social Movements

This section first develops the model outlined above to indicate how the intrusion of regulatory systems into the lifeworld generates struggle around the socio-spatial sites on to which crises are displaced. It then raises two issues central to a Critical Theory of social movements, which were signalled in Chapter 4. First, how might these fragmented and often particularistic conflicts be articulated in emancipatory forms; and secondly, what are the appropriate terms of engagement of key SMOs with broader popular movements and constituencies (which will be illustrated with reference to current debates over the role and organization of the ANC)?

Colonization and Fragmentation

Crisis management involves the over-extension of steering systems into the lifeworld, which creates new sites of resistance, necessitating renewed strategic regulation, since it has been seen already that disengagement from social processes within which the state has become bureaucratically embedded will sooner or later require an extension of intervention elsewhere. Thus the township uprisings in the 1970s and 1980s developed new forms of struggle in social sites newly politicized by mechanisms of crisis displacement. The context for these was provided by the increasing complexity of the economy and segmentation of the Black labour force which placed strains on the classical model of apartheid. The political stability which had been imposed by state repression in the 1960s laid the basis for large-scale (especially foreign) investment in manufacturing. This was capital intensive growth which both repelled labour into the pool of unemployed and attracted labour into expanding economic sectors (where there was an additional labour shortage as a result of the tendency of White workers to move into the tertiary sector). The greatly increased numbers of Black unemployed were banished to the Bantustans, whilst the numbers of skilled and semi-skilled Black workers recruited into industry increased, with three consequences. First, this development presupposed an expansion in Black education, and by the beginning of the 1970s the numbers of Black students had risen to 2.72 million (from 0.75 million in 1953) and by 1976 to 3.75 million (Wolpe, 1988: 72). Secondly, given the shortage of skilled personnel, capital[17] was more interested in labour stabilization than in the maintenance of influx control (which was geared to the supply of cheap labour). Thirdly, it was noted above that labour repression was proving ineffective in preventing strikes, partly because skilled and semi-skilled workers were less easily replaceable, which prompted moves towards legal recognition of (limited) Black trade union rights.[18] However, with the international recession, the falling price of gold and consequent balance of payments problems, the state's resource-base diminished such that the restructuring of apartheid provided the context for administratively driven legitimation crises.

The expansion of Black education created a new site of resistance and mobilization through which the Black Consciousness Movement (BCM) was able to fill the organizational vacuum created by the banning of the ANC (and Pan Africanist Congress[19]) in 1963. Based largely amongst students and focusing on identity politics, BCM had a weak organizational structure but none the less acted as an important catalyst, offering collective identity to a new generation of leaders (Gwala, 1988; Hyslop, 1988).[20] BCM activists, like Steve Biko, came from the first generation of Black students to have been educated in segregated universities (Gwala, 1988), which, although under Afrikaner control, unintentionally produced radical student politics (Nkomo, 1981). Black universities created both grievances (for example, under-resourcing, bureaucratic control, poor staff–student relations) and the social infrastructures through which opposition could mobilize. Hyslop writes of the appearance of a new 'generation . . . at a cultural level . . . the growth of a distinctively urban youth culture . . . [which] began to differentiate out from the . . . rather lumpen, sub-culture of the mapantsula' (1988: 184). In 1969, the South African Students' Organization (SASO) was formed as part of the Black Consciousness Movement, which emphasized consciousness-raising and overcoming subservient psychology and insisted on the autonomy of Black activism from White liberals. Breaking with the ANC's strategy of building broad alliances with the White liberal-Left, BCM and SASO articulated urban frustration and deprivation, especially of the students, at a time when nearly half the population was under 21, and there had been an expansion in educational access (Hyslop, 1988: 186).

Black Consciousness mobilized grass-roots revolt in the townships which represented a new type of resistance from earlier mass defiance or worker-based strategies, since it was concentrated in the schools and universities, where SASO and BCM had made headway. The Soweto revolt (1976), although in part a response to international events,[21] was largely a reaction to state intrusion into education (Wolpe, 1988: 72). First, the arrival of free textbooks in Black schools in 1974 was accompanied by an order to make Afrikaans the language of instruction in state schools. This was met by a boycott of lessons in Afrikaans, the organization of which was facilitated by recent grass-roots democratization in Soweto schools. Secondly, in 1974, Pik Botha had announced the Government's intention to assign all Africans 'national' status in supposedly independent Bantustans, like Transkei, which would render them 'guest workers' in all urban areas. One effect of this was the introduction of a 'pink card' system in 1974, to ensure that only children living 'legally' in urban areas could qualify for places in city schools. When 60,000 out of 111,000 children reporting for enrolment in Soweto were declared 'illegal', mass protest was met by police violence, which in turn created conditions for mass revolt (Holland, 1989: 192–6).

This period saw further political mobilization of the townships consequent on the upgrading of Community Councils to local authorities (in the 1980 Local Government Act). In response to the fiscal crisis of the central state, the new system devolved financial responsibility to newly created local councils, which it was further hoped would defuse discontent (Seekings, 1988). The new structures replaced a system of limited patronage, which had had some local legitimacy, since Community Councils were regarded as arbiters in local disputes who could 'circumvent White authority and preserve an autonomous space in the township' (Seekings, 1988).[22] However, the weakening of influx controls and the adoption of the principle of stabilization rather than residential impermanence resulted in passing control over the allocation of housing, business sites, students' bursaries, and other council funds to the Local Authorities, whilst withdrawing housing subsidies from Pretoria.

The new Local Authorities were not regarded as legitimate, and the old system of clientelism was replaced by commercial patronage, extensive bribes and increasing social distance between councils and residents (that is, an uncoupling of the local state from the lifeworld). Moreover, the new councils were unable to absorb the tension arising from political and financial contradictions. Relaxation of influx controls increased the numbers of shacks (which in Katelhong rose 3000 to 44,000 between 1979 and 1983) which the local authority attempted to evict, resulting in battles with police, and in 1984 7000 troops occupied Vaal townships (Seekings, 1988). Further, attempts to resolve the fiscal crisis of apartheid by raising rents (sometimes by over 50 per cent) interacted with economic differentiation and rising grievances[23] – the average proportion of household income spent on rent in the Eastern Transvaal Development Board rose by 88 per cent (Chaskalson et al., 1987). Thus the restructuring of local government had the effect of focusing resistance against local councillors, in an at times extremely violent struggle, involving necklacing and house burning (Seekings, 1988).

Systemic intrusion of bureaucratic/racial structures into the lifeworld not only regulated the over-arching process of primitive accumulation but also constituted new sites of resistance. Rent boycotts, which on the Witwatersrand involved at least two-thirds of the township (Levin, 1987), occurred largely independently of the ANC, and the Civic Associations were proto-organizations of self-management, spearheading rent strikes, consumer boycotts, mass campaigns, occupying vacant land and establishing street committees. The state's inability to resolve township uprisings by means other than the states of emergency reflected a basic political contradiction of apartheid. To have reduced rents by subsidization, in many ways the obvious solution, would have, first, run counter to policies of fiscal stringency; secondly, violated the ideology of 'separate development', since 'White' revenues would have been paying for 'Black' housing;

and, thirdly, further delegitimized the local councils. The political terrain of struggle in the townships had provoked an administrative crisis which was insoluble within the prevailing mode of politicized regulation.

Workers' Struggle or New Social Movement?

It has been noted already that the relationship between sites of resistance and social movement organization is more complex than Habermasian theory suggests. The foregoing has indicated how multiple sites of resistance emerged along the frontline, as Habermas puts it, between system and lifeworld. However, the anti-apartheid movements have confronted organizational and normative dilemmas, especially over the priority of grass roots *vs* vanguard politics; orientations of 'workerism' *vs* pluralism; and, crucially, over their relationship to the state. The ways in which these dilemmas are resolved within the movement, as a proto-typical social organization, will structure the probability of emancipatory as opposed to regressive outcomes.

Many struggles were decentralized local initiatives, and although the ANC continued underground and in armed camps in the Frontline States, it had for a time lost direct control of resistance and was initially surprised by the fury of the Soweto uprising (Holland, 1989: 200). Pushed into a reactive stance, the ANC was obliged to acknowledge the extent to which autonomous grass-roots organization had created 'no-go areas' and popular democratic structures in the townships. In Soweto, for example, street committees enabled the rent boycotts in 1986 to spread widely after political meetings and other open channels of protest had been banned. Attempting to regain the initiative, the ANC announced its aim as that of building an alternative state from the ruins of state-created structures, and Oliver Tambo's 1985 pamphlet, *Render SA Ungovernable*, called for the transformation of 'these areas into mass revolutionary bases from which Umkhontho We Sizwe [the armed wing of the ANC] must grow as an army of the people'. This view was echoed by Murphy Morabe, Publicity Secretary of the United Democratic Front (UDF), who described the Civic Associations as 'the beginnings of the kind of democracy that we are striving for' (Morabe, 1988).

Initially, these initiatives were largely successful in re-establishing the leading role of the ANC, partly because it was the only opposition movement with an effective organization abroad, which provided sanctuary and training for refugees; partly too, however, because the Wiehahn Report and Riekert Commission increased the scope for trade union organization and hence for the formation of the Congress Alliance.[24] The rise of worker organizations was again the unintended effect of the reform of apartheid from the 1970s since Wiehahn and Riekert, which had intended to diffuse Black and Coloured workers' resistance, actually intensified demands for national liberation (Davies et al., 1984; Greenberg, 1990). By conceding the principle of statutory recognition of Black trade unions, the state reduced the employers' options to threaten police action in industrial disputes. The size of the industrial sector in South Africa, combined with racial segmentation of the labour market, meant that popular democratic struggle has also been a workers' struggle to a degree unparalleled elsewhere in Africa. Further, without the national organization and leadership capacities of the Congress Alliance (not least its ability to project the crisis in South Africa on to the world stage, especially through the 'Free Nelson Mandela' campaign), these localized conflicts might not have escalated into a major legitimation crisis.

However, the origins of the ANC in the milieu of early twentieth-century anti-colonial movements,[25] and its relationship with the South African Communist Party (SACP), have left an organizational legacy which some regard as inappropriate for engagement with broad social movement issues such as gender, ecology and marginalized groups. First, there is the SACP's commitment to a 'two-stage' theory of revolution, the first national-democratic, the second proletarian (a distinction which originated in the 1928 Sixth World Congress of the Comintern). However, after the demise of international communism, the étatist vocabulary of socialist revolution and command economy sounds anachronistic, something Saul (1988) puts down to the ANC leadership's long period of exile. More generally, this debate is in some ways a replaying of the controversy between Marxists and 'new' social movement theorists noted in Chapter 4, although where (in 1980) 69 per cent of the industrial working class was African (a further 13 per cent 'Coloured') and African workers' earnings represented 22.7 per cent of White wages, the notion of a worker-based struggle against apartheid was not implausible. Robert Fine, for example, identifies 'a definite interplay of class forces which, though hidden beneath the surface of political life, are its real social determinants' (1989). However, this is qualified slightly, since the 'great majority of black people appear united by a singular political consciousness *whatever social differences divide them*' (1989; emphasis added). Wolpe argues that whilst there is an African 'middle strata', of proprietors, professionals and managers, 'the subordinate position of black groups is reproduced within each stratum' (1988: 31). However, Cobbett and Cohen find fragmentation within the opposition, class differences and violent conflict between Black groups, which means not only that there is no homogeneous Black nation, but also that the SACP's internal colonialism and two-stage thesis 'tends towards workerism' (Cobbett & Cohen, 1988: 14–16).

Further, anxieties have been voiced by Saul (1988, 1991), Glaser (1989), Adam (1990), Morris and Hindson (1992), and others, about the ANC's continuing commitment to 'vanguardist' politics – anxieties which were expressed in the liberal White press in relation to the trial of Winnie Mandela in 1991.[26] Glaser (1989) argues that the Congress tradition displays a 'lack of resolute commitment to political pluralism and civil liberties', resulting from its origin in 'radical anti-colonial nationalism and orthodox communism'. In response, Fitzgerald (1990) argues that 'the list of ANC activities orientated towards extending and deepening the limits of civil society during the 1980s is lengthy', including dialogue within the churches, community art projects, theatre, establishing women's organizations, a non-racial sports culture, as well as links with White opposition movements such as war resisters, or Jews for Justice. These strategies in turn tap democratic cultural reserves, such as kgotla gatherings, Gandhian satyagraha (civil disobedience) ideas, and struggles against the National Party's repression of civil society in the White core.

This debate directly addresses the western new social movements literature, with Shivji, (1989: 89) for example, citing trade unions, women's, students' and youth organizations and intellectuals as potential emancipatory agencies organized around human rights struggles. Similar views are expressed by Clark (1991) Anyang' Nyong'o (1988) and in Bjorn Beckman's (1989) review of debates on the Nigerian Left. Again, Freyhold notes amongst the African and western new social movements a 'similar concern with democracy, self-organization and the right of people to protect their environment, livelihoods and their cultures in a struggle between state and society', which is attributable to the way 'capitalism is creating a global predicament which provokes similar answers' (1987). Cobbett and Cohen conclude, in relation to South Africa, that the 'slanging match between "workerists" and "populists" can now usefully be superseded' as women's, labour, community, educational and rural struggles coalesce. The Defiance Campaign of the 1950s, Civic Associations, the loose UDF coalition, the National Union of Mineworkers, all indicate 'claims to future involvement and incubators for the practice of democracy in the work-place, home and school' (Cobbett & Cohen, 1988: 16–17).

From one point of view, then, the ANC illustrates how an emancipatory social movement might combine features of classical offensive politics with the new politics of identity and fluidity. However, it was noted above that the impact of such a movement will depend upon its ability to mobilize social resources and infrastructures that permit the articulation of plural politics in a context of equality of speech acts. Moreover, there is a discrepancy between the discursive practices of the leaderships and highly fragmented potentials for organization and mobilization arising from the deep colonization of South African society. The Congress of South African Trade Unions (COSATU) was formed in 1985, and although by 1986 20 per cent of Black labour was unionized, especially in the industrial and mining sectors (for example, the Metal and Allied Workers and National Union of Miners), the township unemployed youth remained largely alienated from the unions (Webster, 1987). This suggests a potential for division between urban squatters, rural dwellers and farm workers and a labour aristocracy (Saul, 1991). However, COSATU has attempted to broaden its work-place activity to develop 'social movement trade unionism', leading campaigns to build a living wage, organizing amongst the unemployed, gaining representation on street committees in townships, supporting students' struggles for democratic control over schools, and campaigning for maternity rights, equal pay for women, childcare facilities, and against sexual harassment.[27] Likewise, the ANC (1991) statement on 'The Emancipation of Women in South Africa' claimed that: 'The prevalence of patriarchal attitudes in South African society permeates our own organizations, especially at decision-making levels, and the lack of a strong mass women's organization has been to the detriment of our struggle.'[28] Even so, at the 1991 conference a resolution from the ANC Women's League demanding a 30 per cent quota for women on all decision-making bodies had to be withdrawn for lack of support. Elaine Unterhalter (1990) points out that despite systematic racial and gender discrimination against Black women students and teachers in South African education, and despite grass-roots demands for an end to sexual abuse of female pupils, movements like People's Education have not given priority to the gender dimension of educational discrimination.

The mode of engagement of emancipatory movements like the Congress Alliance with under-represented constituencies cannot be solved through resolutions (though clearly they provide a focus for further activism). Likewise, Leninist language of working class hegemony through popular fronts, or historical narratives of inexorable stages of struggle, hardly conform with a reality where apartheid has created lifeworlds and conflicts fragmented in terms of space (townships, work-places, urban/rural); intersecting subjectivities (workers in racially segmented labour markets, youth, the unemployed, tenants, and division according to gender and ethnicity); and objects of struggle (national/local state, police, employers). Whether the Congress Alliance is able to construct a sufficiently broad coalition of emancipatory forces to secure a transition to pluralist and socialist multi-racialism, will, in the short term at least, be closely linked with the outcome of constitutional negotiations, on the one hand, and containment of civil war in the Natal, on the other. The impact of emancipatory social movements like ANC/COSATU, then, will depend partly upon outcomes of the regulatory crisis, in that these will structure their ability to mobilize resources on the ground (in townships, schools, work-places, etc.) and this in turn will condition their influence in the constitutional negotiations.

Tactical Retreat and De-regulation

Let us examine this process in more detail. It has been seen that apartheid underwent restructuring during the 1970s – such as modifying influx control, accepting permanent urban African communities, registration of African trade unions – none of which had resolved the crises. Moreover, the aim of these reforms was to protect not undermine the social structures that had formed in the apartheid system. The relaxation of economic apartheid did not ameliorate exploitation, despite a slightly declining trend in income differentials between White and Black workers.[29] By the late 1970s, mechanization had made a local reserve labour supply unnecessary, and farmers wanted large communities removed – which increased the forced population movements, along with attempts to create internally independent homelands, which themselves became sites of intense conflict. Similarly, the abolition of the Pass Laws actually meant an increase in violent evictions of 'illegal' communities, such as that of Thaba'Nchu (Orange Free State) in 1986 in order to create the township of Onverwacht, now renamed Botshabelo.[30] Increasing mechanization was reducing the demand for casual labour, which might suggest that the township exemplified the stabilization of the labour market. It constitutes an extremely large pool of labour, and workers are bussed each day to three employment centres. Moreover, Botshabelo provides an area for investment itself and the state offers investors relocation expenses of up to R.600,000; subsidized capital loans; the cheapest electricity in the country; and 95 per cent of the wage-bill tax free, up to R.100,000 per head per month for seven years (Cobbett & Nakedi, 1987).

However, this limited adjustment had begun to erode the Afrikaner coalition in the core region. Traditionally, acceptance of apartheid had been confined largely to the exclusively White, predominantly Afrikaans, supporters of the NP. However, the escalation of Black militancy during the 1970s had exposed the costs of a narrow base of popular support and initiated amongst the NP leadership a 'search for legitimacy' (Adam, 1984; Posel, 1990). The 'Total Strategy' in the 1970s attempted to achieve three goals: to reduce the scope of state economic management to offset fiscal crisis; to broaden the basis of participation both within the White core and amongst African, Indian and Coloured communities; and to manage the disintegrative effects that this would have on the Afrikaner coalition. The Total Strategy thus involved the deconstruction of former support-bases along with the construction of alliances. However, the ideological framework of Verwoerdian apartheid had appealed to the God-given right of Whites to 'national self-determination', and offered no normative framework within which reforms could proceed without an open renunciation of the past and the de-legitimating consequences that would follow. Within the Afrikaner coalition and state bureaucracy, limited reforms such as the relaxation of influx controls were already meeting with resistance, as the NP fragmented at its ultra-Right periphery, first with Andries Treurnicht's Conservative Party and then Terreblanche's neo-Nazi AWB, both of whom accused the NP of betraying the integrity of the *volk* (Posel, 1990). The architects of Total Strategy, like Wiehahn and Riekert, attempted to avoid political controversy by recommending reform in politically neutral technocratic language.[31] However, the Total Strategy exacerbated rather than diffused conflict in townships, for reasons outlined above, and the state relied increasingly on the military to hold the system together. The failure of structural violence alone as a means of social co-ordination prompted a search within the core coalition for new bases of legitimation.

During the 1980s the Afrikaanse Handelsinstituut Incorporation (AHI) advocated wide-ranging political and economic restructuring, which would replace bureaucratic/racial controls with de-politicized market mechanisms. At the political level the AHI advocated 'consociationalism' with proportional ethnic votes,[32] and attacked public corporations, particularly the Industrial Development Corporation and the Iron and Steel Corporation, as a 'slow subversion of the free enterprise system on which South Africa's growth and prosperity is based'. This new emergent entrepreneurial and professional strata amongst the Afrikaner élite became increasingly dominant amongst the Nationalist leadership which from the early 1980s aligned itself (against the statist pull of party tradition) with free-market supply-side liberalism and privatization. The Bureau for Economic Policy and Analysis (University of Pretoria 1980) claimed that 'failure of socioeconomic growth in the territories of the Black national states . . . is becoming embarrassing . . . separate development is a sinking philosophy'. Again,

> Until fairly recently it was government policy that all Black communities outside the self-governing territories and the TBVC states should satisfy their political aspirations . . . through the institutions of the various territories. . . . By the early 1980s it was clear that the time had come for a reappraisal of the policies in relation to the Blacks . . . especially the urbanized communities. (Republic of South Africa, 1989: 189)

This agenda for a tactical retreat from over-extended and crisis-prone structures made faltering beginnings with P. W. Botha, to be developed under De Klerk. Politics had become an 'explosive trap', and as an anonymous Pretoria economist argued, it is 'of crucial importance for constitutional reform that no major decisions about welfare matters, such as income re-distribution, development assistance, education, health, housing and the like, are taken by the central authority' (quoted by Greenberg, 1990: 394). Politics was an explosive trap because juridification of the lifeworld rendered the exercise of oppressive economic and social power visible, and crisis tendencies entered the administrative sphere in the form of strategic failures (like the Local Authorities fiasco) and legitimation crises (fragile coalition bases falling apart in every direction).

Meanwhile, South Africa's place in the global system is still a source of destabilization. South Africa is more dependent today than before on primary goods exports, and faces falling terms of trade and rising debt, whilst competing with newly developed regions (notably the Pacific Rim) which produce more technologically sophisticated products (Martin, 1991). Thus central to what Saul (1991) describes as the crisis of 'racial Fordism' was not redistribution of consumption so much as redistribution of investment in productive capacity that would have to be increased by drawing funds out of financial markets. This presupposes selective state intervention, and generating new motors of growth such as intensive/employment-producing light industries, township housing, services and infrastructure. This would require the stabilization of new steering media, a mixed economy (which is entering ANC discourse as an alternative to mass nationalization and command economy) and the anchoring of democratic political authority in the socio-cultural system. Only in this way could new learning potentials be released and institutionalized in structures of the lifeworld.

However, at present this is not what is on the agenda. Parastatals, like the Suid Afrikaanse Steenkool Olie en Gaskorporasie (Coal, Oil and Gas Corporation, SASOL), or the Iron and Steel Corporation, are being privatized (the ISCOR flotation alone earning $1.1 billion in 1989). This divestiture is in part a defensive strategy to limit the damage a potential ANC government might do to Afrikaner property, especially since the NP's 'Bottom Line Constitutional Proposals' would write guarantees of marketization and monetarism into the Constitution. This tactical retreat would diminish the direct and visible role of the state in the labour market and work-place, and shift regulation and co-ordination functions to the market, without challenging the systemic identity of the existing mode of domination. This is illustrated by the issue of land compensation. The abolition of the Land Act and Group Areas Act in 1991 has left unresolved the crucial issue of whether Africans (who can now own land in previously 'White' areas) will receive compensation for their dispossession under apartheid. If, as seems likely, they do not, the market, rather than the law, will sustain the spatial structures of oppression and inequality and 'spon-taneously reproduce racial inequalities' (Saul, 1991) by strengthening racial ownership of land. Five million people are without shelter and seven million are in squatter camps.

Indeed the whole process of constitutional negotiation is further threat-ened by the violent effects of de-regulation combined with the resistance of those within the core opposed to change. The de-sublimation of violence that was previously displaced into peripheral social locations has released the 'Third Force', a traditionalistic backlash from those with most to lose from restructuring, which is undermining national negotiations. It was noted above that the Botha reforms of the 1980s, followed by negotiations between De Klerk and the ANC in 1990–1, opened a split within the ruling oligarchy, which produced a defensive reaction amongst sections of the rural Afrikaner petite bourgeoisie in Transvaal, who have followed the Conservative Party or the AWB, both offering the romantic vision of a racially exclusive Boerestaat. The loss of NP hegemony amongst White South Africa has been expressed in the collusion between the apartheid police and bureaucracy with Inkatha attacks on the Congress Alliance in the Natal, where the Bantustan structure has permitted the mobilization of defensive social forces in a form of 'low-intensity conflict'.

Inkatha, the ruling political party in the KwaZulu Bantustan, operates a clientelistic network in which employment is dependent on membership (Mare, 1989). During intense conflict with the Congress Alliance between 1987 and 1992, at least 7000 died and 70,000 were rendered homeless. The underlying causes of the conflict are structural: labour-market segmen-tation (Inkatha supporters tend to be casual migrant labourers), and political competition between ANC and Inkatha supporters. Until 1980,

Inkatha was hegemonic in the Natal, as Chief Buthelezi worked with 'separate development' whilst incorporating the emancipatory rhetoric of ANC. After 1980, Inkatha came into conflict with the national youth, trade union and civic movements, especially as the UDF and COSATU-organized trade union campaigns, commuter and rent boycotts threatened the position of Inkatha Bantustan officials. As the struggle broadened to education, local government, transport, the township uprisings attacked the very services that Inkatha controlled in KwaZulu (Mare, 1989).[33] In response, Inkatha formed the United Workers' Union of South Africa (which supports a free market and opposes sanctions) in competition with COSATU. Following the May 1987 stay-away, assassinations began of Congress Alliance members, who, unlike the Inkatha, never had access to firearms. Following the release of Nelson Mandela and the unbanning of the ANC, Inkatha-led groups attacked UDF communities and the police did not intervene (IDAF, 1990). Using the traditionalist imagery of 'African warlordism' and *impi* soldiers, Inkatha has used its power-base to exploit resentments against more affluent townships, and lead attacks on UDF sections.

Although the underlying causes are structural, this is a systemic crisis in which the previous mode of regulating political cohesion has broken down, the role of the state is changing, and competing power structures have emerged at all levels of society and are struggling for mobilization (Morris & Hindson, 1992). It is not, as is sometimes suggested, a 'tribal', but a profoundly political, conflict, in a region where most residents are Zulu-speaking. However, structural tensions alone do not sufficiently explain why the conflict became so violent in Pietermaritzburg in 1987, nor how it can be 'turned on or off' in periods which coincide with police activity in the townships. There is now extensive evidence of encouragement of Inkatha by the South African Police (SAP), and allegations of ineffective and partial policing include a differential approach to the bearing of arms; failure to prosecute Inkatha members; failure to protect witnesses in trials of Inkatha members; release of 'warlords' on bail; failure to investigate complaints against the SAP; and handing ANC members over to Inkatha 'courts'. In April 1989, the South African Minister of Law and Order blamed the violence on 'revolutionaries' of the Congress Alliance, in response to which Operation Ironfist was to put an end to the violence.

The conflict, which served to justify emergency rule over the townships, was an example of the 'privatization of repression', known in South America as 'low-intensity conflict'. That is, the use of surrogate armed forces, such as death squads, creates a battlefield that dissolves the boundaries between military and society, as a war of counter-organization penetrates into homes and families. Whilst maximum-force policing could not contain the township uprising that began in 1984, in Natal the security forces could use Inkatha's local/particularistic goals while confining the role of the state (IDAF, 1990). As Ajulu (1992) suggests, this violence is the medium through which the apartheid state attempts to define the contours of the future state, in which racial divisions are reproduced through market differentiation.

The crisis which arose in the 1970s represented the disintegration of a mode of co-ordination and regulation on two levels. First, apartheid had only ever achieved partial anchoring in the values and socialization processes of limited locations: mostly amongst Afrikaner landowners and mine-owners, the petite bourgeoisie and industrial workers, and amongst some local Bantustan administrative structures such as Inkatha. Beyond these groups South Africa had been in a protracted legitimation crisis which was offset through racial socio-spatial differentiation and displacement of conflicts to peripheries. Secondly, however, apartheid was losing what legitimacy it had amongst new Afrikaner capital, for whom the statist mode of regulation was increasingly becoming an obstacle to crisis-resolution, and whose interests were better served by more abstract regulatory principles of the market – hence their initiation of the Total Strategy in the early 1980s. On the other side, the emancipatory proto-organizational forms embodied in the Congress Alliance are weakened by two mobilization problems. First, during the period of de-regulation the most marginalized sectors, like hostel dwellers on township peripheries, dependent on the institutional relics of apartheid, are conducting a campaign of mass murder as proxies for the Third Force. Secondly, the National Party has consolidated support within the White core around the concept of transition to de-racialized regulation through the market and legal state (which was indicated in the Whites Only referendum in 1992). Thus the crisis is still displaced to a large degree into the vulnerable peripheral regions, which protects the core from the kind of systemic vacuum witnessed in Eastern Europe. Thus for the ANC, a 'Leipzig Option' of bringing down a de-legitimated government through mass actions and stay-aways will not be effective. These *are* effective in mobilizing grass-roots support, as the summer 1992 stay-aways indicated, but they will not cause the NP to abdicate in the manner of the interim communist governments in Eastern Europe. This case shows more clearly than any of the others discussed that whilst an offensive social movement is capable of sustaining a broad coalition of forces, this signals the prelude to rather than the conclusion of a deep social reconstruction. The demise of apartheid will be followed by possibly fateful conflicts over the mode of appropriation and regional development in southern Africa.

Notes

1. This notion was developed by Barrington Moore (1969) with reference to economies where production is based on a work-force tied to the land through violence, coercion and law, that is, where workers are not free to sell their labour. Since these conditions require strong, undemocratic, political measures, labour-repressive systems point to a distinct type of capitalist development – the 'fascist road to the modern world'. The thesis here, however, is that such systems will ultimately prove unviable because of their inherently implosive tendencies (which does not in any way mitigate their destructiveness whilst extant).

2. Apartheid-like structures – vagrancy laws, local pass systems, manipulation of labour contracts, labour agency laws – have developed elsewhere, to enable settler capital to control the supply of migrant or indigenous labour to minimize competition from more efficient agricultural sectors. See Montejano (1979).

3. The Convention for a Democratic South Africa was to bring relevant political groups into negotiations towards a new constitution. CODESA I concluded in December 1991 with the formation of five working groups to prepare constitutional proposals which would form the basis of CODESA II. In June 1992 the ANC withdrew from CODESA II following the Boipatong massacre, for which the ANC held the Government responsible. Talks hesitantly began again in the autumn of 1992.

4. Which accounted for 60 per cent of export earnings between 1930 and 1937 and 47 per cent thereafter, as the manufacturing sector became more significant (Davies et al., 1984).

5. Largely under British monopoly, mining interests favoured free trade and minimal state intervention. (Davies et al., 1984; Milkman, 1979).

6. A major consequence of apartheid clearly has been to fragment class- or gender-based alliances which might have once been possible. For example, the Garment Workers' Union, one of the largest multi-racial unions of feminized labour, which organized successfully during the 1940s and 1950s, eventually split into racial sections corresponding with highly segmented labour markets (Berger, 1990).

7. According to Lipton, (1986: 104) the laws were evaded in the Northern and Eastern Transvaal, and Upper Natal, where farming was less intensive, which suggests that it was the more heavily capitalized sectors that had most to gain from apartheid.

8. During the 1940s, the pre-war structures of segregation and labour repression had come under sustained assault by the ANC and African and Indian trade union militancy (40 per cent of African labour was unionized). This coincided with spontaneous protests, often involving communal violence, which the formal political organizations could not always control, such as the East London defiance campaign in 1945, or the Durban riots in 1949.

9. The core economy was still heavily dependent on foreign investment, with 60 per cent of workers employed in companies based in the UK, and 25 per cent in companies based in the USA (Davis et al., 1984).

10. For example, the Suppression of Communism Act (1950), removal of 'Coloured' voters from the register, banning or exile of opposition activists, press censorship, and after 1963 the extension of the police state, ninety-day detention, routine use of torture, and state terrorism.

11. General Circular no. 25 of 1967, 'Settling of Non-productive Bantu Resident in European Areas'.

12. Rok Ajulu (1992) objects that Morris and Hindson's analysis follows a 'well-trodden cul de sac' into cultural stereotypes of 'atavistic tribalism'. This criticism might not be justified, since the focus of Morris and Hindson's piece is to explain why violence is occurring on a large scale today, rather than fifteen or twenty years ago. They do not explain this in terms of 'atavistic tribalism', but with reference to the mode of collapse of apartheid, and the NP's attempt to 'reconstitute the society along lines that are . . . non-racial but will continue to exclude a very large section of the population from the major resources and power centres of the society'.

13. The 1922 Stallard Commission laid down the principle that an African should be in the towns to 'minister to the needs of the white man and should depart therefrom when he ceases to minister'. African men over 16 years old had to carry a pass book, a regulation that was systematized in the 1950 Population Registration Act, which classified the whole population by 'race', based on appearance, descent and 'general acceptance'. The 1923 Godley Committee favoured exceptions to these controls and encouraged stratification within the African community, a policy advanced in the 1942 Fagan Report, which argued that the growth of settled Black populations in cities was inevitable.

14. Bophuthatswana (Tswana), Ciskei (Xhosa), Gazankkulu (Shangeans and Tsonga), KaNgwane (Swazi), KwaNdebele (Southern Ndebele) KwaZulu (Zulu), Lebowa (Northern Sotho and Northern Ndebele), QwaQwa (Southern Sotho), Transkei (Xhosa) and Venda (Venda).

15. The converse of this was that White workers might have been expected to resist the easing of the colour bar, although Lipton (1986: 121) concludes that 'White workers' resistance . . . was less effective and fierce than expected', despite some resistance from the Mine Workers' Union and the South African Confederation of Labour in the 1970s. Skilled and professional workers, generally the most in favour of reform, had least to lose in the short-term, because there were relatively few highly qualified African workers.

16. During the 1980s, the White business community made its opposition to apartheid more clear, as, for example, with the business leaders who met with the ANC in Lusaka in 1986.

17. Represented by the Afrikaanse Handelsinstituut Incorporation (AHI), which was to be a major pressure group for the liberalization and eventual abolition of apartheid in the 1980s.

18. Recognition of Black trade unions, under strict state regulation, followed the 1979 Wiehahn Commission, and paved the way for more effective labour organization and relaxation of job-reservation.

19. The Pan Africanist Congress split from the ANC after Sharpville and represents a competing form of nationalism which rejects negotiations with the state, and insists on pan-African separatism in the liberation struggle. See Shabalala (1990).

20. Many BCM members later entered the leadership of the trade unions and new social movements of the 1980s, such as the United Democratic Front (Brewer, 1986).

21. The anti-Vietnam War campaign; recent US civil rights struggles; the defeat of South African forces in Angola, and the victory of Frelimo in Mozambique which had demonstrated the possibilities of Black victory over colonialism; and perhaps European student revolts a few years earlier (Gwala, 1988).

22. For example: 'Our people didn't think of them [Community Councils] playing any active political role . . . they were just like social workers, or marriage councillors.' Tumahhole resident, quoted in Seekings (1988: 62).

23. In the Pretoria–Witwattersrand–Vereeniging region between 1975 and 1985 the proportion of households with incomes below the living wage rose from 22 to 30 per cent.

24. This included principally the ANC, COSATU and the UDF, but also the Azanian People's Organization, Azanian Youth Organization, the Cape Youth Congress, the Detainee Parents' Support Committee, the Soweto Civic Association, the South African Communist Party, and the Western Cape Civic Association. After the release of Nelson Mandela and the unbanning of the ANC and SACP in 1990, the UDF was disbanded.

25. In the 1920s the ANC had close links with the Indian Congress, and Gandhi, who had lived in South Africa since 1893, organized resistance to the Natives' Land Act and pass laws in 1912–13 (Holland, 1989). It also had close links with American Black civil rights leaders like DuBois and Marcus Garvey.

26. Alongside the issues raised directly by the trial, liberal Whites began to question the ANC's broader commitment to civil rights. For example, Glow (Gay and Lesbian Organization of the Witwatersrand) protested to the ANC at the 'level of homophobia that has arisen both within and outside the court'.

27. COSATU's Statement from the National Executive, September 1987.

28. A common story, however, is for women's rights to be given prominence during the liberation struggle but to be sidelined later. See, for example, Arnfed (1988) on the Mozambique women's movement.

29. Ratios of White:Black per capita income have changed only slightly (13.12:1 in 1936; 12.34:1 in 1960; 11.82:1 in 1980; and 11.94:1 in 1987) and overall the 'relative position of Africans, Asians, Coloureds, and Whites has changed very little' (Smith, 1990: 7). Infant mortality rates in 1988, a revealing indicator of socio-economic status, were (per 1000 live births) 62 for Blacks, 9 for Whites; 41 for Coloureds and 14 for Asians.

30. Onverwacht's name had become a synonym for degradation and squalor. With half a million people Botshabelo is, after Soweto, South Africa's second largest township.

31. Nic Wiehahn, chair of the commission which recommended trade union reform, said in an interview with Deborah Posel: 'You can't recommend multi-racial unions. It's too emotive

. . . so you say "keep membership open" . . . You can't speak about freedom, so you call it labour mobility; that's a technical term. When you tell the man in the street about horizontal labour mobility, he won't react' (Posel, 1990: 428).

32. Consociational theory was developed by the Dutch scholar Arend Ljiphart, who became adviser to the Pretoria Government in the 1970s. It advocates a system of multi-ethnic rule and segmental autonomy (power sharing) as opposed to majority rule.

33. Since 1976, there has been frequent violent conflict at the University of Zululand, which Buthelezi, the Chancellor, has tried to bring under the control of the KwaZulu government (i.e. Inkatha) (Gwala, 1988).

Conclusion: Modernity's Unfinished Business

This book has discussed Critical Theory and global social movements around three broad themes, developing a Habermasian theory of social evolution and communicative action. First, a general theory of systemic regulation, collapse and reintegration was developed in relation to social movement formation and impact. It was noted that 'social movements' refers to various forms of collective action, and the term has an elasticity which can blur important distinctions: for example, between pressure groups, proto-political parties and single-issue campaigns. The notion of social movement organization is a little more focused and (despite disagreements with some specific claims of RMT) was used here, with particular reference to movements that through their values and organizational culture constituted proto-typical forms of possible social development. Secondly, the specific analyses of political conflict were conducted with reference to the impact of global forces on local actors within particular historical and cultural contexts. This attempted to show how developmental dynamics and exit routes from crises were structured by both the intermeshing of global with local contexts, and the scope for variation defined by the dominant principle of organization. Thirdly, it was suggested that, following Habermas' 'two-sided' concept of modernity, social movement agendas and systemic crises point towards resolutions in one of two directions: that is, either towards increasingly participatory, decentralized and fluid modernization, or towards repressive modernization, which increases the range of variation of the system whilst minimizing the scope for public sphere activity. The three examples considered in Part 2, the crisis of state socialism, Islamic neo-revivalism and the liberation struggle in South Africa, were each discussed with reference to crisis tendencies of the authoritarian state as a context for social movement formation.

The problem of the authoritarian state was posed more sharply by the Frankfurt Institute than amongst those mid-century Marxists who addressed fascism exclusively with reference to monopoly capitalism. The latter did inform Frankfurt inquiry, but their critique of the flawed project of Enlightenment offered a global frame of analysis which pointed towards an irreconcilable conflict between critical reason and the domination of inner and outer nature. For Adorno and Horkheimer, critical reason was forced to curtail its most subversive aspects so that in the place of *Vernunft* were left the paltry ethics of self-interest and instrumentality which were increasingly enshrined in mass consumption cultures. The core of the thesis, put slightly differently, is that modernity fragments the substantive restraints of traditional norms and institutions, which lose their external status and are challenged by the communicative structures of the public sphere. This releases new communicative and learning potentials which in turn presage a non-authoritarian, more egalitarian social order. However, this logic of cultural pluralization runs counter to the organizational needs of capital and the structural violence presupposed by the extraction of surplus value. The core identity of the system therefore protects itself against the very critical politics to which, from another point of view, it gave rise.

This contradiction is resolved, albeit temporarily, through crisis displacement and state control. Authoritarian states destroy democratic institutions by mobilizing anti-modern resentments amongst constituencies nostalgic for irretrievable pasts, for whom pre-modern happiness has been surrendered to what Adorno (1984: 337) called a 'grey-on-grey future'. Thus beneath violent modernization lurked deep reservoirs of destructiveness which could be mobilized through heroic-charismatic ideologies like fascism. Through analysis of the socio-psychical dynamics of oppression, early Critical Theory raised themes which were to become central to debates in radical theory during the following decades, such as political ecology and the domination of nature, the psycho-dynamics of prejudice and racism, the formation of patriarchy, the relationship between reason and violence, not to mention the future of Marxism without a revolutionary proletariat. Few post-Marxist writers offered such comprehensive or nuanced contributions to understanding problems of modernity.

However, early Critical Theory drew heavily on the Romantic critique of modernity combined with the mass society thesis, which over-emphasized the extent to which revolutionary consciousness was inhibited through manipulation by the culture industry. Further, Adorno and Horkheimer's thesis ultimately presupposed a one-dimensional concept of modernity, or at least projected *Vernunft* beyond any meaningful historical time scale or social practice: like lost mimesis, *Vernunft* could be sensed (for example, in genuinely revolutionary art) but not known in a discursive way. Moreover, early Critical Theory conflated a specific phase in the global organization of capital, namely bureaucratically organized regulation, with the exhaustion of Enlightenment and social contradiction per se. Not distinguishing sufficiently between Fordist regulation in the organic core regions (which involved an interventionist state) and authoritarian-étatist responses located largely at peripheries, Critical Theory was unprepared for the resurgence of social protest later in the century. Further, despite Adorno and Horkheimer's awareness of the relationship between colonialism, the destruction of indigenous peoples and the birth of modernity, there was no systematic attempt to theorize the peripheral state or global dynamics of crisis management. The present volume has attempted to work through some of the implications of this theoretical tradition for understanding struggles for critical politics in the global arena.

Taking his starting point from early Frankfurt Institute themes, Habermas argued that they were ultimately unable to redeem modernity from one-dimensionality or to resolve the dilemmas posed by their theory, because they remained wedded to the philosophy of consciousness. This is a view Habermas reached having left behind his earlier concept of praxis, and its implicit prospect of social transparency through therapeutic-analytical insight. According to his later conception of society as system and lifeworld, traditional forms of integration become unviable as a result of the expansion in technical, economic and communicative possibilities which subject lifeworld horizons to argumentative scrutiny. This 'linguisti-fication of the sacred', however, is accompanied by expansions of steering media – money and power – such that social life increasingly escapes the intuitive knowledge of everyday life, and becomes accessible only to the reconstructive techniques of the social sciences. From this lofty position, the theory of communicative action no longer requires grounding in subject-positions (a view it shares with say Lyotard's postmodernism) but in the capacities inherent in ordinary language for posing *and resolving* validity-questions (a view postmodernists reject). Whilst drawing upon Weber's postulate of the differentiation of cultural value spheres, Habermas none the less turns his theory against Weber by claiming that the formal argumentative properties of language offer the possibility of a comprehensive rationality which links cognition, normative evolution and aesthetics. Thus Critical Theory does not have to settle for what Weber (and Adorno and Horkheimer) saw as an inevitable loss of meaning in modern societies. The present volume has attempted to examine how this reconstructive theory might translate into a Critical Theory of social transformation.

Habermasian universal pragmatics is primarily about clarifying the grounds for critique. It reconstructs a potential for rational discourse through the release of the argumentative power of language, whilst the symmetry requirement – equal chances to deploy speech acts – embeds communication within an expansion of moral as well as cognitive learning. This process finds partial institutional embodiment in modern civil societies which oblige political authority to submit to reasoned justification and legitimation. At an ideal-typical level, the peculiar achievement of modernity has been to release the argumentative power of language by encoding non-authoritarian expectations in lived social fabrics (the life-world). Of course, in modern societies this is no more than a potential, which is undermined by the contrary process of colonization, but by emphasizing this tension Habermas is able to resuscitate the unfinished potential of modernity as a critical presence against the iron cage. Habermas suggests that it is ultimately irrational for the system to colonize the lifeworld and that colonization enforces a false (because impossible) identity between the system's functional requirements and lived experience. By reconstructing emancipatory norms that are implicit in modern communications, the theory of communicative action enables us to envisage a kind of deep democratization of social life inscribed through socialization into cultural learning processes. Concretely this might take the form of non-authoritarian inter-subjective communities, which would subtly restrain power-holders by institutionalizing an anticipation that, at some point, their actions and proposals might be scrutinized by others within the relevant social network. Thus following the style, though not the substance, of Marxism, Critical Theory claims that such emancipatory development is both historically grounded in the evolution of the lifeworld and necessary for the release of culturally latent organizational and cognitive capacities.

In order to situate this emancipatory potential in more concrete sociological processes, the present volume developed a multi-directional model of social evolution based on Habermas' distinction between the logic and dynamics of development. Predicated on an ideal-typical construction of the transition from pre-industrial to capitalist societies, this model reconstructs stages in the evolution of technical, ethical and socio-cultural forms, each with an independent developmental logic. An initial stage of equilibrium is accompanied by an accumulation of cognitive and organizational learning capacities, which are released during crises in the old social order. Through social movements (like those which appeared during the Reformation) new learning capacities appear as proto-typical forms of new social organization. These then struggle for an expansion of social and cognitive-moral communication possibilities, such as markets, formal-rational law, expanded public spheres, democratic participation or citizenship rights. However, the various potentials thrown up in social crisis do not have equal chances of stabilization, and those finally incorporated into the new systemic equilibrium are likely to be isomorphic with the emergent form of system organization (thus Calvinist instrumental ethics were more conducive to the stabilization of capitalist relations than the Anabaptists' ethic of social justice). None the less, there is a tension built into the model, since expansion in capacities for technical and organizational control (system rationalization) do not necessarily entail an expansion of post-conventional socialization (lifeworld rationalization). However, the development of markets and bureaucracies does presuppose *some* lifeworld rationalization (for example, anonymous interactions, social differentiation and the disintegration of traditional solidarity). Thus a new equilibrium both generates new system problems and meets resistance which can tap into suppressed values and communication structures. What is at stake in present conflicts, according to this model, are essentially the limits within which the capitalist system can generate complex forms of systemic organization, whilst holding back the more radical communicative capacities of the socio-cultural sphere.

An advantage of this approach is that 'only a knowledge of structurally anchored developmental trends that run in opposite directions can help one to become aware of possibilities for practical intervention' (Habermas, 1991: 260). Clearly this multi-dimensional perspective rejects theories like systemic functionalism that exclude the autonomous logic of symbolic communication in the lifeworld, and are thus unable to account for pathologies arising from attempts by the system to convert communicative socialization into steering media. But equally, Critical Theory defends the unfulfilled potential of modernity against postmodernist theories that settle instead for diversity, fragmentation or Dionysian innovation, combined with (a perhaps reactionary) disdain for modernist social movements. On the one hand, postmodernist theory risks privileging the instrumental aspect of modernity, against which it presents an equally stereotyped alternative. On the other hand, even Foucault or Lyotard's critical postures tend to replay earlier Critical Theory's inability to locate any persuasive basis of validity, and thereby threaten to become an apologia for dogmatism (for example, celebrating intuition over discursive argument).

Once modernity is understood as releasing the potential for post-conventional communications, and that these structures offer the only rational solution to problems of modernization, then notions of pre- and postmodernity can be viewed in a more nuanced way. This is so for at least three reasons. First, universal pragmatics offers a process of deduction through which the rational potential of social evolution can be reconstructed as a continuous challenge to oppressive social conditions. Secondly, authoritarian-charismatic ideologies are understood as facets of pre-modernity (or at any rate phenomena of a transitional period), thus to regard the eclipse of grand narratives such as Marxism-Leninism as indicative of *post*modernity makes less sense than to regard the present as the beginning of modernity proper. What have been described here as 'heroic' ideologies mobilized against plural public spheres in the name of a transcendent cause are pre-modern in that they are based on a desire for glory, and the cult of warriors upholding 'honour' as prime virtue. The self-aggrandizing willingness to risk oneself for an intrinsic value, or simply for respect and honour, appears in the transition to modernity but is pre-modern in that it blocks off the development of post-conventional public spheres. Further, it tends, like authoritarian state socialism or Islamic neo-revivalism, to appear at the periphery of developed capitalism in response to weaknesses of social regulation and institutional public spheres. Thirdly, although formal rationality offers techniques for negotiating rational consensus, colonization of the lifeworld creates conditions for defensive regressions to heroic populism, where problems of over-complexity are temporarily resolved through quasi-fascistic forms of the state. Modernity, according to this conception, then, is fluid, diverse, dangerous, but also holds out the hope of a rational outcome of the crisis of the global system.

Even so, Critical Theory's case rests on its ability to show, first, that existing forms of domination do not exhaust more varied potentials within modern structures; secondly, that an alternative, suppressed modernity continues to inform new protest potentials; and, thirdly, that these have some realistic expectation of decolonizing the lifeworld. Such demonstration is problematic, because this is a movement of *longue durée* which might form a context for contemporary fields of collective action, but it is difficult to know what time scale would be necessary to see these developments worked through. Moreover, it was suggested that there were a number of further problems with this theory. Despite its global address it has a narrowly West European focus and generalizes the experience of the liberal-democratic welfare state. Its theoretical object is the nation-state, which is assumed to be equivalent to society, thus the boundary between system and lifeworld is understood entirely in terms of conflicts marked out in a national terrain. Meanwhile, however, networks of communicative socialization have global compass and critical conflicts are displaced into peripheral locations of the global arena. Even in its own terms, however, this is at best a theory of social movement genesis rather than impact, and as a theory of genesis it is still (implicitly) tied to the undifferentiated concept of mass society and anomie (reflecting one of a number of largely unacknowledged links between Habermas and earlier Critical Theory).

Further, as a theory of genesis it has difficulty distinguishing amongst the three possible reactions to colonization. That is, colonization provokes reaction-formation and apolitical withdrawal (quietism); nostalgia for lost community (defensive social movement activism); and offensive, emancipatory movements. Critical Theory needs to account for the formation of one rather than another response. There are further difficulties arising from Habermas' idea that emancipatory social movements are concerned primarily with the 'grammar of social life' (symbolic identity politics), since not only is it difficult to separate symbolic from material objectives, but identity politics can involve a privatization of political questions into subcultural movements which eschew engagement with the state and thereby conspire in their own marginalization. On the other hand, the demands of offensive social movements (such as feminism, the liberation struggle in South Africa, or democratic coalitions in state socialism) necessarily point towards fundamental reconstruction of the state, economic and interpersonal relations rather than a mere border dispute between system and lifeworld.

Thus whilst Habermas uses the notion of the unfulfilled potential of modernity to critique postmoderns, his West European focus does not take the argument far enough. A global perspective on the formation of critical politics indicates that far from modernity having been exhausted, the crucial issues dominating the world scene derive from its central contradictions. In each of the cases examined here, social movements were structured by a vortex of problems that involve questions of fundamental rights, access to control of resources, social justice, management of anonymous social interactions, inequalities of power and money, and above all the creation of conditions for social differentiation and political pluralization within which decentred risk-bearing personalities might develop. That is, the conflicts which dominate the world scene are fundamentally modern in origin, nature and orientation and their resolution will require a fulfilment of as yet unrealized potentials of modernity.

The present volume has attempted to develop a more complex theory of crisis management and displacement, which views the lifeworld and system as interpenetrated in complex ways – whereas Habermas tends to over-emphasize the analytical contrast between lifeworld and system. It was argued that power and money inscribe ascriptive identities (for example, gender, 'race') into markets and bureaucracies and thereby preserve and reinforce as well as undermine lifeworld structures. Thus lifeworlds are not in pristine isolation from the system, nor are they simply disorganized by the effects of colonization (into anomie, atomization, etc.). Rather, they are the site of intersections of pre-rational norms, new power relations and segmentations (such as the complex systems of patronage created by Brezhnevite corporatism, or the Pahlavi state). These interlocking relationships will in turn set the conditions for social movement impact, since the latter depends upon the ability of SMOs to mobilize social infrastructures. These infrastructures have been shaped by the effects of global colonization into differing degrees of openness and fluidity (rationalization) or closure and defensiveness (traditionalization). This was illustrated in the contrastive mobilization bases of the ANC (unionized workers) as opposed to Inkatha (marginalized hostel dwellers linked to the patronage networks of the homelands). It was further noted in Iran, with reference to the divergence between the secular liberal or socialist constituencies, as opposed to the *bazaari* and ulama. The latter were successful in gaining control of the crisis, because they could lock into tightly coupled defensive social networks that had been unintentionally strengthened by the over-extension of the Pahlavi state. In each case the resolution of the crisis of the state hinges upon the relative capacities of emancipatory social movements to mobilize constituencies looking to a progressive-participatory, rather than repressive-defensive, outcome.

The conditions for each type of outcome, emancipatory or defensive, were analysed with reference to the impact of the global system at the periphery. Peripheral regions are themselves sites on to which global conflicts are displaced, which, combined with unequal terms of trade, establishes barriers to autonomous development and arrests the formation of functionally differentiated economies, and the regulation of anonymous interactions through public spheres. Rather, the state extends to create the conditions for capital accumulation, often by attempting to self-consciously re-create the 'modernization' that occurred unself-consciously in the organic core, as was the case with forced secularization in Iran. This over-extension of the state creates a complex conjuncture in which two factors are particularly important. First, lifeworlds are structured by clientelistic relations, where the roles of client/worker/citizen are not clearly differentiated. Second, the penetration of transnational capital in peripheral societies actually preserves pre-modern life-forms which are harnessed to global capital accumulation, and this runs counter to the modernized sectors of the society. The consequent state/society divisions tend to result in chronic legitimacy-deficit, where state agencies (for example, mass organizations that channel participation) have insufficient anchoring in the lifeworld. These legitimation crises can be offset to some extent depending on factors like the state's resource-base (for example, export earnings), type of coalition-base (extensive or restricted) and mechanisms of co-optation. Thus, following the terroristic-charismatic phase, Soviet systems traded off repressive corporatism against mass acquiescence, but this could hold together only so long as the state could mobilize sufficient resources and balance the needs of capital investment against consumer demand and a shortage command economy. In Iran state patronage was organized through bodies like the Pahlavi Foundation along with an extensive bureaucratic and military structure that created a loyal stratum. In South Africa authoritarian control was sustained through a complex blending of labour repression, socio-spatial displacement, the ideology of separate development, and clientelist networks in the core and homelands.

However, each of these involves the over-extension of bureaucratic steering media in ways which create new sites of resistance, since the over-extended state (like the White Revolution or Resurgence Party in Iran) runs up against endemic administrative and legitimation crises. These attest to the ultimate failure of systemic colonization to effectively convert the socio-cultural sphere over to systemic media. Moreover, endogenous crisis tendencies were exacerbated by exogenous crises arising from restructuring of the global economy. The end of the Cold War signalled the beginning of a re-alignment in which multi-peripheries and semi-peripheries emerge around at least three centres (the USA, Japan and the EC). Combined with de-regulation and privatization of local state capital this has resulted in the erosion of clientelistic corporatist bases of peripheral states.

However, the present volume has argued that crises in the political system, or even administrative failure, do not necessarily spell the end of the core structure of appropriation. In a major strategy of crisis regulation, the state itself (which has become a vehicle for capital accumulation) can shift its mode of legitimation from repressive corporatism to de-politicized, repressive modernization, especially through marketized regulation (described here as a tactical retreat). This might not be successful, of course, since in a systemic vacuum multiple lines of development are released and new social movements and identities compete for mobilization of resources. A decisive factor for future development is the extent to which proto-public spheres have matured within the former system and are institutionalized through social movements capable of sustaining a participatory rather than repressive outcome. Attachments to the past, conventional communication structures embedded in clientelistic networks vie with social movements embodying alternative communication structures.

For example, it was seen that in post-socialism a crucial question for the future will be the ability of social movements to regulate the privatization and marketization processes, within a framework of civil law, and in such a way as to limit the destructive effects of the transition on social infrastructures.

The three cases considered here illustrate different potential modes of intersection between the global system and local structures. The systemic vacuum in post-socialism combined with a weak social movement base has increased the regenerative capacities of accumulation amongst the former nomenklatura. However, the destruction of clientelistic institutions combined with fast-track marketization inhibits the stabilization of pluralistic structures and could still result (in some cases) in a reversion to statist authoritarianism. In Iran the route of tactical retreat through disengaging the state from the lifeworld was precluded partly because the Pahlavis had reinforced the resource-base of an alternative élite (the ulama) by closing off other avenues of public identity formation and participation. Whilst this successfully undermined the secular opposition, the leading ulama were capable of using the crisis in 1978–9 as a basis for further extending the state through Terror combined with organizational charisma, to a degree that would have been impossible under the Pahlavis. In South Africa the outcome will depend upon the ability of the Congress movement to consolidate a sufficiently strong coalition to resist both Inkatha and the intransigence of the National Party over crucial issues of constitutional reform and compensation. The consolidation of racial divisions within marketized relationships, a repressive modernization, would solve none of the crisis tendencies of the apartheid system, and would mark a descent into further violence.

Critical Theory cannot determine which directions will be taken, although it can evaluate the outcomes of social conflicts against an underlying tow of modernity, and thereby clarify what is at stake in global conflicts. The theory of communicative action predicts an underlying movement of modernity towards more differentiated and plural structures of integration, and underpins the concept of legitimation crisis, which has been central to the analysis here. It insists that communicative areas of social life cannot be successfully incorporated within systems of power and money, which in the long term precludes the stabilization of repressive socialization. Consequent disruptions in systems of regulation release multiple innovations from stored interpretive and cognitive resources of the lifeworld. Whilst in these senses communicative action could be said to be primary to social evolution, in order to explain the directions taken by social development (the dynamics rather than the logic of evolution) the theory must refer in addition to the complex interactions between system and lifeworld. Critical Theory can demonstrate what is at stake as global systemic organizations restructure and seek new bases of integration and consensus through repressive or participatory institutions. This creates a context for crisis-logics where outcomes are determined by struggles, but where the resources available to the contending parties are structured by the extent and type of rationalization that has taken place. These lifeworld–system interactions create a circuit in which the potential for emancipation is still historically grounded in the unfolding project of modernity. However, the context of crisis is precisely that – a context, the stuff of life from which social identities are formed, and not an implacable fate which controls the destiny of social actors.

Bibliography

Abdel-Malek, A. (1968) *Egypt: Military Society*, New York: Random House.

Abercrombie, N., Hill, S., & Turner, B. (1980) *The Dominant Ideology Thesis*, London: Allen & Unwin.

Abrahamian, E. (1981) 'Strengths and Weaknesses of the Labour Movement in Iran 1941–1953' in Bonine & Keddie, *Modern Iran*, pp. 211–32.

Abrahamian, E. (1982) *Iran Between Two Revolutions*, Princeton, NJ: Princeton University Press.

Abrahamian, E. (1991) 'Khomeini: Fundamentalist or Populist?' *New Left Review*, 186:102–19.

Ackerman, N., & Jahoda, M. (1950) *Antisemitism and Emotional Disorder*, New York: Harper & Bros.

Adam, H. (1984) 'South Africa's Search for Legitimacy', *Telos*, 59:45–68.

Adam, H. (1990) 'Transition to Democracy: South Africa and Eastern Europe', *Telos*, 85:33–55.

Adler, F. (1990–1) 'Politics, Intellectuals and the University', *Telos*, 86:103–9.

Adorno, T. (1968) 'Spätkapitalismus oder Industriegesellschaft?' *Soziologische Schriften*, 1:354–70.

Adorno, T. (1973) *Negative Dialectics*, trans. E. B Ashton, London: Routledge & Kegan Paul.

Adorno, T. (1974) *Minima Moralia*, trans. E. Jephcott, London: New Left Books.

Adorno, T. (1977) 'The Actuality of Philosophy (1931)', *Telos*, 31:120–33.

Adorno, T. (1982) *Prisms*, trans. S. & S. Weber, Cambridge, Mass.: MIT Press.

Adorno, T. (1984) *Aesthetic Theory*, trans. C. Lenhardt, London: Routledge & Kegan Paul.

Adorno, T., Freukel-Brunswick, E., Levinson, D., & Sanford, R. (1969) *The Authoritarian Personality*, New York: Norton. (First published, 1951.)

Adorno, T., & Horkheimer, M. (1973) *Dialectic of Enlightenment*, trans. E. Cumming, London: New Left Books.

Agger, B. (1991) *A Critical Theory of Public Life*, London: Falmer Press.

Aglietta, M. (1979) *A Theory of Capitalist Regulation*, London: New Left Books.

Ajulu, R. (1992) 'Political Violence in South Africa: A Rejoinder to Morris & Hindson', *Review of African Political Economy*, 55:67–71.

Akhavi, S. (1980) *Religion and Politics in Contemporary Iran*, Albany: State University of New York Press.

Akhtar, S. (1987) *Reason and the Radical Crisis of Faith*, New York: Lang.

Alavi, H. (1972) 'The Over–Developed Post–Colonial State', *New Left Review*, 79:59–82.

Alavi, H. (1982) 'State and Class Under Peripheral Capitalism' in H. Alavi and T. Shanin (eds), *Introduction to the Sociology of Developing Societies*, London: Macmillan, pp. 289–307.

Alexander, J. (1991) 'Habermas and Critical Theory' in Honneth & Joas, *Communicative Action*, pp. 49–73.

Alexander, N. (1986) 'Approaches to the National Question in South Africa', *Transformation*, 1.

al-Mahdi, S. (1978) 'The Concept of the Islamic State' in A. Ganhar (ed.), *The Challenge of Islam*, Islamic Council of Europe.

Amin, Q. (1899) *Tahrir al-Mar'a [The Liberation of Women]* reprinted in M. 'Imara (1976) *Qasim Amin: Al-a'mal al-kamila*, Beirut.

Amin, S. (1989) *Eurocentrism*, London: Zed Books.

Amin, S. (1990) *Delinking: Towards a Polycentric World*, London: Zed Books.

Amin, S. (1991) 'The State and Development' in Held, *Political Theory Today*, pp. 305–29.

Anderson, B. (1988) *Imagined Communities*, London: Verso.

Andrusz, G. (1990) 'Housing Policy in the Soviet Union' in J. Sillince (ed.), *Housing in Eastern Europe and the USSR*, London: Routledge.

Anyang' Nyong'o, P. (ed.) (1988) *Popular Struggles for Democracy in Africa*, London: Zed Books.

Arato, A. (1981) 'Civil Society Against the State: Poland 1980–81', *Telos*, 47:23–47.

Arato, A. (1982) 'Critical Sociology and Authoritarian State Socialism' in Thompson & Held, *Habermas: Critical Debates*, pp. 196–218.

Arjomand, S. A. (1980) 'The State and Khomeini's Islamic Order', *Iranian Studies*, 13, 1–4:147–64.

Arjomand, S. A. (ed.) (1984) *From Nationalism to Revolutionary Islam*, London: Macmillan.

Arnason, J. P. (1990) 'Nationalism, Globalization and Identity' in Featherstone, *Global Culture*, pp. 207–36.

Arnason, J. P. (1991) 'Modernity as Project and Field of Tensions' in Honneth & Joas, *Communicative Action*, pp. 181–213.

Arnfed, S. (1988) 'Women in Mozambique: Gender Struggles and Politics', *Review of African Political Economy*, 45/46:5–16.

Aronowitz, S. (1981) *The Crisis in Historical Materialism*, New York: Praeger.

Aronowitz, S. (1989) *Science as Power: Discourse and Ideology in Modern Society*, Basingstoke: Macmillan.

Arrighi, G. (1990) 'Marxist Century, American Century: The Making and Remaking of the World Labour Movement', *New Left Review*, 179:29–63.

Arrighi, G. (1991) 'World Income Inequalities and the Future of Socialism', *New Left Review*, 189:39–65.

Arrighi, G., Hopkins, T., & Wallerstein, I. (1989) *Anti–Systemic Movements*, London: Verso.

Ascherson, N. (1987) *The Struggles for Poland*, London: Pan Books.

Ash, T. G. (1990) *We the People: The Revolutions of '89*, London: Granta Books.

Austin, J. L., (1962) *How to Do Things With Words*, Oxford: Oxford University Press.

Az (pseud.) (1981) 'The Women's Struggle in Iran', *Monthly Review*, 32, 10:22–30.

Azad, S. (1981) 'Workers' and Peasants' Councils in Iran', *Monthly Review*, 32, 5:14–29.

Babu, A. (1991) 'A New Europe: Consequences for Tanzania', *Review of African Political Economy*, 50:75–8.

Badie, B. (1986) *Les deux états: Pouvoir et société en occident et en terre d'Islam*, Paris: Fayard.

Bahro, F. (1984) *From Red to Green*, London: Verso.

Baker, R. (1982) 'Clientelism in the Post-Revolutionary State: The Soviet Union', in Clapham, *Private Patronage and Public Power*, pp. 36–52.

Bakhash, S. (1985) *The Reign of the Ayatollahs*, New York: Basic Books.

Balibar, E. (1991) '*Es Gibt Keinen Staat in Europa*: Racism and Politics in Europe Today', *New Left Review*, 186:5–19.

Bangura, Y. (1987) 'The Recesssion and Workers' Struggles in the Vehicle Assembly Plants: Styr – Nigeria', *Review of African Political Economy*, 39:4–22.

Batt, J. (1991) *East Central Europe from Reform to Transition*, London: Pinter.

Baudrillard, J. (1981) *For a Critique of the Political Economy of the Sign*, trans. C. Levin, St Louis: Telos Press.

Bauman, Z. (1984) in the 'Review Symposium on Soviet-type Societies', *Telos* 60:173–8.

Bauman, Z. (1989a) *Modernity and the Holocaust*, Cambridge: Polity.

Bauman, Z. (1989b) 'Poland: On Its Own', *Telos*, 79:47–62.

Bayat-Philipp, M. (1981) 'Tradition and Change in Iranian Socio-Religious Thought' in Bonine & Keddie, *Modern Iran*. pp. 37–58.

Beck, U. (1992) *Risk Society*, trans. M. Ritter, London: Sage.

Beckman, B. (1981) 'Imperialism and the National Bourgeoisie', *Review of African Political Economy*, 22:5–13.

Beckman, B. (1988) 'Peasants and Democratic Struggles in Nigeria', *Review of African Political Economy*, 41:30–44.

Beckman, B. (1989) 'Whose Democracy? Bourgeois vs Popular Democracy', *Review of African Political Economy*, 45/46:84–97.

Beetham, D. (1991) *The Legitimation of Power*, London: Macmillan.

Behdad, S. (1989) 'Winners and Losers of the Iranian Revolution: A Study in Income Distribution', *International Journal of Middle East Studies*, 21:327–58.

Bell, D. (1974) *Cultural Contradictions of Modernity*, New York: Basic Books.

Benard C., & Khalilzad, Z. (1984) *'The Government of God': Iran's Islamic Republic*, New York: Columbia University Press.

Bence, G., & Kis, J. (1980) 'On Being a Marxist: A Hungarian View', *Socialist Register*, London: Merlin Press, pp. 139–65.

Ben-David, J. (1962–3) 'Professions in the Class-System of Present-Day Societies', *Current Sociology*, XII:247–330.

Benhabib, S. (1981) 'Modernity and the Aporias of Critical Theory', *Telos*, 49:38–61.

Benhabib, S. (1986) *Critique, Norm and Utopia*, New York: Columbia University Press.

Benjamin, J. (1978) 'Authority and the Family Revisited: or A World Without Fathers?', *New German Critique*, 13:35–57.

Berger, I. (1990) 'Solidarity Fragmented: Garment Workers of the Transvaal, 1930–1960' in Marks & Trapido, *Politics of Race, Class and Nationalism*, pp. 124–56.

Berger, J. (1991) 'The Linguistification of the Sacred and the Delinguistification of the Economy' in Honneth and Joas (eds.), *Communicative Action*, pp. 165–80.

Bergmann, B. R. (1986) *The Economic Emergence of Women*, New York: Basic Books.

Bernstein, H. (1977) 'Notes on Capital and the Peasantry', *Review of African Political Economy*, 10:60–73.

Bernstein, H. (1979) 'African Peasantries – a Theoretical Framework', *Journal of Peasant Studies*, 6:421–42.

Bernstein, H. (1981) 'State and Economy in Tanzania', *Review of African Political Economy*, 21:44–62.

Bernstein, R., (ed.) (1985) *Habermas and Modernity*, Cambridge: Polity.

Billig, M. (1978) *Fascists*, London: Academic Press.

Billig, M. (1982) *Ideology and Social Psychology*, London: Sage.

Blackburn, R. (1991) 'Fin de Siècle: Socialism After the Crash', *New Left Review*, 185:5–66.

Blumenberg, H. (1985) *Work on Myth*, trans. R. Wallace, Cambridge Mass.: MIT Press.

Blumenfeld, J. (1986) 'Class, Race and Capital in South Africa Revisited', *The Political Quarterly*, 57, 1:74–82.

Boella, L. (1979) 'Eastern European Societies', *Telos*, 41:59–75.

Boguszak, M., Gabal, I., & Rak, V. (1990) *Czecho-Slovakia – Survey Report*, Prague: Association for Independent Social Analysis.

Bonine, M. E., & Keddie, N. R. (eds) (1981) *Modern Iran: The Dialectics of Continuity and Change*, New York: State University Press.

Bourdieu, P. (1979a) 'The Disenchantment of the World' in *Algeria 1960*, trans. R. Nice, New York: Cambridge University Press, pp. 205–26.

Bourdieu, P. (1979b) *The Inheritors: French Students and their Relation to Culture*, trans. R. Nice, Chicago: Chicago University Press.

Bourdieu, P. (1989) 'Intellectuals in the Modern World', *Telos*, 81:99–110.

Brand, A. (1990) *The Force of Reason: An Introduction to Habermas' Theory of Communicative Action*, London: Allen & Unwin.

Brenner, R., & Glick, M. (1991) 'The Regulation Approach: Theory and History', *New Left Review*, 188:45–120.

Brett, E. A. (1988) 'States, Markets and Private Power' in Cook & Kirkpatrick, *Privatization in Less Developed Countries*, pp. 47–67.

Brewer, J. D. (1986) *After Soweto: An Unfinished Journey*, Oxford: Clarendon.

Bubner, R. (1982) 'Habermas's Concept of Critical Theory' in Thompson & Held, *Critical Debates*, pp. 42–56.

Buck-Morss, S. (1977) *The Origin of Negative Dialectics*, Brighton: Harvester.

Bujra, J. (1990) 'Taxing Development: Why Must Women Pay? Gender and the Development Debate in Tanzania', *Review of African Political Economy*, 47:44–63.

Bunce, V. (1983) 'The Political Economy of the Brezhnev Era: The Rise and Fall of Corporatism', *British Journal of Political Science*, 13:129–158.

Burnham, J. (1962) *The Managerial Revolution*, Harmondsworth: Penguin. (First published, 1941.)

Callaghy, T. M., & Wilson, E. J. (1988) 'Africa: Policy, Reality or Ritual' in R. Vernon (ed.), *The Promise of Privatization*, New York: Council on Foreign Relations.

Callinicos, C. (1989) *Against Postmodernism: A Marxist Critique*, Cambridge: Polity.

Campbell, J. (1992) 'Reflections on the Fiscal Crisis of Post-Communist States', paper presented to the 'Post-Socialism: Problems and Prospects' Conference, Charlotte Mason College, Cumbria, UK, July.

Cancian, F. (1964) 'Functional Analysis of Change' in A. & E. Etzioni (eds), *Social Change*, New York: Basic Books, pp. 112–25.

Carlebach, J. (1978) *Karl Marx and the Radical Critique of Judaism*, London: Routledge.

Carlo, A. (1989) 'Contradictions of Perestroika', *Telos*, 79:29–48.

Carré, O. (1983) 'The Impact of the Muslim Brotherhood's Political Islam since the 1950s' in G. R. Warburg & U. M. Kupferschmidt (eds), *Islam, Nationalism and Radicalism in Egypt and the Sudan*, New York: Praeger.

Casanova, J. (1984) 'The Politics of Religious Revival', *Telos*, 59:3–34.

Charney, C. (1987) 'Political Power and Social Class in the Neo-Colonial African State', *Review of African Political Economy*, 38:48–65.

Chaskalson, M., Jochelson, K., & Seekings, J. (1987) 'Rent Boycotts in South Africa', *Review of African Political Economy*, 40:47–64.

Chomsky, N. (1965) *Aspects of the Theory of Syntax*, Cambridge, Mass.: MIT Press.

Clapham, C. (ed.) (1982) *Private Patronage and Public Power*, London: Pinter.

Clapham, C. (1985) *Third World Politics*, Beckenham: Croom Helm.

Clapham, C. (1989) 'State and Revolution in Ethiopia', *Review of African Political Economy*, 44:5–17.

Clark, J. (1991) *Democratizing Development*, London: Earthscan.

Clegg, S. (1991) 'Max Weber's Relevance for the Sociology of Organizations', paper presented to the 'Weber, Work, Organizations and Bureaucracy' Conference, Lancaster University, UK, April.

Cliffe, L. (1977) 'Class Formations as an Articulation Process', *Journal of Peasant Studies*, 4, 2:195–224.

Cobbett, W., & Cohen, R. (1988) *Popular Struggles in South Africa*, London: James Currey with ROAPE.

Cobbett, W., Munslow, B., & Szeftel, M., (eds) (1987) 'Southern Africa – The Crisis Continues', *Review of African Political Economy*, 40.

Cobbett, W., & Nakedi, B. (1987) 'Behind the "Curtain" at Botshabelo', *Review of African Political Economy*, 40:32–46.

Cohen, J. (1979) 'Why More Political Theory?', *Telos*, 40:70–94.

Cohen, J. (1982a) 'Between Crisis Management and Social Movements', *Telos*, 52:21–40.

Cohen, J. (1982b) *Class and Civil Society*, Cambridge, Amherst, Mass.: University of Mass. Press.

Cohen, W. (1991) 'From Victim to Shylock and Oppressor: The New Image of the Jew in the Trotskyist Movement', *Journal of Communist Studies*, 7 (1):46–68.

Collins, R. (1983) 'The Weberian Revolution of the High Middle Ages' in A. Bergsen (ed.), *Crisis in the World-System*, London: Sage, pp. 205–26.

Collins, R. (1986) *Weberian Sociology*, Cambridge: Cambridge University Press.

Cook, L. (1992) 'Brezhnev's Social Contract and Gorbachev's Reforms', *Soviet Studies*, 44, 1:37–56.

Cook P., & Kirkpatrick, C. (eds) (1988) *Privatization in Less Developed Countries*, Brighton: Harvester.

Copans, J. (1991) 'No Shortcuts to Democracy: The Long March towards Modernity', *Review of African Political Economy*, 50:102–14.

Coulter, J. (1979) *The Social Construction of Mind*, London: Macmillan.

Cowen, M. (1981) 'The Agrarian Problem: Notes on the Nairobi Discussion', *Review of African Political Economy*, 20:57–73.

Cowen, M., & Kinyanjui, K. (1977) 'Some Problems of Capital and Class in Kenya', *Occasional Paper*, 26, Nairobi: IDS.

Craib, I. (1989) *Psychoanalysis and Social Theory: The Limits of Sociology*, Brighton: Harvester.

Csaszi, L., & Kullberg, P. (1985) 'Reforming Health Care in Hungary', *Social Science and Medicine*, 21, 8:849–55.

Cudsi, A., & Dessouki, A. (eds) (1981) *Islam and Power*, London: Croom Helm.

Currie, K., & Ray, L. J. (1987) 'State, Peasants and Agri-Business in Kenya', *Review of African Political Economy*, 38:89–96.

Dallmayr, F. (1984) *Polis and Praxis: Exercises in Contemporary Political Theory*, Cambridge, Mass.: MIT Press.

Dangschat, J. (1987) 'Social Disparities in a "Socialist City" – Warsaw', *International Journal for Urban and Regional Research*, 11:37–60.

Davies, R., O'Meara, D., & Dlamini, S. (1984) *The Struggle for South Africa*, Vols 1 & 2, London: Zed Books.

Davies, T. (1988) 'A Framework for Relating Social Welfare Policy to Economic Change: Evidence from Hungarcity' in F. Millard (ed.), *Social Welfare and the Market*, London: LSE, pp. 36–80.

Davies, W. (1990) *We Cry for Our Land: Farm Workers in South Africa*, Oxford: Oxfam.

Dews, P. (1986) 'Adorno, Post–Structuralism and the Critique of Identity', *New Left Review*, 28–44.

Djilas, M., (1957) *The New Class: An Analysis of the Communist System*, London: Thames & Hudson.

Doornbos, M. (1991) 'Linking the Future to the Past: Ethnicity and Pluralism', *Review of African Political Economy*, 52:53–65.

Doyal, L. (1979) *Political Economy of Health*, London: Pluto.

Dresler, Z. (1991) 'The Enterprise as a Field for the Conflict of Interests' in Hausner, (ed.), *System of Interest Representation in Poland*, Cracow: Cracow Academy of Economics, pp. 11–26.

Dubiel, H. (1985) *Theory and Politics*, Cambridge, Mass.: MIT Press.

Dubula, S., & Slovo, J. (1981) 'The Two Pillars of Our Struggle: Reflections on the Relationship between the ANC and SACP', *The African Communist*, 87:36–8.

Dummett, M. (1976) 'What is a Theory of Meaning?' in G. Evans and J. McDowell (eds), *Truth and Meaning*, Oxford: Oxford University Press, pp. 67–130.

Dunleavy, P., & Husbands, C. (1983) *British Democracy at the Crossroads*, London: Allen & Unwin.

Durkheim, É. (1979) Review of G. Simmel, *The Philosophy of Money*, *Social Research*, 46:321–8.

Dux, G. (1991) 'Communicative Reason and Interest' in Honneth & Joas, *Communicative Action*, pp. 74–96.

Dwyer, K. (1991) *Arab Voices*, London: Routledge.

Eder, K. (1982) 'A New Social Movement?', *Telos*, 52:5–20.

Eder, K. (1985) *Geschichte als Lernprozess?* Frankfurt: Suhrkamp.

Ehrenreich, B., & English, D. (1973) *Witches, Midwives and Nurses: A History of Women Healers*, New York: Feminist Press.

Eisenstadt, S. N, (1980) 'Comparative Analsyis of State Foundation in Historical Contexts', *International Social Science Journal*, 4, 23:624–5.

Eisenstadt, S. N., & Lemarchand, R. (eds) (1981) *Political Clientelism, Patronage and Development*, London: Sage.

Elkins, S. (1989–90) 'The Politics of Mystical Ecology', *Telos*, 82:52–70.

Elshtain, J. B. (1981) 'Feminist Discourse and its Discontents: Language, Power, and Meaning' in N. Keohane, M. Z. Rosaldo, B. C. Gelp (eds), *Feminist Theory*, Chicago: Chicago University Press, pp. 127–45.

Elson, D., (1988) 'Market Socialism or Socialization of the Market?' *New Left Review*, 172:3–44.

Engels, F. (1973) *The Condition of the Working Class in England*, Moscow: Progress Publishers.

Esposito, J. L. (ed.) (1983) *Voices of Resurgent Islam*, Oxford: Oxford University Press.

Evans, A. (1986) 'The Decline of Developed Socialism? Some Trends in Recent Soviet Ideology', *Soviet Studies*, 38, 1:1–23.

Fay, B. (1987) *Critical Social Science: Liberation and Its Limits*, Ithaca, NY: Cornell University Press.

Featherstone, M. (ed.) (1990) *Global Culture: Nationalism, Globalization and Modernity*, London: Sage.

Feher, F. (1982) 'Paternalism as a Mode of Legitimation in Soviet-type Societies' in Feher & Rigby, (eds.) *Legitimation in Communist Societies*, pp. 64–81.

Feher, F. (1986) 'In the Bestarium: A Contribution to the Cultural Anthropology of "Real Socialism" ' in Feher & Heller, *Eastern Left – Western Left*, pp. 260–78.

Feher, F., & Arato, A. (eds) (1989) *Gorbachev: The Debate*, New York: Humanities Press.

Feher, F., & Heller, A. (1982) 'The Antinomies of Peace', *Telos*, 53:5–16.

Feher, F., & Heller, A. (1986) *Eastern Left–Western Left*, Cambridge: Polity.

Feher, F., Heller, A., & Markus, G. (1984) *Dictatorship Over Needs: An Analysis of Soviet Societies*, Oxford: Blackwell.

Feher, F., & Rigby, T. H. (eds) (1982) *Legitimation in Communist Societies*, Oxford: Oxford University Press.

Fichte, J. (1971) 'Ueber die Würde des Menschen (1794)' *Werke* I:412–16.

Fields, G. (1991) 'The Road from Gdansk: How Solidarity Found a Haven in the Marketplace', *Monthly Review*, 43:95–121.

Fine, R. (1989) 'The Antinomies of Nationalism and Democracy in the South African Liberation Struggle', *Review of African Political Economy*, 45/46:98–106.

Fischer, M. M. J. (1980a) 'Becoming Mollah: Reflections on Iranian Clerics in a Revolutionary Age', *Iranian Studies*, 13, 1–4:83–117.

Fischer, M. M. J. (1980b) *Iran, from Religious Dispute to Revolution*, Cambridge: Harvard University Press.

Fischer, M. M. J. (1982) 'Islam and the Revolt of the Petit-Bourgeoisie', *Dedalus*, 1, 3:101–25.

Fischer, M. M. J. (1983) 'Imam Khomeini: Four Levels of Understanding' in Esposito, *Voices of Resurgent Islam*, pp. 150–74.

Fitzgerald, P. (1990) 'Democracy and Civil Society in South Africa: A Response to Daryl Glaser', *Review of African Political Economy*, 49:94–110.

Flaherty, P. (1988) 'Restructuring the Soviet State: Organizational Politics in the Gorbachev Era', *Socialist Register*, 90–131.

Forbes, H. D. (1985) *Nationalism, Ethnocentrism and Personality*, Chicago: University of Chicago Press.

Forester, J. (1985) *Critical Theory and Public Life*, London: MIT Press.

Forrest, J. (1987) 'The Contemporary African State: A Ruling Class?', *Review of African Political Economy*, 38:66–70.

Foster, M. B. (1934, 1935) 'Christian Theology and Modern Science of Nature', *Mind* 43:446–68 and 44:439–66.

Foucault, M. (1977) *Discipline and Punish – the Birth of the Prison*, trans. A. Sheridan, London: Allen Lane.

Frank, G. (1991) 'No Escape from the Laws of World Economics', *Review of African Political Economy*, 50:21–32.

Fraser, N. (1989) *Unruly Practices: Power, Discourse, and Gender in Contemporary Social Theory*, Cambridge: Polity.

Freedman, H., & Molteno, R. (1982) *Pan Africa Handbook*, London: Zed Books.

Freire, P. (1980) *Pedagogy of the Oppressed*, Harmondsworth: Penguin.

Freire, P., & Shor, I. (1987) *A Pedagogy for Liberation*, London: Macmillan.

Freyhold, M. von (1987) 'Labour Movements or Popular Struggles in Africa', *Review of African Political Economy*, 39:23–33.

Friedgut, T., & Siegelbaum, L. (1990) 'Perestroika from Below: the Soviet Miners' Strike and its Aftermath', *New Left Review*, 181:5–32.

Friedman, G. (1981) *The Political Philosophy of the Frankfurt School*, London: Cornell University Press.

Gadamer, H. (1975) *Truth and Method*, New York: Seabury Press.

Geertz, C. (1968) *Islam Observed*, New Haven: Yale University Press.

Gellner, E. (1974) 'The Unknown Apollo of Biskra: The Social Base of Algerian Puritanism', *Government and Opposition*, Summer: 277–310.

Gellner, E. (1983) *Nations and Nationalism*, Oxford: Blackwell.

Gellner, E. (1991) 'Nationalism in Eastern Europe', *New Left Review*, 189:127–37.

George, T. (1988) *Theology of the Reformers*, Nashville: Broadman.

Geras, N. (1987) 'Post-Marxism', *New Left Review*, 163:40–82.

Geras, N. (1988) 'Ex-Marxism Without Substance: Being a Real Reply to Laclau and Mouffe', *New Left Review*, 169:34–62.

Gerry, C., & Birkbeck, C. (1983) 'Petty Commodity Producers in Third World Cities' in F. Bechoffer & B. Elliot (eds), *The Petty-Bourgeoisie: Comparative Studies on the Uneasy Stratum*, London: Macmillan.

Getty, J. A. (1985) *Origins of the Great Purges: The Soviet Communist Party Reconsidered, 1933–38*, Cambridge: Cambridge University Press.

Giddens, A. (1991) *Modernity and Self-Identity*, Cambridge: Polity.

Gifford, P. (1991) 'Christian Fundamentalism and Development in Africa', *Review of African Political Economy*, 52:9–20.

Glaser, D. (1989) 'Liberating Liberal Freedoms', *Work in Progress*, 61.

Glenny, M. (1990) *The Rebirth of History?* Harmondsworth: Penguin.

Gonzales, M./Piccone, P. (1989) 'Exorcising Perestroika', *Telos*, 81:30–54.

Gorlice, J. (1986) 'Introduction to the Hungarian Democratic Opposition', *Berkeley Journal of Sociology*, 31:111–65.

Gorz, A. (1982) *Farewell to the Working Class: an Essay on Post-Industrial Socialism*, London: Pluto Press.

Gouldner, A. (1976) *The Dialectic of Ideology and Technology*, London: Macmillan.

Graham, R. (1978) *Iran: The Illusion of Power*, London: Croom Helm.

Green, J. D. (1980) 'Pseudo-Participation and Counter-Mobilization: Roots of the Iranian Revolution', *Iranian Studies*, 13, 1–4:31–54.

Greenberg, S. B. (1990) 'Ideological Struggles within the South African State' in Marks & Trapido, *The Politics of Race, Class and Nationalism*, pp. 389–418.

Grendmann, R. (1991) 'The Ecological Challenge to Marxism', *New Left Review*, 187: 103–20.

Guber, A. (1985) *Intensified Economy and Programmes in Science and Technology*, Moscow: Novosti.

Gusdorf, G. (1982) *Fondements du savoir romantique*, Paris: Payot.

Gwala, N. (1988) 'State Control, Student Politics and the Crisis in Black Universities' in Cobbett & Cohen, *Popular Struggles in South Africa*, pp. 163–82.

Habermas, J. (1970) 'Summation and Response', *Continuum*, 8.

Habermas, J. (1971) *Knowledge and Human Interests*, trans. J. Shapiro, London: Heinemann.

Habermas, J. (1972) *Towards a Rational Society*, London: Heinemann.

Habermas, J. (1974) *Theory and Practice*, London: Heinemann.

Habermas, J. (1976) *Legitimation Crisis*, trans. T. MacCarthy, London: Heinemann.

Habermas, J. (1979a) *Communication and Evolution of Society*, London: Heinemann.

Habermas, J. (1979b) 'Interview with Detlev Horster and Willem van Reijen', trans. R. Smith, *New German Critique*, 18:43.

Habermas, J. (1982a) 'Entwinement of Myth and Reason: Re-Reading *Dialectic of Enlightenment*', *New German Critique*, 26:13–30.

Habermas, J. (1982b) 'Reply to My Critics' in Thompson & Held, *Habermas: Critical Debates*, pp. 219–83.

Habermas, J. (1984) *The Theory of Communicative Action: Reason and the Rationalization of Society*, Vol. 1, trans. T. McCarthy, London: Heinemann.

Habermas, J. (1986) *Autonomy and Domination*, ed. and trans. P. Dews, London: Verso.

Habermas, J. (1987) *The Philosophical Discourse of Modernity*, trans. T. McCarthy, Cambridge, Mass.: MIT Press.

Habermas, J. (1989a) *The New Conservatism: Cultural Criticism and the Historians' Debate*, trans. S. Weber Nicholsen, Cambridge: Polity.

Habermas, J. (1989b) *The Theory of Communicative Action: Lifeworld and System: A Critique of Functionalist Reason*, Vol 2, trans. T. McCarthy, Cambridge: Polity.

Habermas, J. (1990) 'What Does Socialism Mean Today? The Rectifying Revolution and the Need for New Thinking on the Left', *New Left Review*, 183:3–22.

Habermas, J. (1991) 'A Reply' in Honneth & Joas, *Communicative Action*, pp. 214–64.

Haddad, Y. (1983) 'Sayyid Qutb' in Esposito, *Voices of Resurgent Islam*, pp. 70–98.

Halfmann, J. (1985) 'The German Left and Democracy', *New German Critique*, 35:165–86.

Halliday, F. (1979) *Iran: Dictatorship and Development*, Harmondsworth: Penguin.

Hankiss, E. (1990) *East European Alternatives*, Oxford: Clarendon.

Hart, N. (1989) 'Gender and the Rise and Fall of Class Politics', *New Left Review*, 175:19–47.

Hartmann, H. (1979) 'Capitalism, Patriarchy and Job Segregation by Sex' in Z. Eisenstein, (ed.), *Capitalist Patriarchy and the Case for Socialist Feminism*, New York: Monthly Review Press pp. 206–47.

Hauslohner, P. (1989) 'Gorbachev's Social Contract' in Feher & Arato, *Gorbachev: The Debate*.

Hausner, J., & Nielsen, K. (1992) 'The Post-Socialist Transformation Process: Systemic Vacuum, Search Processes, Implementation Problems and Social Struggle', paper presented to the 'Post-Socialism: Problems and Prospects' Conference, Charlotte Mason College, Cumbria, UK, July.

Hausner, J., & Wojtyna, A. (1991) 'Trends and Perspectives in the Development of a System of Interest Representation in Post-Socialist Society' in J. Hausner (ed.), *System of Interest Representation in Poland*, Cracow: Cracow Academy of Economics, pp. 71–94.

Havel, V. (1988) 'Anti-Political Politics' in Keane (ed.), *Civil Society*, pp. 381–98.

Hay, C. (1993) 'Environmental Security and State Legitimacy', *Capitalism, Nature, Scialism*, forthcoming.

Hegedus, J. (1987) 'Reconsidering the Roles of State and Market in Socialist Housing Systems', *International Journal of Urban and Regional Research*, 11:79–97.

Held, D. (1980) *Introduction to Critical Theory*, London: Hutchinson.

Held, D. (1989) 'The Decline of the Nation State' in S. Hall & M. Jacques (eds), *New Times*, London: Lawrence & Wishart.

Held, D. (ed.) (1991) *Political Theory Today*, Cambridge: Polity.

Heller, A., (1982) 'Habermas and Marxism' in Thompson & Held, *Habermas: Critical Debates*, pp. 21–41.

Henley, N. (1977) *Body Politics*, Englewood Cliffs: Prentice Hall.

Hill, R. S. (1988) 'The *Apparatchiki* and Soviet Political Development' in P. Potichnyj (ed.), *The Soviet Union Party and Society*, Cambridge: Cambridge University Press, pp. 3–25.

Hiro, D. (1989) *Islamic Fundamentalism*, London: Paladin.

Hoffman-Ladd, V. J. (1987) 'Polemics on the Modesty and Segregation of Women in Contemporary Egypt', *International Journal of Middle East Studies*, xix:23–50.

Holland, H. (1989) *The Struggle: A History of the African National Congress*, London: Grafton.

Holub, R. (1991) *Jürgen Habermas: Critic in the Public Sphere*, London: Routledge.

Honneth, A, & Joas, H. (eds) (1991) *Commmunicative Action: Essays on Jürgen Habermas's 'The Theory of Communicative Action'*, trans. J. Gaines & D. L. Jones, Oxford: Polity.

Honneth, A., Knodler-Bunte, E. & Windmann, A. (1981) 'The Dialectics of Rationalization: An Interview With Jürgen Habermas', *Telos*, 49:3–31.

Hoogvelt, A. (1990) 'Debt and Indebtedness: The Dynamics of Third World Poverty', *Review of African Political Economy*, 47:117–27.

Horkheimer, M. (1972) *Critical Theory: Selected Essays*, trans. M. O'Connell et al., New York: Herder & Herder.

Horkheimer, M. (1973) 'The Authoritarian State', *Telos*, 15: 3–20.

Horkheimer, M. (1974a) *Notizen 1950 bis 1969 und Dämmerung*, Frankfurt: Verlag.

Horkheimer, M. (1974b) *Eclipse of Reason*, New York: Seabury Press.

Horkheimer, M. (1982–3) 'Egoism and the Freedom Movement (1936)', *Telos*, 54:10–60.

Hosking, A. (1990) *A History of the Soviet Union*, London: Fontana.

Hourani, A. (1968) 'Ottoman Reform and the Politics of the Notables' in W. Polk & R. Chambers (eds), *The Beginnings of Modernization in the Middle East*, Chicago: Chicago University Press, pp. 41–68.

Hullot-Kentor, R. (1989) 'Back to Adorno', *Telos*, 81:5–29.

Huyssen, A. (1981) 'The Search for Tradition – The Avant-Guard and Post-Modernism in the 1970s', *New German Critique*, 22:23–40.

Hyman, R. (1983) 'André Gorz and His Disappearing Proletariat', *Socialist Register*, London: Merlin Press, pp. 272–95.

Hyslop, J. (1988) 'School Student Movements and State Education Policy, 1972–87' in Cobbett & Cohen, *Popular Struggles in South Africa*, pp. 183–209.

IDAF (International Defence and Aid Fund for Southern Africa) (1990) 'The Natal Violence', *Information*, 90, 1–8.

Issawi, C. (1978) 'The Iranian Economy 1925–1975', in G. Lenczowski, (ed.) *Iran Under the Pahlavis*, Stanford: Hoover Institute Press, pp. 129–66.

Jacoby, R. (1987) *The Last Intellectuals*, New York: Basic Books.

Jameson, F. (1990) *Late Marxism, Adorno, or the Persistence of the Dialectic*, London:Verso.

Jansen, G. H. (1979) *Militant Islam*, Harmondsworth: Penguin.

Jay, M. (1973) *Dialectical Imagination: A History of the Frankfurt Institute of Social Research*, London: Heinemann.

Jay, M. (1980) 'The Jews and the Frankfurt School: Critical Theory's Analysis of Anti-Semitism', *New German Critique*, 19:137–49.

Jay, M. (1982–3) 'Introduction to Horkheimer', *Telos*, 54:5–9.

Jay, M. (1988) *Fin de Siècle Socialism*, London: Routledge.

Jencks, C. (1991) 'New World Order: Stones, Paper, Scissors', *Marxism Today*, February pp. 14–18.

Jessop B. (1990) *State Theory: Putting Capitalist States in Their Place*, Oxford: Polity.

Joas, H. (1991) 'The Unhappy Marriage of Hermeneutics and Functionalism', in Honneth & Joas, *Communicative Action*, pp. 97–118.

Jowitt, K. (1983) 'Soviet Neotraditionalism: The Political Corruption of a Leninist Regime', *Soviet Studies*, 35, 3:275–97.

Kagarlitsky, B. (1988) 'The Dialectic of Reform', *New Left Review*, 169:63–84.

Kagarlitsky, B. (1990) *Farewell Perestroika: A Soviet Chronicle*, trans. R. Simon, London: Verso.

Kamrava, M. (1990) *Revolution in Iran and the Roots of Turmoil*, London: Routledge.

Keane, J. (ed.) (1988) *Civil Society: New European Perspectives*, London: Verso.

Keat, R. (1981) *The Politics of Social Theory*, Chicago: Chicago University Press.

Kecskemeti, P. (1969) *The Unexpected Revolution*, Stanford: Stanford University Press.

Keddie, N. (1972) *Sayyid Jamal ad-Din 'al-Afcghani': A Political Biography*, Berkeley: University of California Press.

Keddie, N. (1980) *Iran: Religion, Politics and Society*, London: Frank Cass.

Keddie, N. (1981) 'Religion, Society and Revolution in Modern Iran', in Bonine & Keddie (eds), *Modern Iran*, pp. 21–36.

Keddie, N. (ed.) (1983) *Religion and Politics in Iran*, New Haven: Yale.

Kelidar, A. (1981) 'Ayatollah Khomeini's concept of Islamic government', in Cudsi & Dessouki, *Islam and Power*, pp. 75–94.

Kellner, D. (1989) *Critical Theory, Marxism and Modernity*, Cambridge: Polity.

Kellner, D., & Roderick, R. (1981) 'Recent Literature on Critical Theory', *New German Critique*, 23:141–70.

Kershaw, I. (1989) *The Nazi Dictatorship*, London: Edward Arnold.

Khalid, D. H. (1978) 'The Phenomenon of Re-islamization', *Aussen Politik*, 29, 4:433–53.

Kitschelt, H. (1986) 'Political Opportunity Structures and Political Protest: Anti-Nuclear Movements in Four Democracies', *British Journal of Political Science*, 16:58–85.

Kohlberg, L. (1971) 'From Is to Ought', in T. Mischel (ed.), *Cognitive Development and Epistemology*, New York: Academic Press, pp. 151–235.

Kowalik, T. (1991) 'Marketization and Privatization: The Polish Case', *Socialist Register*, London: Merlin Press, pp. 259–77.

Konrad G., & Szelenyi, I. (1979) *Intellectuals on the Road to Class Power*, Brighton: Harvester.

Kornai, J. (1986) 'The Hungarian Reform Process: Visions, Hopes, and Reality', *Journal of Economic Literature*, 24:1687–2037.

Krizan, M., (1988) ' "Civil Society" and the Modernization of Soviet-Type Societies', *Praxis International*, 8, 1:90–110.

Laclau, E. (1991a) 'What Comes After 1991?' , *Marxism Today*, October: 16–19.

Laclau, E. (1991b) 'God Only Knows', *Marxism Today*, December: 56–9.

Laclau, E., & Mouffe, C. (1985) *Hegemony and Socialist Strategy*, London: Verso.

Laclau, E., & Mouffe, C. (1987) 'Post-Marxism without Apologies', *New Left Review*, 166: 79–106.

Lal, D. (1987) 'The Political Economy of Economic Liberalization', *World Bank Economics Review*, 1, 2:273–99.

Lambert, R., & Webster, E. (1988) 'The Re-emergence of Political Unionism in Contemporary South Africa?' in Cobbett & Cohen, *Popular Struggles in South Africa*, pp. 20–41.

Lasch, C. (1978) *Culture of Narcissism*, New York: Norton.

Lash, S., & Urry, J. (1988) *The End of Organized Capitalism*, Oxford: Polity.

Lauret, L. (1940) *Marxism and Democracy*, London.

Lemarchand, R. (1981) 'Comparative Political Clientelism' in R. N. Eisenstadt & R. Lemarchand, *Political Clientelism*, pp. 1–26.

Leonard, S. T. (1990) *Critical Theory and Political Practice*, Princeton, NJ: Princeton University Press.

Levin, R. M. (1987) 'Democratic Struggles in South Africa', *Review of African Political Economy*, 40:7–31.

Levitas, A., & Strzalkowski, P. (1990) 'What does "Vwlaszczenie Nomenklatury" (Propertization of the Nomenklature) Really Mean?', *Communist Studies*, 2:413–16.

Leys, C. (1976) 'The Overdeveloped Post-Colonial State – a Re-evaluation', *Review of African Political Economy*, 5.

Lipietz, A. (1989) 'The Debt Problem, European Integration and the New Phase of the World Crisis', *New Left Review*, 178:37–50.

Lipset, S. (1959) *Political Man*. New York: Doubleday.

Lipton, M. (1986) *Capitalism and Apartheid – South Africa 1910–84*, Aldershot: Wildwood.

Loewy, M. (1979) *Marxisme et Romantisme Revolutionnaire*, Paris: Le sycomore.

Loewy, M. (1982) 'Le marxisme rationaliste de l'école de francforte', *L'homme et la société*, 65–6:45–66.

Lovas, I., & Anderson, K. (1982) 'State Terrorism in Hungary: The Case of Friendly Repression', *Telos*, 54:77–86.

Lovenduski, J., & Woodall, J. (1987) *Politics and Society in Eastern Europe*, London: Macmillan.

Lovibond, S. (1989) 'Feminism and Postmodernism', *New Left Review*, 178:5–28.

Luhmann, N. (1982) *The Differentiation of Society*, New York: Columbia University Press.

Lukács, G. (1968) *History and Class Consciousness*, Cambridge, Mass.: MIT Press.

Lukács, G. (1980) *The Destruction of Reason*, trans. P. Palmer, London: Merlin Press.

Luke, T. (1988) 'The Dreams of Deep Ecology', *Telos*, 76:65–92.

Luke, T. (1990) *Social Theory and Modernity*, London: Sage.

Lyotard, J.-F. (1991) *The Postmodern Condition: A Report on Knowledge*, trans. G. Bennington & B. Massumi, Manchester: Manchester University Press.

McCarney, J. (1990) *Social Theory and the Crisis of Marxism*, London: Verso.

McCarthy, J. D. (1987) 'Pro-Life and Pro-Choice Mobilization: Infrastructure Deficits and New Technologies' in Zald and McCarthy, *Social Movements*, pp. 49–66.

McCarthy, T. (1973) 'A Theory of Communicative Competence', *Philosophy of the Social Sciences*, 3:135–56.

McCarthy, T. (1978) *The Critical Theory of Jürgen Habermas*, London: Hutchinson.

McCarthy T. (1985) 'Complexity and Democracy, or the Seducements of Systems Theory', *New German Critique*, 35:27–55.

McCarthy, T. (1991) 'Complexity and Democracy: or the Seducements of Systems Theory' in Honneth & Joas, *Communicative Action*, pp. 119–40.

Mahdavy, H. (1964) 'The Coming Crisis in Iran', *Foreign Affairs*, 44:134–46.

Majkowski, W. (1985) *People's Poland: Patterns of Social Inequality and Conflict*, London: Greenwood.

Malek, M. (1989) 'Kurdistan and the Iran–Iraq War', *New Left Review*, 175:79–94.

Mandel, D. (1988) 'Economic Reform and Democracy in the Soviet Union', *Socialist Register*, London: Merlin Press, pp. 132–53.

Mandel, D. (1991) 'The Struggle for Power in the Soviet Economy', *Socialist Register*, London: Merlin Press, pp. 95–127.

Mardin, S. (1978) 'Youth and Violence in Turkey', *Archives Européen de Sociologie*, I:229–54.

Mare, G. (1989) 'Inkatha and Regional Control: Policing Liberation Politics', *Review of African Political Economy*, 45/46:179–89.

Marks S., & Trapido, S. (1990) *Politics of Race, Class and Nationalism in Twentieth-Century South Africa*, London: Longman.

Markus, M. (1982) 'Overt and Covert Modes of Legitimation', in T. H. Rigby & F. Feher, *Political Legitimation in Communist Societies*, London: Macmillan, pp. 82–93.

Marody, M. (1991) 'On Polish Political Attitudes', *Telos*, 89:109–13.

Martin, W. (1991) 'The Future of Southern Africa: What Prospects After Majority Rule?', *Review of African Political Economy*, 50:115–34.

Marx, K. (1844) *Critique of Hegel's Philosophy of Right*, in D. McLelland (ed.) (1977), *Karl Marx: Selected Writings*. Oxford: Oxford University Press.

Marx, K. (n.d.) *The Poverty of Philosophy* (1846), Moscow: Progress.

Marx, K. (1972) *Theories of Surplus Value*, 2 vols, London: Lawrence & Wishart.

Marx, K. (1973) *Grundrisse*, London: Penguin.

Marx, K. (1977) *Karl Marx: Selected Writings*, D. McLelland (ed.), Oxford: Oxford University Press.

Marx, K., & Engels, F. (1969) *The Manifesto of the Communist Party*, Moscow: Progress.

Marx, K., & Engels, F. (1974) *Capital*, Vol. I, London: Lawrence & Wishart.

Marx, K., & Engels, F. (1975) *Collected Works*, Vol 3, London: Lawrence & Wishart.

Medvedev, R. (1991) 'Politics After the Coup', *New Left Review*, 189:91–110.

Meillassoux, C. (1972) 'From Reproduction to Production: A Marxist Approach to Economic Anthropology', *Critique of Anthropology*.

Meillassoux, C. (1978) *Maids, Meal and Money*, London: Cambridge University Press.

Melucci, A. (1989) *Nomads of the Present*, London: Radius.

Menashri, D. (1980) 'Shi'ite Leadership: In the Shadow of Conflicting Ideologies', *Iranian Studies*, 13, nos 1–4:119–46.

Merchant, C. (1983) *The Death of Nature: Women, Ecology and the Scientific Revolution*, San Francisco: Harper and Row.

Meyer, J. W., & Rowan, B. (1977) 'Institutionalized Organizations: Formal Structure as Myth and Ceremony', *American Journal of Sociology*, 83, 2:340–63.

Mies, M. (1989) *Patriarchy and Accumulation on a World Scale*, London: Zed Books.

Milkman, R. (1979) 'Contradictions of Semi-Peripheral Development – The South African Case', in W. Goldfrank, (ed.), *The World-System of Capitalism: Past and Present*, London: Sage. pp. 261–84.

Misgeld, D. (1984) 'Critical Theory and Sociological Theory', *Philosophy of the Social Sciences*, 14:97–105.

Misgeld, D. (1985) 'Education and Cultural Invasion: Critical Social Theory, Education as Instruction and the "Pedagogy of the Oppressed" ', in Forester, *Critical Theory and Public Life*, pp. 77–120.

Mitscherlich, A., & Mitscherlich, M. (1975) *The Inability to Mourn*, trans. B. Placzek, New York: Free Press.

Molyneux, M. (1990) 'The "Woman Question" in the Age of Perestroika', *New Left Review*, 183:23–49.

Montejano, D. (1979) 'Frustrated Apartheid: Race, Repression, and Capitalist Agriculture in South Texas, 1920–1930', in W. Goldfrank (ed.), *The World-System of Capitalism: Past and Present*, London: Sage. pp. 131–70.

Moore, B. (1969) *The Social Orgins of Dictatorship and Democracy*, London: Penguin.

Morabe, M. (1988) 'Towards a People's Democracy: The UDF View', *Review of African Political Economy*, 40:81–7.

Morris M., & Hindson, D. (1992) 'South Africa: Political Violence, Reform and Reconstruction', *Review of African Political Economy*, 53:49–59.

Mouzelis, N. (1985) *Politics in the Semi-Periphery*, London: Macmillan.

Mouzelis, N. (1988) 'Marxism or Post-Marxism?', *New Left Review*, 167:117–21.

Mouzelis, N. (1990) *Post-Marxist Alternatives*, London: Macmillan.

Možný, I. (1992) *Proč tak snadno?* ['Why So Easy?'] *Sociologický Časopis*, Prague: SLON.

Mukaru-Ny'ang'a, D. (1981) 'What is Happening to the Kenyan Peasantry?', *Review of African Political Economy*, 20:7–16.

Musil, J. (1987) 'Housing Policy and the Sociospacial Structure of Cities in a Socialist Country', *International Journal of Urban & Regional Research*, 11:27–36.

Nafisi, R. (1982) 'The Genesis of the Clerical State in Iran', *Telos*, 51:197–205.

Nashat, G. (1980) 'Women in the Islamic Republic of Iran', *Iranian Studies*, 13, 1–4:165–214.

Needham, J. (1979) *The Grand Titration*, London: Allen Lane.

Nettler, R. (1987) *Past Trials and Tribulations: A Muslim Fundamentalist's View of the Jews*, Oxford: Pergamon.

Neumann, F. (1944) *Behemoth: The Structure and Practice of National Socialism*, London: Victor Gollancz.

Nicholson, L. (1986) *Gender and History: The Failure of Social Theory in the Age of the Family*, New York: Basic Books.

Nikazmerad, N. (1980) 'A Chronological Survey of the Iranian Revolution', *Iranian Studies*, 13, 1–4:327–68.

Njonjo, A. L. (1981) 'The Kenyan Peasantry: A Re-assessment', *Review of African Political Economy*, 20:27–40.

Nkomo, C. (1981) 'Contradications in Bantu Education', *Harvard Educational Review*, 51, 1.

Nove, A. (1975) 'Is There a Ruling Class in the USSR?', *Soviet Studies*, 27:615–38.

Nzongola-Ntalaja (1987) *Revolution and Counter-Revolution in Africa*, London: Zed Books.

O'Connor, J. (1973) *The Fiscal Crisis of the State*, London: Macmillan.

O'Connor, J. (1987) *The Meaning of Crisis*, London: Macmillan.

Offe, C. (1976) 'Crisis of Crisis Management', *International Journal of Politics*, 6.

Offe, C. (1984) *Contradictions of the Welfare State*, Cambridge, Mass.: MIT Press.

Offe, C. (1985) *Disorganized Capitalism*, Oxford: Polity.

Okin, S. M. (1991) 'Gender, the Public and the Private' in Held, *Political Theory Today*, pp. 67–90.

O'Neill, J. (1985) 'Decolonization and the Ideal Speech Community', in Forester, *Critical Theory and Public Life*, pp. 57–76.

Ortega y Gasset, J. (1951) *The Revolt of the Masses*, London: Allen & Unwin. (First published, 1930.)

Ost, D. (1989) 'The Transformation of Solidarity and the Future of Central Europe', *Telos*, 79:63–94.

Ost, D. (1990) *Solidarity and the Politics of Antipolitics: Opposition and Reform in Poland since 1968*, Philadelphia: Temple University Press.

Ost, D. (1991) 'The Crisis of Liberalism in Poland', *Telos*, 89:85–95.

Outhwaite (forthcoming) *Habermas*, Cambridge: Polity.

Pahl, J. (1990) 'Household Spending, Personal Spending and the Control of Money in Marriage', *Sociology*, 24, 1:119–38.

Parsons, T. (1991) *The Social System*, London: Routledge.

Pateman, C. (1988) *Sexual Contracts*, Cambridge: Polity.

Piaget, J. (1965) *Moral Judgement of the Child*, trans. M. Cook, Harmondsworth: Penguin.

Piccone, P. (1989) 'Introduction to the Special Issue on Eastern Europe', *Telos*, 79:2–8.

Piccone, P. (1990–1) 'Artificial Negativity as a Bureaucratic Tool?', *Telos*, 86:127–41.

Piccone, P. (1991) 'Paradoxes of Perestroika', *Telos*, 84:3–33.

Pickvance C. G. (1992) 'Social Movements in the Transition from State Socialism', paper presented to the BSA Conference, April, University of Kent, UK.

Pokrovsky, M. (1924) *Ocherki russkovo revolytsionnovo dvizheniya* [Outline of the Russian Revolutionary Movement], Moscow.

Pollock, F. (1944) *Behemoth: The Structure and Practice of National Socialism 1933–1944*, rev. ed., London: Victor Gollancz.

Popper, K. (1979) *Objective Knowledge*, Oxford: Oxford University Press.

Posel, D. (1990) 'The Language of Domination, 1978–1983' in Marks & Trapido, *Politics of Race, Class and Nationalism*, pp. 419–44.

Postone, M., & Brick, B. (1982) 'Critical Pessimism and the Limits of Traditional Marxism', *Theory & Society*, 11:617–58.

Qotb, S. (1970) *Social Justice and Islam*, New York: Octagon Press. (First published, 1949.)

Quandt, W. B. (1969) *Revolution and Political Leadership: Algeria 1954–68*, Cambridge, Mass.: MIT Press.

Rabinbach, A. (ed.) (1988) Special Issue on the *Historikerstreit*, *New German Critique*, 44.

Rahman, F. (1982) *Islam and Modernity: Transformation of an Intellectual Tradition*, London: University of Chicago Press.

Rakovski, M./János Kis (1978) *Towards an East European Marxism*, London: Allison & Busby.

Rasmussen, D. M. (1990) *Rereading Habermas*, Oxford: Blackwell.

Raulet, G. (1979–80) 'What Good is Schopenhauer? Remarks on Horkheimer's Pessimism', *Telos*, 42:98–106.

Raulet, G. (1983) 'The Agony of Marxism and the Victory of the Left', *Telos*, 55:163–78.

Ray, L. J. (1986) 'Protestant Ethic Debate' in R. J. Anderson, J. A. Hughes and W. Sharrock (eds), *Classic Disputes in Sociology*, London: Allen & Unwin, pp. 97–125.

Ray, L. J. (1989) 'Foucault, Critical Theory and the Decomposition of the Historical Subject', *Philosophy and Social Criticism*, 14, 1:69–110.

Republic of South Africa (1989) *Official Yearbook*, Pretoria: Bureau for Information.

Rigby, T. H. (1988) 'Staffing the USSR Incorporated: The Origins of the Nomenklatura System', *Soviet Studies*, 40:523–37.

Rigby, T. H., & Feher, F. (eds) (1982) *Political Legitimation in Communist Societies*, London: Macmillan.

Rittersporn, I. (1989) 'Reforming the Soviet Union', *Telos*, 79:9–28.

Rizzi, B. (1985) *Bureaucratization of the World*, trans. A. Westoby, New York: Free Press. (First published, 1939.)

Rorty, R. (1979) *Philosophy and the Mirror of Nature*, Princeton, NJ: Princeton University Press.

Rose, G. (1978) *The Melancholy Science – An Introduction to the Thought of Theodor Adorno*, London: Macmillan.

Roseneil, S. (1992) 'The Origin of Women's Collective Action: The Case of Greenham'. Paper presented to the BSA Conference, University of Kent, April.

Ruane, J., & Todd, J. (1988) 'The Application of Critical Theory', *Political Studies*, 36:533–8.

Rudebeck, L. (1988) 'The Effects of Structural Adjustment in Kandjadja, Guinea-Bissau', *Review of African Political Economy*, 49:9–21.

Rupnik, J. (1988) 'Totalitarianism Revisited' in Keane, *Civil Society: New European Perspectives*, pp. 263–89.

Ruthven, M. (1984) *Islam in the World*, London: Penguin.

Ryan, M. (1981) 'French Theory in New German Critique', *New German Critique*, 22 Winter, pp. 145–61.

Said, E. (1985) *Orientalism*, New York: Pantheon.

Sampson, S. (1985–6) 'The Informal Sector in Eastern Europe', *Telos*, 66:44–66.

Sarlvik, B., & Crew, I. (1983) *Decade of Dealignment*, Cambridge: Cambridge University Press.

Saul, J. (1979) 'The State in Postcolonial Societies' in *The State and Revolution in Africa*, London: Heinemann. pp. 167–99.

Saul, J. (1988) 'Class, Race and the Future of Socialism' in Cobbett & Cohen, *Popular Struggles in South Africa*, pp. 210–28.

Saul, J. (1991) 'South Africa between "Barbarism" and "Structural Reform" ', *New Left Review*, 188:3–44

Scambler, G. (1987) 'Habermas and the Power of Medical Expertise' in Scambler (ed.), *Sociological Theory and Medical Sociology*, London: Tavistock, pp. 165–93.

Schmid, M. (1982) 'Habermas' Theory of Social Evolution', in Thompson & Held, *Habermas Critical Debates*, pp. 162–80.

Schmied-Kowarzik, W. (1984) *Das Dialektische Verhältnis des Menschen zur Natur*, Freiburg: Alber.

Schnadelbach, H. (1991) 'The Transformation of Critical Theory' in Honneth & Joas, *Communicative Action*, pp. 7–22.

Schroyer, T. (1973) *The Critique of Domination: The Origins and Development of Critical Theory*, New York: George Braziller.

Schutz, A., & Lukmann, T. (1974) *The Structures of the Lifeworld*, London: Heinemann.

Sciulli, D. (1992) *The Theory of Societal Constitutionalism: Foundations of a Non-Marxist Critical Theory*, Cambridge: Cambridge University Press.

Scott, A. (1990) *Ideology and the New Social Movements*, London: Unwin Hyman.

Searle, J. R. (1969) *Speech Acts*, Cambridge: Cambridge University Press.

Seekings, J. (1988) 'The Origins of Political Mobilization in the PWV Townships, 1980–84' in Cobbett & Cohen, *Popular Struggles in South Africa*, pp. 59–76.

Seel, M. (1991) 'Two Meanings of "Communicative Rationality" ' in Honneth & Joas, *Communicative Action*, pp. 36–48.

Seldon, M. (1983) 'Imposed Collectivization and the Crisis of Agrarian Development in the Socialist States', in A. Bergesen (ed.) *Crisis in the World System*, London: Sage.

Shabalala, S. (1990) *An Africanist's View of Economic Emancipation*, Cape Town: Skotaville Publishers.

Shariati, A. (1979) *Red Shi'ism*, Tehran: The Shariati Foundation.

Shivji, I. G. (1989) *The Concept of Human Rights in Africa*, London: Codesria Books.

Shlapentokh, V. (1988) 'The XXVII Congress: A Case Study of the Shaping of a New Party Ideology', *Soviet Studies*, 40, 1:1–20.

Silvers, P. von. (1984) 'National Integration and Traditional Rural Organization in Algeria

1970–80: Background for Islamic Traditionalism?' in Arjomand (ed.) *From Nationalism to Revolutionary Islam*, pp. 94–118.

Simmel, G. (1990) *The Philosophy of Money*, trans, D. Frisby & T. Bottomore, London: Routledge.

Sivan, E. (1990) 'The Islamic Resurgence: Civil Society Strikes Back', *Journal of Contemporary History*, May–June, 25, 2–3:353–62.

Sklair, L. (1991) *Sociology of the Global System*, London: Harvester.

Skocpol, T. (1982) 'Rentier States and Shi'a Islam in the Iranian Revolution', *Theory & Society*, 11, 3:265–83.

Smart, B. (1983) *Foucault, Marxism & Critique*, London: Routledge.

Smith, A. D. (1979) *Nationalist Movements*, London: Macmillan.

Smith, A. D. (1990) 'Towards a Global Culture?' in Featherstone, *Global Culture*, pp. 171–92.

Smith, A. D. (1991) 'National Identity and the Idea of European Unity', *International Affairs*, 68, 1:55–76.

Smith, D. E. (1983) 'Women, Class and Family', *The Socialist Register*, London: Merlin Press, pp. 1–44.

Smith, G, (1991) 'The State, Nationalism and the Nationalities Question in the Soviet Republics' in C. Merridale & C. Ward (eds), *Perestrioka: The Historical Perspective*, London: Edward Arnold.

Soper, K. (1989) 'Feminism as Critique', *New Left Review*, 176:91–114.

Soper, K. (1991) 'Postmodernism, Subjectivity and the Question of Value', *New Left Review*, 186:120–8.

Spivak, G. C. (1987) *In Other Worlds: Essays in Cultural Politics*, London: Methuen.

Stadler, A. (1987) *The Political Economy of Modern South Africa*, London, Croom Helm.

Stame, F. (1984) 'The Crisis on the Left and the New Social Identities', *Telos*, 60:3–14.

Standbrook, R. (1988) 'Patrimonialism and the Failing of Parastatals' in Cook & Kirkpatrick, *Privatization in Less Developed Countries*, pp. 162–79.

Staniszkis, J. (1989) 'The Obsolescence of Solidarity', *Telos*, 80:37–50.

Stockman, N. (1983) *Anti-positivist Theories of the Sciences*, Reidel: Dordrecht.

Strydom, P. (1990) 'Habermas and New Social Movements', *Telos*, 85:156–63.

Szamuely, T. (1988) *The Russian Tradition*, London: Fontana.

Szelenyi, I. (1979) 'Social Inequalities in State Socialist Redistributive Economies', *International Journal of Comparative Sociology*, XIX, 1/2:63–87.

Szelenyi, I. (1980) 'Whose Alternative?', *New German Critique*, 20:117–34.

Szelenyi, I. (1983) *Urban Inequalities Under State Socialism*, Oxford: Oxford University Press.

Szelenyi, I. (1988) *Socialist Entrepreneurs: Embourgeoisiement in Rural Hungary*, Oxford: Polity.

Szelenyi, I., & Mankin, R. (1987) 'Social Policy under State Socialism', in M. Rein et al., *Stagnation & Renewal in Social Policy*, New York: Sharpe.

Szelenyi, I., & Szelenyi, S. (1991) 'The Vacuum in Hungarian Politics: Classes and Parties', *New Left Review*, 187:121–38.

Tabari, A., & Yeganeh, N. (1982) *In the Shadow of Islam*, London: Zed Books.

Tar, Z. (1977) *The Frankfurt School*, New York & London: John Wiley.

Tarkowska, E., & Tarkowski, J. (1991) 'Social Disintegration in Poland: Civil Society or Amoral Familism?', *Telos*, 89:103–9.

Tarkowski, J. (1981) 'Political Clientelism in Poland' in Eisenstadt & Lemarchand, *Political Clientelism*, pp. 173–90.

Taylor, C. (1991) 'Language and Society', in Honneth and Joas, *Communicative Action*, pp. 23–35.

Taylor, R. (1990) 'South Africa: Consocation or Democracy?', *Telos*, 85:17–32

Tehranian, M. (1980) 'Communication and Revolution in Iran: The Passing of a Paradigm', *Iranian Studies*, 13, 1–4:5–30.

Thompson, E. P. (1967) 'Time, Work-Discipline and Industrial "Capitalism" ', *Past and Present*, 38:56–97.

Thompson, J. B. (1982) 'Universal Pragmatics' in Thompson & Held, *Habermas: Critical Debates*, pp. 116–33.

Thompson, J. B., & Held, D. (eds) (1982) *Habermas: Critical Debates*, London: Macmillan.

Tokei, F. (1972) 'Lukács and Hungarian Culture', *New Hungarian Quarterly*, 13:109–12.

Tosics, I. (1988) 'Inequalities in East European Cities: Can Redistribution Ever Be Equalizing . . .?', *International Journal for Urban and Regional Research*, 12:133–6.

Touraine, A. (1977) *The Self-Production of Society*, Chicago: University Press.

Touraine, A. (1981) *The Voice and the Eye*, trans. A. Duff, New York: Cambridge University Press.

Touraine, A., Hegedus Z., & Wieviorka, M. (1983) *Anti-Nuclear Protest*, Cambridge: Cambridge University Press.

Trimberger, E. K. (1978) *Revolution from Above*, New Brunswick: Transaction Books.

Turner, B. (1981) *For Weber: Essays on the Sociology of Fate*, London: Routledge & Kegan Paul.

Turner, B. (1984) *Capitalism and Class in the Middle East: Theories of Social Change and Economic Development*, London: Heinemann Educational Books.

Turok, B. (1987) *Africa – What Can Be Done?*, London: Zed Books.

Ulam, A. (1985) 'Surviving in Strength', *Times Literary Supplement*, 13 Sept., p. 1010.

Unterhalter, E. (1990) 'The Impact of Apartheid on Women's Education in South Africa', *Review of African Political Economy*, 48:66–75.

Urry, J. (1981) 'Localities, Regions and Social Class', *International Journal of Urban and Regional Research*, 5, 4:455–74.

Vatikiotis, P. J. (1981) *Politics in the Middle East*, London: Croom Helm.

Vatin, J.-C. (1981) 'Religious Resistance and State Power in Algeria' in Cudsi & Dessouki, *Islam and Power*, pp. 119–57.

Vergopoulos, K. (1978) 'Capitalism and Peasant Productivity', *Journal of Peasant Studies*, 5, 4:446–65.

Vieille, P. (1984) 'L'État péripherique et son héritage', *Peuples Méditerranéen*.

Voll, J. (1983) 'Renewal and Reform in Islamic History' in Esposito, *Voices of Resurgent Islam*, pp. 32–47.

Voskamp, U., & Wittke, V. (1991) 'Industrial Restructuring in the Former GDR', *Politics & Society*, 19, 3:341–71.

Voslensky, M. (1984) *Nomenklatura – Anatomy of the Soviet Ruling Class*, London: Bodley Head.

Waines, D. (1988) 'Political Activism and the Islamic Revolution', *Awraq*, IX:179–201.

Walby, S. (1986) *Patriarchy at Work*, Cambridge: Polity.

Walicki, A. (1991) 'From Stalinism to Post-Communist Pluralism: The Case of Poland', *New Left Review*, 185:92–121.

Walker, M. (1988) *The Walking Giant: The Soviet Union Under Gorbachev*, London: Sphere.

Wallerstein, I. (1980) 'States in the Institutional Vortex of the Capitalist World Economy', *International Social Science Journal*, 32, 4:743–89.

Warde, A., Savage, M., Longhurst, B., & Martin, A. (1987) *Class Composition and Voting*, Lancaster Regionalism Group Working Paper 23. Lancaster University.

Watt, M. (1988) *Islamic Fundamentalism and Modernity*, London: Routledge.

Weber, M. (1974) *The Protestant Ethic and the Spirit of Capitalism*, trans. Talcott Parsons, London: Unwin.

Weber, M. (1976) *The Protestant Ethic and the Spirit of Capitalism*, London: Allen & Unwin.

Weber, M. (1978) *Economy and Society*, 2 vols, trans. G. Roth & C. Wittich, Berkeley: University of California.

Weber, M. (1981) *General Economic History*, London: Transaction Books.

Webster, E. (1987) 'The Two Faces of the Black Trade Union Movement in South Africa', *Review of African Political Economy*, 39:33–41.

Wellmer, A. (1971) *Critical Theory of Society*, New York: Seabury Press.

White, S. K. (1990) *The Recent Work of Jürgen Habermas*, Cambridge: Cambridge University Press.

White, S., Gardner, J. and Schopflin, G. (1984) *Communist Political Systems*, London: Macmillan.

Whitebook, J. (1984) 'Reason and Happiness: Some Psychoanalytical Themes in Critical Theory', *Praxis International*, 4, 1:15–31.

Wieriorka, M. (1984) *Les Juifs, la Pologne, et Solidarnosc*, Paris: Denoël.

Wiles, P. (1982) *The New Communist Third World*, New York: St Martin's Press.

Wollstonecraft, M. (1982) *Vindication of the Rights of Woman*, Harmondsworth: Penguin.

Wolnicki, M. (1989) 'Self-Government and Ownership in Poland', *Telos*, 80:63–78.

Wolpe, H. (1988) *Race, Class and the Apartheid State*, London: James Currey.

World Bank, (1981) *Accelerated Development in Sub-Saharan Africa* (The Berg Report), Washington, DC: World Bank.

Wright, M. (1989) *Iran*, Harlow: Longman.

Wuthnow, R. (1980) 'World Order and Religious Movements' in A. Bergesen, (ed.), *Studies of the Modern World System*, New York: Academic, pp. 52–72.

Wuthnow, R. (1983) 'Cultural Crises' in A. Bergesen (ed.), *Crisis in the World System*, London: Sage, pp. 57–75.

Young, R. (1991) 'Privatization in Africa', *Review of African Political Economy*, 51:50–62.

Zald, M. N., & McCarthy, J. D. (eds) (1987) *Social Movements in an Organizational Society*, New Brunswick: Transaction Books.

Zaslavskaya, T. (1984) 'The Novosibirsk Report', trans. T. Cherfas, *Survey*, Spring 28, 1:88–108.

Zaslavsky, V. (1982) *The Neo-Stalinist State: Class, Ethnicity and Consensus in Soviet Society*, New York: Sharpe.

Zaslavsky, V. (1985) 'The Soviet World System: Origins, Evolution, Prospects for Reform', *Telos*, 65:3–22.

Zilsel, E. (1942) 'Genesis of the Concept of Law', *Philosophical Review*, 51:245–79.

Zloch-Christy, I. (1987) *Debt Problems of Eastern Europe*, Cambridge: Cambridge University Press.

Zon, H. van (1992) *Alternative Scenarios for Central Europe*, Brussels: Commission of the European Communities, Science Research and Development.

Zubaida, S. (1989) *Islam, the People and the State: Essays on Political Ideas and Movements in the Middle East*, London: Routledge.

Index

Adorno, T., vii, viii, ix, 1, 2–16 *passim*, 88, 172, 173
African National Congress (ANC), 85, 152, 155, 158, 160–2, 163, 166, 167, 168, 178, 180
Afrikaanse Handelsinstituut Incorporation, 164–5, 170
agrarian social relations, 87
Alliance of Free Democrats, 119
Anabaptists, 44, 45, 55, 175
antisemitism, 8–10
apartheid, 85, 151–6, 158, 159, 163, 164, 168
art, 4
austerity programmes, 100–1
authoritarian state, 5–11, 88, 89, 172, 173
autonomy, 32–3

Babism, 136–7
bazaari, 135, 136, 137, 139, 142, 143, 149, 178
Black Consciousness Movement (BCM), 158
bureaucratic socialism, *see* state socialism

Calvinism, xv, 42, 44, 175
capital, transnational/international, 91–2, 99, 178–9
capital accumulation, 83, 87, 178, 179
capitalism, xii, 45, 88, 89; and gender relations, 69–70; political, 110; state, 6
charisma, 8, 128, 180
civil society, xi
class conflict, xiv
class, 71–2; formation, 92
clientelism, political, 92, 93–8, 112, 113, 139, 178
CODESA talks, 152, 169
cognitivism, 29
colonialism, 130, 132; in Iran, 135–6
colonization of the lifeworld, 46–7, 50–4, 57, 57–75, 82, 174–5, 177
commodification, 3–4, 14, 46–7
communicative action, vii, xvi, 24–34, 38–9, 57–8, 79, 80–1, 130, 151, 174, 175, 180

Communist Party: Iran, *see Tudah* party; South Africa, 161
Congress of South African Trade Unions (COSATU), 162–3, 167
conscientization, 22
consciousness-raising, 22–3, 61
consensus, 87, 89, 90
conservatism, 20–1
conspiracy theories, 10
consumer capitalism, xii
corporatist strategies, 111–12
Council of Mutual Economic Assistance (CMEA), 115
counter-culture politics, 13, 20, 67
crisis, systemic, 102–5
crisis displacement, xii–xiii, 151, 173
crisis management, 108, 156, 157
critical pedagogy, 22
cultural knowledge, xiv, xv–xvi
culture, popular, 2–4
culture industry, 3, 4, 173
Czech Association for Independent Social Analysis, 123

de-regulation in South Africa, 163–8
debt, 99, 100, 101
decentration, 32, 33
defensive social movements, 57, 62, 63
dependent states, 98–101, 105
development: logic and dynamics of, 39, 41–6; *see also* social evolution
Dialectic of Enlightenment (Adorno & Horkheimer), 1, 2, 10, 11, 11–15, 19
domestic relations, 68, 69, 70

Eastern Europe, 84, 108–9; *see also individual countries*
ecology movements, 63
education: higher, 66; in South Africa, 157, 158
Enlightenment, 6, 7, 19
ethics, 43–5
expert cultures, 49–50, 51, 54, 73
exploitation, 15–16